Rediscovering
Sacred Science

# Rediscovering Sacred Science

Edited by Christopher Bamford

Floris Books

First published in this form in 1994 by Lindisfarne Press and Floris Books

"What is Sacred in Architecture?" and "The Platonic Tradition on the
Nature of Proportion" by Keith Critchlow and "Ancient Temple Architec-
ture" by Robert Lawlor were previously published in *Lindisfarne Letter 10:
Geometry and Architecture.* Copyright © The Lindisfarne Association, 1980.
"Twelve Criteria for Sacred Architecture" by Keith Critchlow was previously
published in *Lindisfarne Letter 12: The Lindisfarne Chapel.* Copyright © The
Lindisfarne Association, 1981. "Introduction: Homage to Pythagoras" by
Christopher Bamford; "Pythagorean Number as Form, Color and Light" by
Robert Lawlor; "The Two Lights" by Arthur Zajonc; "Apollo: The
Pythagorean Definition of God" by Anne Macaulay; and "Blake, Yeats and
Pythagoras" by Kathleen Raine were previously published in *Lindisfarne Let-
ter 14: Homage to Pythagoras.* Copyright © The Lindisfarne Association, 1982.

Drawings for "Pythagorean Number as Form, Color, and Light" and
for "Apollo: The Pythagorean Definition of God" by Rachel Fletcher

Front cover art: Pythagoras, Royal Portal, Chartres Cathedral
(from *An Illustrated Monograph of Chartres Cathedral,* Etienne Houvet)

British Library CIP Data on request

ISBN 0-86315-197-3

Printed in the United States of America

# CONTENTS

PUBLISHER'S NOTE

The present compilation has been assembled from three previous publications now out-of-print and no longer available: *Lindisfarne Letter 10: Geometry and Architecture* (1980); *Lindisfarne Letter 12: The Lindisfarne Chapel* (1981); and *Lindisfarne Letter 14: Homage to Pythagoras* (1982). The first and last of these were both "conference books"—collections made up of oral presentations within a specific context and to a particular audience. *Letter 10* contained the major presentations from a Lindisfarne Fellows Conference held at Zen Center's Green Gulch Farm in 1979. This was a small, intimate gathering whose main function was to bring together for the first time Keith Critchlow from London and Robert Lawlor from Tasmania, both of whom, continents apart, had been simultaneously approaching a similarly contemporary "reimagining" of ancient metaphysics, cosmology, and geometry. The meeting was fruitful, and the following year, 1980, both came together again, with William Irwin Thompson and Rachel Fletcher, to teach in the Lindisfarne Institute's Summer Program in Sacred Architecture. It was this program that provided the context for the design and building of the Lindisfarne Chapel. Critchlow's *Twelve Criteria for Sacred Architecture* derives from a lecture given at this time. The following year, 1981, a gathering of about fifty members of the Lindisfarne Association met in Crestone, Colorado, under the sign of *Homage to Pythagoras* to celebrate the rebirth of the idea of science as a sacred, sacramental activity. As such, it marked a historic moment. Besides those whose presentations are included here, Robert Bly, Jocelyn Godwin, John Michell, and Ernest McClain were also present and made valuable contributions. In reading the various talks printed here these different contexts should be borne in mind.

*All such disciplines, theories, and scientific investigations, as truly invigorate the eye of the soul, and purify the intellect from blindness introduced by studies of a different kind, so as to enable it to perceive the true principles and causes of the universe, were unfolded by Pythagoras to the Greeks.*

IAMBLICHUS, *Life of Pythagoras*

*What he said to his disciples, no man can tell for certain, for they preserved an exceptional silence. However, the following facts in particular became universally known: first, that he held the soul to be immortal, next that it migrates into other kinds of animals, further that events repeat themselves in a cyclical process and nothing is new in an absolute sense, and finally that one must regard all living things as kindred. These are the beliefs that Pythagoras is said to have been the first to introduce into Greece.*

PORPHYRY, *Life of Pythagoras*

*At this point we may ask the question: since we are distinguished from all other existing things, for what particular purpose have nature and God brought us into being? Pythagoras, when asked this question, replied, "To view (or contemplate therein) the heavens." And he added that he was a viewer of nature, and had come into life for this purpose.*

ARISTOTLE, *Protrepticus*

*Then comes the most difficult of all questions, whether unity or being, as the Pythagoreans and Plato said, is not a particular something at all, but is the very being of any being.*

ARISTOTLE, *Metaphysics*

*Indeed, no one can doubt that the soul of Pythagoras was sent to mankind from the empire of Apollo, either being an attendant on the God, or co-arranged with him in some other more familiar way: for this may be inferred both from his birth, and the all-various wisdom of his soul. And thus much concerning the nativity of Pythagoras.*

*But after his father Mnesarchus had returned from Syria to Samos, with great wealth, which he had collect from a prosperous navigation, he built a temple to Apollo, with the inscription of Pythius; and took care to have his son nourished with various and the best disciplines, at one time by Creophilus, at another by Pherecydes the Syrian, and at another by almost all those who presided over sacred concerns, to whom he earnestly recommended Pythagoras, that he might be as much as possible sufficiently instructed in divine concerns. He, however, was educated in such a manner, as to be fortunately the most beautiful and godlike of all t hose that have been celebrated in the annals of history. On the death of his father, likewise, though he was still but a youth, his aspect was most venerable and his habits most temperate, so that he was even reverenced and honored by elderly men; and converted the attention of all who saw and heard him speak, on himself, and appeared to be an admirable person to every one who beheld him. Hence it was reasonably asserted by many, that he was the son of a God. But he being corroborated by renown of this kind, by the education which he had received from his infancy, and by his natural deiform appearance, in a still greater degree evinced that he deserved his present prerogatives. He was also adorned by piety and disciplines, by a mode of living transcendently good, by firmness of soul, and by a body in due subject to the mandates of reason. In all his worlds and actions, his discovered an inimitable quite and serenity, not being subdued at any time by anger, or laughter, or emulation, or contention, or any other perturbation or precipitation of conduct; but he dwelt at Samos like some beneficent daemon.*

IAMBLICHUS, *Life of Pythagoras*

*Introduction*
# Homage to Pythagoras

.................................................................. *Christopher Bamford*

Oh! Friend, we come too late. True the gods live,
  But above our heads, up there in another world.
Endlessly they act there, and seem to care little
  Whether we live, that much the heavenly ones spare us.
For a weak vessel is not always able to retain them,
  And only occasionally is man able to bear the heavenly fullness.
A dream of them is life after that. But wandering helps,
  And slumber, and need and night make us strong.
Until heroes enough in the brazen cradle have grown
  Hearts strong as the heavenly ones', like before.
Thundering they come then. Meanwhile, it often seems to me
  Better to sleep than to be so without friends,
So to wait; and what to do or say meanwhile
  I do not know; and what are poets for in a destitute time?
But they are, you say, like the holy priests of the winegod,
  Who moved from country to country in the holy night.[1]

ALCMAEON OF CROTON, who lived in the old age of
Pythagoras himself, said that "men die because they cannot join their
beginning and their end." It is therefore extremely auspicious, I feel,
that we have come together to consider Pythagoras, who in so many ways
is the presiding genius of our culture and the originator of so many of
its governing principles. Indeed, a good case may be made not only that
everything which we consider of value derives from the enigmatic spirit

---

1. The idea to use this stanza of Holderlin's "Bread and Wine" as an epigraph came from Robert Bly, who recited his translation of it as a response to my talk. He was quite right, and therefore I decided to include it here, but in my own translation. —C.B.

we are here to invoke but also that in fact the entire epoch or evolutionary moment whose end we are now witnessing began with the birth of
Pythagoras and represents but a continuing metamorphosis of the
teaching whose seeds he was called upon to plant. I am overstating the
case; nevertheless it is certain, as Simone Weil for one made very clear,
that Pythagorean thought is the seminal mystery of Greek civilization
and recurs everywhere, impregnating almost all religion, poetry, philosophy, music, architecture, not to mention the 'sciences' which in many
ways are still those of today. And not only Greece: since then every critical moment in the development of our civilization has witnessed a
revival, a deepening even in some way, and certainly a metamorphosis,
of principles related to this Pythagoras who at each instant—at the time
of Christ, in the twelfth century, during the Renaissance, in the Romantic period and now today—is invoked by name. When we come to
consider him, then, we have in many ways to consider the destiny of our
culture, that culture, for better or worse, whose vessels of transformation
we have chosen to be. In other words, to render homage to Pythagoras
is to ask who we are, where we have come from and where we are going.
It is to seek the meaning of our culture, and hence an answer to Joseph
Needham's question, put so forcefully in his *Science and Civilization in
China,* namely: "Why did modern technological science develop only in
the West?" Not for nothing therefore was Pythagoras assimilated to
Apollo, whose injunction "Know Thyself" he taught to the fullest degree.

Let me interject here a personal note. My first guide in these matters
was probably Charles Olson, who taught the need and possibility of
thinking the whole earth and its history. By the old principle—actually,
of course, Pythagorean—that "a one is only if it produces a one," he
showed that the world, the earth, was a knowable, sizable, single and *our*
thing. If the universe is a whole, that is, it must produce a whole, and we
are it—*imago mundi, anima mundi*—which means that we can know it.
Myth thus became for Olson history in the sense of a finding out for oneself, as the way man, estranged from that with which he is most familiar,
namely himself, could return to himself. Following Olson, Bateson gave
me a more philosophical, epistemological way of thinking about these
things, about the universe, that is, viewed from the side of the primacy of
mind, or rather viewed as mind. He taught me about the dynamic, recur-
sive, self-organizing pattern-nature of the mental world of relations,
which is the world we live, calling his path or approach Pythagorean and
giving it a lineage: Pythagoras, the Gnostics, Alchemists, Goethe, Blake,
Lamarck, Samuel Butler—and made it very clear that if we did not understand and fully achieve this way of thinking the consequences would

be appalling. I therefore began to study deeply in this tradition he had proposed and at the same time, having learned the valuable lesson that epistemologies or world-views were not irrevocable, I found myself led both to the school of Guénon, Schuon and the other 'traditionalists', and to scholars and teachers like Corbin, Heidegger, Ricoeur, Barfield, Steiner, de Lubicz and many others, some of whom are gathered here. All these showed me that this so-called Pythagorean thinking which Bateson was trying to recover, in its epistemology at least, was common to all the spiritual traditions of the world. In other words, it was in the very nature of things, which led me to the study of nature and of Christianity.

I say all this both to excuse in advance the mixture of languages I shall be using and to confess that what in all this has remained most elusive for me is the actual mission, meaning, contribution of Pythagoras himself. That is, though pythagoreanism, as it were with a small 'p' and in the broadest possible sense, is an easily graspable notion—we know what it is and can talk about music, number, pattern, form, relationship, geometry, etc., as primary and invoke the great traditions of Egypt, Vedic India, Islam, as well as find apparent echoes among such contemporaries as Heisenberg, Wheeler, Eigen, Spencer-Brown, etc., who seem to inquire after pattern rather than after substance—what Pythagoreanism with a capital 'P' is, what he stands for, what I have suggested is the very essence and mystery of our culture, is much more obscure. In fact the closer one examines the Western lineage of pattern-seekers, from the early Neo-Pythagoreans and Neo-Platonists on through, the harder it is to grasp the archetype. One traces the evolution of an ecology of ideas, but the central idea continually evades one. Today, I am going to suggest this is because Pythagoreanism, though revolutionary, is not original. Just as its history shows evidence of metamorphosis, a continuous change of form or understanding—a changing framework of application of the principles if you will—so Pythagoras himself instituted just such a change. As we are the seeds generated from the plant which sprung from the seed which was Pythagoras, so Pythagoras, too, a seed, sprang from another plant.

To discover, then, what it is that we are destined to carry forth into the future—should we have a future, by which Alcmaeon would mean, can we join our beginning and our end, our seed and our fruit—we must examine the past. The problem here is that the so-called past is obscure, uncertain, ambiguous; our memory is defective; things are forgotten, confused, misattributed. In a word, it is difficult to recall what we are trying to remember. To help us do so, as in this conference, a kind of crabwise procedure is necessary. By circling around the point of oblivion, now turning this way, now that, by connotation, not denotation, by waiting, as Heidegger would say, not pointing, the point will perhaps come to meet us.

Now, for the ancients, though Pythagoras had travelled and learned much of God, nature and humanity in Egypt, Babylon, Crete (and perhaps even India, whence he would have acquired the designation Pitta Guru), from the Greek point of view what he taught and practiced was a form of Orphism. Indeed, from quite early on a number of Orphic texts were even attributed to him, both confirming his Orphism and suggesting the nature of Orpheus to be an angelic, initiatic state perhaps similar to that of Hermes Trismegistus. Thus to understand the riddle of Pythagoras we must confront the prior riddle of Orpheus, from whom tradition asserts that Pythagoras derived most of what we associate with the idea of Pythagoreanism, including the Numbers. Witness Iamblichus, who writes: "If anyone wishes to learn what were the sources whence these men derived so much piety, it must be said that a perspicuous paradigm of Pythagoric theology according to Numbers is in a certain respect to be found in the writings of Orpheus. Nor is it to be doubted that Pythagoras, receiving auxiliaries from Orpheus, composed his *Treatise Concerning the Gods . . .* [which] contains the flower of the most mystical place in Orpheus." Indeed, according to this sacred discourse it was Orpheus who, learning from his mother on Mount Pangaeum, said that the eternal essence of number is the most providential principle of the universe, of heaven and earth, and the intermediate nature. In other words, as Syrianus says: "The Pythagoreans received from the theology of Orpheus the principles of intelligible and intellectual numbers, assigning them an abundant progression and extending their dominion as far as sensibles themselves." And not only numbers, of course, but the entire religious framework of their study was Orphic from the Greek point of view. That is, we can find the whole of Pythagorean number theory in Orpheus, but embodied in mythological, symbolic, religious language.

Indeed, we must never forget that, from many points of view, Pythagoras was primarily a 'religious' teacher. Aristoxenus, a pupil of Aristotle and friend of the Pythagoreans of his day, wrote of them: "Every distinction they lay down as to what should be done and not done aims at conformity with the divine. This is their starting-point: their whole life is ordered with a view to following God, and it is the governing principle of their philosophy."

Note here the identity of philosophy with following God. Pythagoras, who was traditionally the first to call himself a philosopher, clearly meant something different by it than we. Men come to life, he said, as to a festival: most come to buy and sell and compete in the many competitions that are offered, but some come simply to observe, revere and contemplate the order, beauty and purpose of what is occurring, the golden unifying thread of essential wisdom that holds, binds all together. As Heidegger suggests, the philosopher is thus one who loves—*philein*—this wisdom—*sophia*. Love here having the connotation of amity, harmony, correspondence—Platonic friendship almost—rather than the striving yearning which is *eros* or the purely spiritual identity which is *agape*. Though these three loves are all one Love, the Greek can distinguish without separating, and I think that *philein* definitely has a friendly feeling of cooperation and community, of familial affection between equals and codependents. The philosopher is the friend, the intimate, of wisdom—holds amicable discourse with her. We may recall Philolaus' definition of harmony as the common thought of separate thinkers or the agreement of disagreeing elements, the reciprocal unity or third in which two things are brought together. The philosopher, then, is one whose thinking is in accord or harmony with wisdom, and whose practice of philosophy is devotion and dedication to it. This is why Heidegger says that *philein* here means *homolegein*, to speak in accordance with the wisdom which for Pythagoras, since only like can know like, is itself a harmony and a *philia*—in other words with the wisdom which is the Kosmos, that divine, true and beautiful order held together harmoniously by bonds of amity, reciprocity and affection or sympathy. The Pythagorean philosopher thus strove to align his being, unite his thinking—though these are one, not two—with the thinking and being sources of the Kosmos, i.e., the Gods, Numbers or Archetypes. Assimilation to the divine, then, imitation of it, by the practice of a way of life—*philosophy* a word meaning in its beginning a right relationship with the universe and with God—the famous "Pythagorean way of life," was what Pythagoras taught. Pythagoras' teaching is thereby 'religious' rather than scientific or philosophical, though these three of course are one for him, perhaps distinguishable—though this is not clear—but certainly not divisible. By the same token all three are quite different from what we usually consider them. Indeed, his bringing of these together, in a new way, with a social and artistic vision also, is what from ancient times accorded him the status, quite specifically, of a religious genius, one blessed with a religious revelation or mission. "A greater good never came, nor ever will come to mankind," wrote Iamblichus, "than that which was imparted by the Gods through this Pythagoras." And what he had in mind was not that Pythagoras inaugurated a new approach to nature or to mind, though he would have agreed these were important if he had had the language to articulate them. What Iamblichus means is a little different. Just before making this statement he has said that Pythagoras was associated by many with Apollo—Pythian and Hyperborean. And just after it he invokes Aristotle to the effect that one of the principal arcana of Pythagorean philosophy was the division of beings into three kinds: Gods, humans and such as Pythagoras. In other words, Pythagoras was felt to augur a new kind of being, the possibility of a new kind of being. Or rather that consciousness manifested a new religious or *redemptive* possibility in Pythagoras. And it is this religious aspect, at once Orphic and Apolline, that I want to look at first.

> A tree rose up. O pure over-rising!
> O Orpheus sings! O high tree in the ear!
> And all was quiet. Yet even in that quiet
> came forth a new beginning, sign and transformation.
>
> Animals of stillness pushed from the clear,
> opened wood of lair and nest;
> and it happened that not from cunning
> and not from fear were they so quiet,
>
> but from listening. Bellow, cry, roar
> seemed small in their hearts. And where hardly
> even a hut had been to receive this,
>
> a shelter from darkest desire,
> with an entry, whose posts shake—
> there, in hearing, you made a temple for them.

(Rilke, *The Sonnets to Orpheus*, First Series, 1.
Trans. C. Bamford.)

Rilke clearly realized the mystery and the magic, the dream, the presence and the premonition which is Orpheus, sensing in him more than myth and history, something akin perhaps to consciousness itself. For Goethe, too, this was the case, and Orpheus, and Orphic 'Archetypal Words'—*Urworte*—came to stand for the very archetypes of organic being. Thus, for the Renaissance, Orpheus was of the 'prisci theologi'— the Greek representative of 'ancient theology', the peer of Moses, Zoroaster, Hermes Trismegistus. And this was the view of the Greeks themselves for whom, as Proclus said all theology—Homer, Hesiod,

Pythagoras, Plato—was the "child of Orphic mystagogy." Yet Orpheus is a mystery, and in many ways has always been so, from the beginning, that is, from the time of Pythagoras and Plato, who while tacitly proclaiming themselves Orphics changed Orphism so much that a hiatus—what Bachelard would call "an epistemological rupture"—was placed between them and their founder that we, Pythagoreans and Platonists, have not yet succeeded in overcoming. There, indeed, is our task.

Briefly, the problem is and was twofold. Firstly, the Orphic teaching which is mythological, symbolic, connotative, concrete and synthetic was incompatible and increasingly incomprehensible to the rising analytic, denotative and abstract self-conscious mentality. Secondly, his history was odd. No one knew anymore where Orpheus had come from. As a 'person' he was dated sometime between 1500–1200 B.C., for he had supposedly sailed, after a visit to Egypt, with Jason on the *Argo*, eleven generations before the Trojan War, in search of the Golden Fleece. The search for the Fleece, of course, suggests an alchemical or Hermetic association, while the visit to Egypt, if at that time, brings Orpheus and the Orphic impulse tantalizingly into association with Akhenaton (c. 1377), the creator of a radical, solar theism that rejected not only the subtle theology of Amun-Ra-Prah but also the ancient canons of proportion and measure, substituting for them a kind of naturalism, in which Akhenaton and his family were portrayed in 'androgynous' form. This is interesting because esoterically Akhenaton is considered a premonition of the coming Solar Age—a mixed, androgynous principle mediating between the passing Osirian and the rising Horian emphases. The relevance here lies in the fact that Osiris and Horus, according to Plutarch, were Dionysus and Apollo of the Greeks, between whom, as we shall see, Orpheus is precisely the mediator.

The historical manifestation of Orphism, however, does not occur until about half a millennium after this, when Orpheus appears as a prophet or priest of Dionysus, a reformer of the ancient mysteries, who at the same time paradoxically is an initiate of Apollo and a proclaimer of a solar monotheism. And it is this Orphism which, while clearly constituting a movement of religious renewal or reform, is actually more of a revolution. For what Orphism seemed to have proclaimed was the Orphic way of life, the possibility of any individual attaining by his own effort, together with the action of grace, a transcendent purity synonymous with divinity. The revolutionary aspect lay both in the fact that the Orphic way was open to all and so universalized the Mystery and hieratic initiations of the past epoch, releasing the one from determination by sacred geography and the other from determination by caste and Temple, and also in that, as far as one can gather, Orphism taught the possibility or promise of resurrection: the idea of a transcendent, unfallen aspect of the soul, which we may call the Daimon.

Who then was this founder? Looking more closely at the myth we discover the following. Orpheus was the son of the Muse Calliope—that is, the Muse of *Poetry*, the Leader of the Muses—either by Apollo, their chief, or by Oeagrus, A Dionysian River-Water-Wine God. In any event, then, his grandmother would have been Mnemosyne, Memory, the mother of the Muses, and Zeus himself would have been his grandfather. It was Apollo on the other hand who gave him his lyre, which had originally belonged to Hermes who had exchanged it for the *Caduceus*. Apollo and Hermes (and so Orpheus) are brought into the closest connection, as are the Caduceus and the Lyre; and we may therefore associate Orpheus with the Hermetic tradition, that is, with the science, cosmology (alchemy) and perfection of the intermediate or human realm, the realm mediating between Heaven and Earth.

Orpheus then, taught to play on his lyre by the Muses—and so too we may imagine by Mnemosyne and Apollo—created or introduced the arts of prophetic poetry (under which head we may include theology, mythology, hymns), song and dance, so excelling at these that by the beauty of his harmonies all nature—trees, stones and animals—joined together in peace and joy. His science, in other words, was a magical one which brought all nature to some kind of blessed consummation. And in the same spirit other sciences and inventions, medicine, agriculture, ritual, astrology, architecture, mathematics were all attributed to Orpheus.

This is the figure, then, whom we must see married to the fateful Eurydice who, bitten by a snake, was taken down to Hades. Orpheus, descending after her, implored Pluto to permit her return. This was granted him, of course, on condition that he not look back upon her until she stood in the full sunlight. Later versions say that Orpheus failed; earlier versions have him completely successful. Here we may note, without comment for the moment, that according to Heraclitus Hades and Dionysus are one and the same; we may further note the similarity of this story and the gnostic one of Christ and Sophia—a similarity borne out by the more timid medieval mind's interpretation of the story in terms of spirit and soul. This last interpretation is supported by the most recent etymological findings concerning the Greek word *nous* or spirit/mind as derived from a whole cluster of words having to do with the return to life and light from death and darkness.

Finally, it is told of Orpheus that he rose daily to greet the sun on Mount Pangaeum, calling Helios whom he named Apollo the greatest of the Gods, for which the Maenads, followers of Dionysus, dismembered him, casting his head into the River Hebros, whence it floated out to sea, coming to land on Lesbos where it long continued to prophesy. Alternatively it is said that Orpheus, having introduced the rites of Dionysus into Greece, had to suffer the death of his God. As Rilke wrote:

> Finally they tore you, impelled by vengeance,
> while your sound still lingered in rock and lions,
> in trees and birds. You still sing there now.
>
> O you lost God! You endless trace!
> Only because in the end hate divided you
> are we now nature's mouth and listeners.

(Rilke, *The Sonnets to Orpheus:* First Series, 26.
Trans. C. Bamford.)

But before getting into that, and to the question of the relations between Apollo and Dionysus, and to the mythology, we must first consider something else.

Namely, that there is an echo in this Orphic story of something extremely archaic, of an almost primordial tradition and time. It comes at us from almost every aspect, and if we had to give it a name we would call it "Shamanic." And certainly Orpheus is that, as Eliade points out, not only in his descent into Hades, but in his healing, his love of music, his charms, his powers of divination. Indeed from that point of view, as Giorgio de Santillana says, "Shamanism is not primitive at all but belongs, as all our civilizations do, to the vast company of ungrateful heirs of some almost unbelievable near-Eastern ancestor who first dared to understand the world as created according to number, measure and weight." And that is true, but I think it confuses the issue. In a sense the key word here is music, for though Orpheus was the "divine musician" his music primarily and primordially was prophetic, divinely inspired *song*, that is, *poetry*. Orpheus harks back to an ancient time when words and things were not yet separated but were united in a kind of melodic chant. Naming, singing, was identical with creation, with making reality. Or rather, in naming, the Gods spoke through the name. To sing was to invoke the Gods, for only the God, the Archetype had a name. In this sense poetry was science; language was knowledge and power: at least in the mouth of the prophet-poet-shaman, language was the language of the Gods. As it says in the Vedas: "The gods created the hymns first, then the fire, then the burnt offering. . . ." The essence of this view, which Owen Barfield has termed "original participation," is that there stands behind phenomena, on the other side of them from us, something which is of the same nature as humanity. Of this vision, music is the privileged model, both as to cosmology and as to communication. Of this *urkultur* of poetry, prophecy, theology and inspired knowledge Nora Chadwick writes: "Everywhere the gift of poetry is inseparable from divine inspiration. Everywhere this inspiration carries with it knowledge. . . . Always this knowledge is uttered in poetry which is accompanied by music. . . . Music is everywhere the medium of communication with spirits." In other words, behind every sensible phenomenon there lies a reality of an animistic, super-sensible order, and just as one can make an open string vibrate by sounding its own note on a nearby instrument, so one may conjure up and communicate with a spirit by providing it with a song or tone. The universe, which is body, is song from this point of view, and Orpheus is the child of what he teaches. "Song is being," says Rilke. Marius Schneider writes in *The New Oxford History of Music*: "To produce a sound, effort must be made. The bowstring has to be stretched, and the breath must impinge on a sharp resisting edge. The ground must be stamped down. All life arises solely from stamping, from the tension of two opposing factors, which have to sacrifice their strength, if need be their life, for the birth of new life. . . ." This is a fundamental Orphic notion as we shall see—enacted typically in the polarity of Aether and Chaos, Apollo and Dionysus—that in creation a sacrifice has been made, a debt must be paid. Life is a gift, imposing certain duties and obligations, behind which as Cause and Origin lies a cosmic, universal primordial sacrifice that must be atoned, harmonized. This is what Plato refers to when he says that we are prisoners of the Gods—an idea which seen in Orphic perspective and with Christian hindsight is clearly not primitive at all.

With all this in mind, then, let us consider the Orphic theology or cosmogeny, from which Pythagoras reputedly derived his philosophy and to which, in fact, all transcendent, symbolic imaginal philosophy may trace its roots.

We begin with an ineffable First Principle or Principle of Principles, *Chronos*, conceived under the aspect of Infinite Time. Proclus describes it as "Once-Beyond": it is in fact irreducible, indescribable, incomprehensible. Why under the aspect of Time? This is very difficult. I will hazard two suggestions. First, this is a dynamic cosmogeny of action in which action is anterior to time-space-movement-matter in any form. Second, this primacy of Infinite Time suggests the possibility of conceiving of the Orphic Gods, which after all become the Pythagorean Numbers, as, in some sense, Rhythms. In any event, Chronos, this Ineffable First, polarizes, that is, adds itself to itself, presents itself to itself, doubles itself, giving rise to two principles: *Aether*, that is Heaven or Fire, a male principle, and *Chaos*, that is, What is Poured or Water, a female principle. Demythologizing these two principles, the Platonic Pythagoreans will call them *Peras*, a Principle of Limitation or Distinction, and *Apeiron*, a Principle of Unlimitedness or Lack of Distinction or Indefinitude. That is to say, as an Islamic source has it: "When from the Cause emanates One, there emanates from it Not-One," that is: Two. Thus it is between One and Two that creation occurs, and Plato will call the Principle of Intelligible Matter, the *Apeiron*, the Indefinite Dyad. What is important is not to confuse this Principle of the Unlimited with anything related to matter as we know it. Indeed one of the first things to be overcome in these questions is, as Coleridge says, the obsession with matter, the need for a Matter as a datum. "As soon as this gross prejudice," he writes "is cured by the appropriate discipline, and the Mind is familiarized to the contemplation of Matter as a product in time, the resulting phenomenon of the equilibrium of two antagonist forces, Attraction and Repulsion . . . the idea of creation alone remains." Coleridge, in fact, is very good on these things. As what he calls a "transcendental philosopher" he says not "Give me matter and motion and I will construct you the universe," as Descartes does, but rather: "Grant me a nature having two contrary forces, one of which tends to expand infinitely, while the other strives to apprehend or find itself in this infinity, and I will call up the world of intelligences with the whole system of their representations to arise before you." In other words: "Every power in nature and in spirit must evolve an opposite as the sole means and conditions of its manifestation: and all opposition is a tendency to reunion." This is true universally. Even God, the Unknowable Cause without Cause, must evolve an opposite by the necessity of Himself, and that opposite can only be Himself, so that the principle of polarity becomes the principle of identity. In other words, to manifest Himself to Himself, to know Himself, to take form, Chronos must place Himself as Aether before Himself as Chaos: or rather, must flow forth from Himself as Chaos to return to Himself as Aether. Thus even the Nothing before itself becomes Something: in fact as we shall see becomes Seed, Light, Power, Vision: which we might call with Schwaller de Lubicz the "Cosmic or Divine Ego," the Divine "I am."

This is the teaching from the beginning. As Philolaus, the first Pythagorean to write anything down, said: "Nature in the Universe was fitted together [i.e. harmonized] from the Limiting and the Unlimited, both the Universe as a whole and everything in it." Just so Plato, in his unwritten doctrines, affirmed that the One and the Indefinite Dyad were the principles of all things, even of the Eide, the Forms, themselves. And in the *Philebus* he calls it a gift from the Gods, a gift passed on in the form of a saying, namely: "All things that are ever said to be consist of a one and a many, and have in their nature a conjunction of limit and unlimitedness." Note the language: everything is formed, fitted together, by a conjunction, a marriage: "Great is the mystery of marriage," says the Gospel of Philip, "for by it the world is created."

This is the Orphic version, too. Chronos, polarized by addition into Aether and Chaos, forms an Ellipse, an Egg: silver, bright, shining. This we may say is the Golden Germ, seed, womb and embryo of all things, in Sanskrit the *Hiranyagharba*, which is but another name for *Prajapati*, the Creator, the Lord of Produced Beings. So, too, in Orphism the Egg cracks, revealing the perfected manifestation of the conjunction of the two principles, called *Phanes*. Here we must note that while Chronos must in some sense have contained these two natures, It did so in utter darkness of potentiality, while Phanes in some sense manifests them— for Phanes, Protogonos, First-born of beings, is threefold. He-She is Phanes, first of all, who first shone forth and appeared in a blaze of light, illuminating, lighting, creating. This name was said to derive from *pheinein*, to shine; from which we derive phenomenon or what is illuminated. But to begin with Phanes only illuminates himself, that is, Chronos, giving to him an ineffable body of light. He is thus the knower-known, the Creator-created, Fiat Lux and Logos: the primordial cosmic divine Anthropos. As threefold First Adam, he is also Erikapaius, power, masculine, and Metis, intelligence, feminine. In other words, the first form or salt, conjunction of Aether and Chaos, Fire and Water, is Light-Intelligence-Power, a triple being also called in the cosmogeny Eros, Pan and Dionysus, the first of three.

This Phanes-Dionysus is symbolized as a God without a body—he is entirely spiritual—with golden wings on his side, bulls' heads about him and a monstrous serpent encircling his head, with every form of creature engraved upon it. Accordingly he is, as Proclus has shown, the model or paradigm of the universe, the seed of all. As Plato teaches in the *Timaeus*, the universe is one single, visible living being made by the Demiurge after the model of the most perfect intelligible living being. And what difference is there, Proclus asks, thinking of the Orphic Egg, between calling it an Egg or Seed or that which is unfolded from it, namely Phanes, a being or animal. In fact, as the Pythagoreans knew, the difference is most important, for between Egg and Animal, between seed and fruit, the stages or logic of development unfold. Hence Phanes, unfolding from the Egg, as Proclus says, "antecedently comprehends or unfolds in himself the Causes of the secondary orders." That is, in this process of the coming into mediated identity of Unspeakable Chronos as Phanes there is contained the idea of logical development. In Phanes, as Unity, all Numbers, that is, relations or phases of development, are contained. However, since at this stage there is not yet any space-time-movement-matter, these numbers or activities are identical with what undergoes them: they are what they know and govern. At this point we must recall that this Phanes is at once the Divine Self-Identity and Cosmic I am. "Keep these things in thy mind, dear son, and in thy heart," says Orpheus in a fragment to his student Musaeus, "well knowing all the things of long ago, even from Phanes." Here then we have the basis of a Pythagorean theory of knowledge. The innate consciousness of humanity is total.

Continuing this cosmogeny which is at once anthropogeny and epistemology, Phanes, having his own daughter-consort aspect Nyx, or Night, produces Ouranos and Gaia, Ouranos, according to Plato, meaning "looking upward" and so signifying the pure intelligible world of Nous or mind, the level of contemplation according to Olympiodorus.[2] This level now produces in turn, by contemplation Plotinus will say, besides the Fates and Karmic Powers, the Titans: Chronos (Time/Saturn), Rhea (Earth), Okeanos (Space) and Tethys (Disposer). Chronos, of course, takes over from Ouranos, castrating him and marrying his own sister, Rhea. The age of Chronos now begins which is paradoxically at once the Golden Age of Saturn or "the urn of Being"—Chronos is said to mean sated "intelligence" and purification—and also the beginning of time. In this sense it marks a fall, indeed a fall into the body of both reason/discourse, i.e., soul, and birth and death. It is the realm of *dianoia* and marks the moment when, as Plotinus so beautifully puts it, the soul, through self-will temporalizes herself: "There was a nature which was forward and wished to own and rule itself and had chosen to strive for more than was present to it. Thus it started to move, and along with it also moved time, and the movement was towards the ever-still-coming and later, not towards the self-same but towards the ever and again other.

2. Interestingly, in the *Cratylus* Plato also gives "looking upwards" as the meaning of *anthropos* or human being. Thus we are reminded that each level is human. Indeed, as Olympiodorus says of these four reigns of Orpheus—by which he means the reigns of Ouranos, Chronos, Zeus, and Dionysus (Phanes, the First Adam of Light being entirely spiritual and of the First Day, the Beginning)—they are "not sometimes existent, sometimes non-existent, but they are always there and they represent in mystical language the several degrees of virtue that our soul can practice. . . ."

. . . Thus also the Soul, when she made the sensible world. . . first of all temporalized herself, generating time as a substitute for eternity. . . . As the Soul imparts her activities in portions—one succeeding another and succeeded by a different one—she generated succession as such along with her being active; and at one with discursive thought which is each time different from the preceding one, there came forth what had not been before. . . ." Or, as the Orphic Hymn to Chronos says:

> Unbreakable is the hold you have on the boundless cosmos,
> O Chronos, begetter of time, Chronos of contrasting discourse,
> Child of Earth and Starry Heaven,
> In you there is birth and decline, august and prudent Lord of Rhea
> Who, as progenitor, dwell in every part of the world. . . .

Although with Chronos time and death arose, to begin with—one imagines for the duration of the Golden Age or Earthly Paradise—he ate all his children, that is kept them within himself, until Rhea concealed Zeus from him, giving him a stone instead. Zeus, then, attaining sovereignty, overthrows his father, casting the Titans into Tartarus, and the Age of Zeus thus begins. However, we must not forget that each contains the whole. Zeus, for instance, is said to swallow Phanes, thereby making himself the beginning, middle and end of the Universe. That is, the whole is still wholly present. Then, cutting a long story short, Zeus conjoins with his syzygy to produce Dionysus, Bakchos, also called Zagreus. The story now goes that Hera, another aspect of the consort Rhea-Demeter-Persephone, jealous of the child Dionysus, releases the Titans from Tartarus. These, whitening their faces, lure the child, engrossed in his own image in a mirror, away from his guardians, tear him to pieces, roast him and eat him. Zeus, arriving on the scene too late, strikes the Titans with his lightning bolt. From the ashes then, or the smoke, Zeus creates humankind, a mixed creature of Dionysian and Titanic elements. That is one ending: in the other Apollo comes and gathers up the pieces.

Here again, of course, we are faced with the relation between Dionysus and Apollo, than which, as Jane Harrison says, "mythology has left us no tangle more intricate and assuredly no problem half so interesting." Orpheus himself is clearly an Apolline figure, yet his God, the God of Orphism, is equally clearly Dionysus. Orpheus, and Orphism, then, lead from one to the other. However, we must not imagine any opposition between these, rather a kind of complementarity. The universe is of one piece—it is a "one only": one humanity, one nature, one universe, one God—and there is no more an opposition between Apollo and Dionysus than between the Sun and the Moon, or between Principles of Transcendence and Immanence. Plutarch, in his Essay on the meaning of *Ei* engraven over the Gate of Apollo's Temple at Delphi, at one point speaks of the "E" as representing the five or quinary, the primordial marriage of even and odd, two and three. At the same time, he says, five represents nature, for just as nature taking a grain of wheat for seed will diffuse and produce many forms and species of growth, to return once again to seed which once more will contain that same potentiality, so the number five will always return to itself, that is when multiplied will produce either itself or ten.

> And this as far as all number can extend, this number imitating the beginning or First Cause which governs the universe. For as that First Cause, preserving the world by itself, does reciprocally perfect itself by the world, as Heraclitus says of fire . . . so the congress of five with itself is framed by Nature to produce nothing imperfect or strange, but has limited changes. . . . Now if anyone shall say, What is all this to Apollo? we will answer, that it concerns not Apollo only, but Bacchus also, who has no less to do with Delphi than Apollo himself. For we have heard the divines . . . saying and singing that God is of his own nature incorruptible and eternal, but yet, through a certain decree and reason, suffers changes of himself, having sometimes his nature kindled into a fire, and making all things alike, and otherwhiles becoming various, in different shapes, passions and powers, like unto the World, and is named by this best known of names. But the wiser, concealing from the vulgar the change . . . call him both Apollo from his unity, and Phoebus from his purity and unpollutedness. But as for the passion and change of his conversion into winds, water, earth and stars. . . plants and animals . . . this they obscurely represent as a certain distraction and dismembering; and they now call him Dionysus, Zagreus . . . exhibiting and chanting forth certain corruptions, disparitions, deaths and resurrections. . . .

Dionysus thus is the Divine Principle in its genesis or becoming; torn to pieces, sacrificed by the Titans, it must be reassembled, remembered; Apollo is the transcendent principle, that aspect of the Divine whereby this is made possible, whereby nature or becoming is made supernatural once again. At the same time, as transcendent presence, Apollo is the directing wisdom of becoming, simultaneously present and ineffable in all natural processes as the other principle of wisdom.

From another point of view, Dionysus stands rather for the descent of the Soul, Apollo for its ascent or return—the one suggesting immanence or reincarnation, the other transcendence and resurrection.[3] "The souls of men, seeing their images in the mirror of Dionysus, as it were have entered into that realm in a downward leap from the Supreme; yet even they are not cut off from their origin, from the Divine Intellect," so writes Plotinus. The Dionysian fallen soul may have forgotten its Apolline, Daimonic nature, but it is not cut off from it. That is, there is a part of the soul that remains, or remained, forever unfallen, out of time. In this sense, Apollo is the Savior of Dionysus. Damascius writes: "When Dionysus had projected his reflection in the mirror, he followed it and thus was scattered over the universe. Apollo gathers him and brings him back to heaven, for he is the purifying God and truly the Savior of Dionysus, and therefore he is celebrated as the 'Dionysus-giver'. Like Kore, the soul descends into generation, like Prometheus and the Titans she is chained to the body. She frees herself by acquiring the strength of Hercules, gathers herself through the help of Apollo and Athena . . . that is, by truly purifying philosophy."

Therewith we return to Pythagoras, who, as we said, 'invented' this notion of philosophy that Damascius teaches, and whose God, as we said, was Apollo. Or rather: whose teaching, and practice and way was that of Apollo. First it must be stressed that these notions that Orphism introduced, whether they derived primarily from Egypt, Crete, Thrace or even Babylon (and an equally convincing case may be made for all four) were new to Greece. Apollo is always remembered as a 'late-comer' into the company of Gods, and the idea of a transcendent self was not known in Homeric times. More than a late-comer, however, I think we should think of Apollo as one who was 'still arriving'. Where from? He was called Hyperborean, and though through Thrace and Crete the idea may have come from the North, as Anne Macaulay will suggest, we should not necessarily consider him as arriving only from the geographic north but

---

3. But what is resurrection? It is the uncovering at any given time of the elements that have "arisen."

Now if you should recall having read the Gospel that Elias appeared—and Moses—in His company, do not suppose that resurrection is an apparition. It is not an apparition; rather it is something real. Instead one ought to maintain that the world is an apparition rather than resurrection. . . . But let me not deprecate the circumstances of this world. . . . Simply: resurrection is not of this sort, for it is real.

It is what is constant:
and the revealing of what truly exists.
And it is what one receives in exchange for the circumstances of this world:
and a migration into newness.
For incorruption is streaming down upon corruption:
And light is streaming down upon darkness, swallowing it.
And the fulness is filling up its lack.
"The Gnostic Treatise on Resurrection" from *The Nag Hammadi Library*

rather also from the Cosmic North, the Sacred or Transcendent Peak of the Cosmic Mountain, the pole and focus of all true orientation. Another similar interpretation makes him a 'Shepherd God', another a messenger or mediator, like the Archangel Michael. All these bespeak his transcendent origin, from which point of view we may take his bow and lyre to symbolize projection, emanation into immanence.

Against this base, then, Pythagoras carries out his mission. But in fact things are moving very fast and he institutes some very radical changes. Let us pick him up as he arrives in Crotona, having passed his years of wandering and apprenticeship: in Phoenicia, on Mount Carmel, in Egypt, Babylon, Crete. He arrives, as C. J. de Vogel says, in Italy with certain definite views: views on the structure of the universe, on the nature of man and his place in it, and views on his own calling. The ancient sources are unanimous. "All show us Pythagoras as a man who, because of his views on cosmic order, felt called upon to form and lead a human community to teach people to take their appropriate place in the cosmos."

We have had philosophy as a Pythagorean innovation, and now we have cosmos, again a word we must rethink to understand it as he meant it. Cosmos is much more than just the universe. It includes the idea of beauty, order or goodness, and structural perfection which we might call truth. All of these are held together by the prior principle of unity, which, manifesting as Cosmos—one mass of Life and Consciousness as the *Corpus Hermeticum* will say—becomes a teaching of the harmony, sympathy and kinship of all things—a universal interrelationship and interdependence: a harmony, which in the broadest sense we may take to be the void of God, the *a priori* law and divine order, incomprehensible in itself but presiding over all things. As Phanes we said was the model of the cosmos, so the process of unfoldment he resumed and contained within himself—all the Numbers, Gods, Archetypes—is Harmony: the relationship between phases.

Thus in his public speeches Pythagoras affirmed as cosmic law the primary principle of universal amity or friendship, whose embodiment could be achieved by temperance, responsibility, affection, honesty, respect and spontaneity. And at the center of these he placed a religious emphasis: for the young, philosophy; for the Elders, the Temple of the Muses; and for the women, leadership in devotion.

As for the Pythagorean School, the heart of this was constituted by the *Mathematici*, those who practiced disciplines, *mathesis*. First, an oral interview; next, a probationary period of observation; then, a period of neglect, a three year residency on the periphery of the community;

then, finally, entrance into the community, which began with a five-year silence. During this period one could listen, but not question; one began to practice the various disciplines of recollection, temperance, memory—memory was much stressed; music and chanting were daily employed, both as purification (hence recollection) and as worship—these would be the "Orphic hymns"—and there was dancing, also; goods were held in common, in a cenobitic life. This was the first stage. Next came the real mathematics or practices; arithmetic, geometry, theory of music, stereometry, astronomy, music. These were still a means and not an end. Proclus says that the Pythagoreans recognized that everything we call learning is remembering, and that through awakened sense-perception learning has its source within us, in our understanding's attending to itself. The explanation is, he says, that what remembers is the understanding—dianoia, the level of Chronos in the cosmology—which is that part of the soul having its source and essence in the divine spirit, Ouranos, where the Archetypes or Numbers have their being, and so it has prior knowledge of these, even when not using it. Possessing them all in a latent fashion, it can bring them to light when set free of hindrances, all of which stem from objectification by the senses. Every divisible thing, everything divided from us, is an obstacle to our returning upon ourselves. "Consequently," Proclus writes, "when we remove these hindrances we are able to know by understanding itself the ideas that it has, and then we become knowers in actuality, that is, producers of genuine knowledge."

There, then, is one end of Pythagorean philosophy, to become a producer of genuine knowledge. The implication at one level is that the forms of thought are the laws of form, and that that through which the mind understands is one with that through which the world is created, so that knowledge of mind is knowledge of creation. "You see, then, my friend," writes Plato in the *Republic*, "that this branch of study really seems indispensable to us, since it plainly compels the soul to employ pure thought with a view to truth itself." The soul's self-knowledge in pure thought thus becomes its knowledge of the universe. In other words, the intention seems to have been for the student entering the Pythagorean school by means of various disciplines to become one — A-pollo, not many—and by becoming one enter into relation with the all—Dionysus.

That was the intention, but, as Proclus' description shows perhaps only too well, there was a tendency in the intention to isolate the knowing and the knower from what was known, a tendency containing its shadow, or opposite, namely the isolation and separation of the known.

By the known, here, I mean the sense world. Though Pythagoras himself seems to have taken great care not to separate Numbers from things, this was a vision the consciousness of the time did not seem to be able to hold, for by Plato, who is a Pythagorean, the Numbers, which he calls forms or ideas, are already in some sense separated from the sense world: they are no longer things; nor are things, as they were for Thales, hieroglyphs, full of Gods. They are and they aren't, and Plato is suspicious both of the senses and of the sense world. Consequently *epistime/* knowledge/the world of ideas becomes separated from the sense-perceptible world—not that the senses do not mislead, but the idea that the senses can be transformed begins to be doubted. Also the ethical/moral nature of the sense-perceptible world begins to be lost. Though Philolaus says that "everything that can be known has a number, for without number nothing can be thought or known" and that "number fits all things into the soul through sense-perception, making them recognizable and comparable with one another, in that Number gives them body," the emphasis in later Pythagoreanism is increasingly one-sidedly turned upon the soul or mind, its laws, and there is little suggestion of friendly congress—philo-sophia—with the wisdom of 'nature' or the so-called sense world. There is no give and take, or rather there is nothing given in turn for what the 'senses' have provided. And in fact the form of Pythagoras' School makes clear why this occurred.

Original Orphism, however, equally clearly harked back to something different, at least held the promise of something different. Meaning and experience are still one in the sense-object; what a thing is, its meaning, is revealed in the perception of it. Through sense-images, which are names, words, songs, the Gods are spoken. So knowledge is concrete, something seen, witnessed, lived. By the time of Pythagoras, however, it seemed as though meaning and object were coming apart, the Gods were growing silent, meaning seemed to be moving to another dimension. As it did so, the senses were increasingly seen to betray and mislead.

Here we are almost faced with the story of Orpheus again—the *Urgesang aller Wesen*, the Archetypal Story of All Beings, as Herder called it. Orpheus lost the world, the beautiful soul of manifestation, and he descended down after it into Hades, which Heraclitus tells us is one with Dionysus, the granulated world of birth and death. He failed, in the version taught in Greece, to raise her up, but he forever holds the promise of so doing, of the reunion of mind and nature, being and becoming, humanity and the universe. In other words, he presents the possibility of a non-objectifying perception, an imaginal thinking.

Pythagoras seems to stand for, or rather, at a turn in the story. He seems to stand, in some ways, for the transformation, the development of pure thinking, of a thinking, again, in some ways free of the senses. In this sense, he opens the door to Docetism and idealism, to the kind of rational mysticism, mystical rationality that culminates perhaps in Hegel. But this is only one side of Pythagoras' dream; the other is purely Orphic and has to do with the redemption and transfiguration of the Cosmos. It is time, I think, to return to that, to the world of the senses, to re-spiritualize it. From another point of view, this is to return to art—the speaking, disclosing, embodying of truth—as the origin of culture. We are just at the beginning. As Heidegger says,

> We are too late for the gods and too early
> for Being. Being's poem,
> just begun, is man.

Bateson struggled with this. And Goethe, as in this characteristic piece:

In observing the cosmic structure from its broadest expanse down to its minutest parts, we cannot escape the impression that underlying the whole is the idea that God is operative in Nature and Nature in God, from eternity to eternity. Intuition, observation, and contemplation lead us closer to these mysteries. We are presumptuous and venture ideas of our own; turning more modest, we merely form concepts that might be analogous to those primordial beginnings.

At this point we encounter a characteristic difficulty—one of which we are not always conscious—namely, that a definite chasm appears to be fixed between idea and experience. Our efforts to overbridge the chasm are forever in vain, but nevertheless we strive eternally to overcome this hiatus with reason, intellect, imagination, faith, emotion, illusion, or—if we are capable of nothing better—with folly.

By honest persistent effort we finally discover that the philosopher might probably be right who asserts that no idea can completely coincide with experience, nevertheless admitting that idea and experience are analogous, indeed must be so.

In all scientific research the difficulty of uniting idea and experience appears to be a great obstacle, for an idea is independent of time and place but research must be restricted within them. Therefore, in an idea, the simultaneous and successive are intimately bound up together, whereas in an experience they are always separated. Our attempt to imagine an operation of Nature as both simultaneous and successive, as we must in an idea, seems to drive us to the verge of insanity. The intellect cannot picture united what the senses present to it separately, and thus the duel between the perceived and the ideated remains forever unsolved.

From the primordial beginnings of time until now it seems as though the whole cosmic process has been moving towards a point where it is, as it were, turned inside out. We are at that turning, really that same turning still that Pythagoras was on and situated. We are still doing what he did, only we are a little further on, and so it is clearer to us that having arisen out of the cosmic process it is time to return it, to give back what we have received. Heidegger speaks of art as creation, as the bringing forth of the unconcealedness of what is; as the projecting of the unconcealedness (truth) of what is. As a letting be and a letting speak, as the setting-into-work of truth, bestowing, grounding and beginning. This is a new birth of the Orphic word, a return of Pythagoreanism into Orphism, a new directive from Apollo. It is a return to "language" as that which brings what is into the open.

> Earth, Is not this what you want: to resurrect
> in us invisibly? Is it not your dream
> to be invisible one day? Earth! Invisible!
> What's your urgent charge, if not transformation?

So Rilke in the Ninth Duino Elegy; and in the last Sonnet to Orpheus:

> In this vast night, be the magic power
> at your senses' intersection,
> the meaning of their strange encounter.
>
> And if the earthly has forgotten
> you, say to the still earth: I flow.
> To the rushing water speak: I am.

# Bibliography

Athanassakis, Apostolos N., trans. *The Orphic Hymns*. Society of Biblical Literature, Graeco-Roman Series 4. Missoula, Mont.: Scholars Press, 1977.

Barfield, Owen. *What Coleridge Thought*. Middletown, Conn.: Wesleyan University Press, 1971.

Burkert, W. *Lore and Science in Ancient Pythagoreanism*. Cambridge, Mass.: Harvard University Press, 1972.

Chadwick, Nora K. *Poetry and Prophecy*. Cambridge: At the University Press, 1942.

de Santillana, Giorgio and von Dechund, Hertha. *Hamlet's Mill*. Boston: Gambit, 1969.

de Vogel, C. J. *Pythagoras and Early Pythagoreanism*. Assen and New York: Van Gorcum, 1966.

Eliade, Mircea. *Shamanism: Archaic Techniques of Ecstasy*. Translated by Willard R. Trask. Bollingen Series LXXVI. Princeton: Princeton University, Press, 1964.

Findlay, J. N. *Plato: The Written and Unwritten Doctrines*. New York: Humanities Press, 1974.

Goethe, Johann Wolfgang von. *Goethe's Botanical Writings*. Translated by Bertha Mueller. Honolulu: University of Hawaii Press, 1952.

Guthrie, W.K.C. *Orpheus and Greek Religion*. New York: W.W. Norton & Company, 1966.

———. *The Earlier Presocratics and the Pythagoreans*. Vol. I in *A History of Greek Philosophy*. Cambridge: Cambridge University Press. 1962.

———. *The Greeks and Their Gods*. Boston: Beacon Press, 1954.

Harrison, Jane. *Prolegomena to the Study of Greek Religion*. New York: Meridian Books, 1955.

Heidegger, Martin. *Poetry, Language, Thought*. Translated by Albert Hofstadter. New York: Harper & Row, 1971.

Iamblichus. *Life of Pythagoras*. Translated by Thomas Taylor. London: John M. Watkins, 1965.

Isenberg, Wesley W., trans. "The Gospel of Philip." In *The Nag Hammadi Library*, edited by James M. Robinson. San Francisco: Harper & Row, 1977.

Mead, G.R.S. *Orpheus*. London: John M. Watkins, 1965.

Plato. *The Collected Dialogues of Plato*. Edited by Edith Hamilton and Huntington Cairns. Bollingen Series LXXI. Princeton: Princeton University Press, 1963.

Plotinus. *The Enneads*. Translated by Stephen MacKenna. 4th ed., rev. .London: Faber and Faber Limited, 1969.

Plutarch. *Plutarch's Essays and Miscellanies*. Vol. 4 in *Plutarch's Lives and Writings*, edited by A.H. Clough and William W. Goodwin. New York: The Colonial Company, Limited, 1905.

Proclus. *The Commentaries of Proclus on the Timaeus of Plato*. Translated by Thomas Taylor. London: Printed for and sold by author, 1820.

———. *Diadochus, A Commentary on the First Book of Euclid's Elements*. Translated by G. R. Morrow, Princeton: Princeton University Press, 1970.

Rilke, Rainer Maria. *Duino Elegies and The Sonnets to Orpheus*. Translated by A. Poulin, Jr. Boston: Houghton Mifflin Company, 1977.

Schwaller de Lubicz, Isha. "Akhenaton," Chapter 39 in *Her-Bak, 'Chick-Pea'*. Translated by Charles E. Sprague. New York: Inner Traditions International, 1978.

Schneider, Marius. "Primitive Music." In *The New Oxford History of Music*. London: Oxford University Press, 1957.

Spencer-Brown, G. *Laws of Form*. New York: The Julian Press, 1972.

Weil, Simone. *Intimations of Christianity among the Ancient Greeks*. Edited and translated by Elizabeth Chase Geissbuhler. London: Routledge & Kegan Paul, 1976.

——. *Notebooks*. Translated by Arthur Wills. London: Routledge & Kegan Paul, 1956.

Westerink, L. G. *The Greek Commentaries on Plato's Phaedo*: Vol. I, *Olympiodorus*; Vol. II, *Damascius*. Amsterdam: North-Holland Publishing Company, 1976, 1977.

# 2 | Ancient Temple Architecture

..........................................................*Robert Lawlor*

I N THESE TALKS I WOULD LIKE to look at ancient, and particularly Egyptian, Temple Architecture, not from the point of view of art history nor even from the point of view of religion, but instead from that of the history of science. I would like to show that Temple Architecture was symbolic language, chosen by a hieroglyphic culture for the purpose of recording its scientific philosophy and epistemological technique.

This approach should have the advantage both of revealing the relevance of the ancient position with regard to the problems facing the philosophy of science today and of preventing our exposition of Temple geometry from remaining simply a historical curiosity. Symbols have to be slain in order to resurrect, and I feel most strongly that the ancient wisdom can only gain relevance for us if it accepts the challenge of verification within the terms and data of modern science.

For this to happen, however, it will be necessary first to place the Temple in the broad context of the scientific beliefs which have appeared throughout history. Therefore, so as not to be accused of wandering away from the agreed upon topic, I would like to state right at the beginning that I feel that the title, "Ancient Temple Architecture," authorizes, and even necessitates, that we discuss four areas of thought: namely, Time, Perception, Resonance, and Symbolization.

This is my reasoning. The first word, "Ancient," implies the idea of history, which implies a particular way of perceiving and recording the passage of Time, while the second word, "Temple," is derived from the Latin, *tempus*, meaning "temporal order," and *templum*, meaning "spatial order," and the third word, "Architecture," means in Greek "the way or method of structuring what is archetypal." Temple Architecture is therefore the structuring or symbolizing of the archetypal concepts of Time and Space and thus "Ancient Temple Architecture," as our title, includes three out of our four areas of thought. The selection of "Resonance" as our fourth will become more obvious later on.

Before approaching the meaning of ancient Temple structures, then, an attempt should be made to examine the ways in which Time and Space might have been perceived, experienced and symbolized by their builders. For this reason I would like to begin by outlining certain models for these concepts which I feel are suggested by the architecture, mythology and geometry contained particularly in the Egyptian Temple of Luxor, using as a guide the voluminous work on this edifice by R.A. Schwaller de Lubicz, *Le Temple de L'Homme, Apet du Sud a Louqsor.*

In the talks that follow I shall present scientific, mythological and geometric data that may act as support for these models.

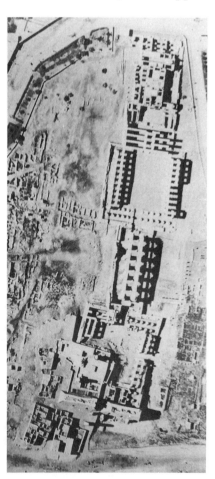 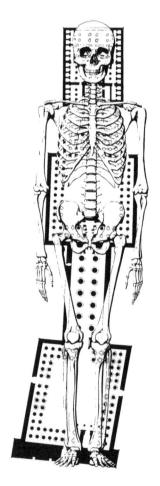

# INTRODUCTION
## Time, Perception, Resonance, Symbolization

. 1 .

It is relatively easy to demonstrate spatial concepts in relation to architecture, but Time is very difficult to conceptualize, let alone discuss, in any context. Nevertheless, those cultures which are steeped in myth generally have a model of Time which is not only cyclical but re-cyclical, one of whose essential premises is that Light is the carrier of the messages of Time, an idea which is supported by modern research in bioclocks and helio-biology.

According to this mythic perception, time, in the form of light, formed, filtered and resonated through the effects of celestial law, is drawn towards earth, "Earth" here meaning a field of objectification or manifestation.

Reaching earth, it forms, energizes, particularizes, drives, animates, creates and destroys; and is itself absorbed, assimilated, reflected, refracted, distorted, captivated, transfigured and transformed; before finally being released back again towards its celestial origin, modified, and carrying in pattern form a record of all the events that occurred during its given moment of interaction with the forces of manifestation.

From this point of view, time, like light, as it recedes from the earth towards the heavens and moves away from its phenomenal condition back towards its original condition of order based upon laws of celestial configuration, may be said to diffuse, expand and shift its spectral tonality relative to the viewing point from which it was perceived as an objective event. It follows from this that since every event in time is only the result of a complex momentary relation between a viewer and a viewed, the more an event recedes in time the more it recedes in space, and conversely. In other words, the quality of time, like that of light, changes as it recedes in space-time; and the red-shift in light has a parallel in the mythic shift in time.

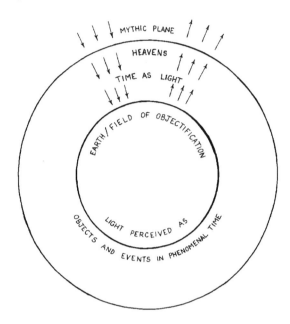

We are given an image, then, in which time is cycled and re-cycled in a volley-like exchange between a celestial organization and an earthly or manifest organization; in which there is an unfolding of a pre-pattern energy within the contingencies of emerging forms and structures; a movement in which time-light descends from a mythic to a phenomenalized level, undergoes a modification within the varied yet limited possibilities of a material state, and then returns again to the realm of potentiality.

Thus to the mythic mind an event in time may never be retrieved as a factual replication but only in its new quality as it recedes towards, or returns from, its origins in Mythic Time. History is then always either a deduction or an intuition based upon a residue of receding light in space and memory—which can only act as a symbol, not a fact, for thought. When the Egyptian priest told Herodotus that the first kings in Egypt were preceded by the gods, he was saying that phenomenal time before the period of the kings had already been absorbed back into the archetypal field of celestial organization, called in Egypt the realm of the *Neters*. In this sense, we will be considered gods to some future generation—that is, our phase and formation of light will have become a recurring influence within the possibilities of future evolution.

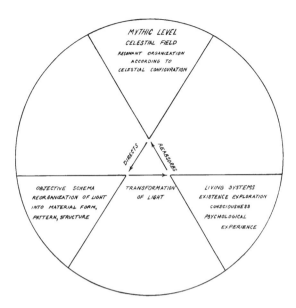

This cosmic dialogue between the existing—the changing—and the pre-existing is expressed in Egyptian mythology by the linguistic play of modulations on the verb "to become" or "to come into existence," *Kheper*, while the *Neter* of the rising sun, whose symbol is the scarab, is called *Khepri*. One text reads:

> When I manifested myself into existence, existence existed. I came into existence in the form of the Existent, which came into existence at the First Time. Coming into existence according to the mode of existence of the Existent, I therefore existed. And it is thus that the existent came into existence, for I was anterior to the two Anteriors, for my name was anterior to theirs, for I made them thus anterior to the Two Anteriors.

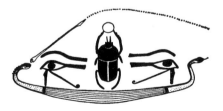

Such a cyclic and interwoven time-space metaphor, depending upon a continuous, oscillating movement in duration, in which time is conceived of as a modulation shifting through variations in tendency and intensity, is a particularly difficult image of time for us, both because we have very few terms in our language to express these types of concepts, and because we have the linguistic habit of objectifying time by applying formal, spatial, or quantitative terms to describe it. For example, we say a "long" time or a "short" time, or break it into quantified segments, such as "ten days," etc. But time, of course, is not an object, nor is it measurable in the sense that we measure space.

Thus in Egyptian, as in many languages of myth-imbued cultures, there is no absolute grammatical segmentation of time into past, present and future tenses. Such languages, on the contrary, are structured according to a continuous, graduated movement—first into a particularized condition, then out again—just as light moves in and out of phenomenal perception. For example, in hieroglyphic writing, the verb "to listen" includes, like other verbs, modulations which indicate a process of moving through various states of actualization. One form means "approaching the state of being able to listen," and another means "the state of being able to listen," and finally there is "listen." A further form indicates a continuing present: "all the time that he is listening." The future, however, may only be indicated by a sort of conditional.

It is evident, then, that each language reformulates in different ways (auditory, visual, symbolic) the experience of the mind's perception of light; and it is these language patterns which permit the experience of vibratory arrays to manifest in the realms of thought and embodied consciousness. To quote Benjamin Whorf:

> Western culture has made, through language, a provisional analysis of reality and, without correctives, holds resolutely to that analysis as final. The only correctives lie in all those other tongues which by aeons of independent evolution have arrived at different, but equally logical, provisional analyses.

The mythic analysis of reality is summarized in the essential concept underlying the Egyptian "Book of Transformations," called *The Book of what is in the Dwat*, the *Dwat* being the "inversed" or netherworld: Re, who is Consciousness in the form of light, symbolized by the Sun, becomes flesh (*Uf*), in order to know himself as embodiment. The universe of time and space is thus the field through which Light can know itself as flesh and, ultimately, flesh can know itself as Light. I would like to propose in these talks that Temple Architecture is a particularly synthetic language which describes this cosmic unfolding—a language that is a logical, even scientific, envisioning of the mythic analysis of reality.

But before we can approach the language of the Temple directly, we must acknowledge that we have been drawn into a consideration of the question of perception in general through the shifting interdependency that we have found to exist between the concept of time and the perception of time.

. 2 .

In his new book, *Mind and Nature*, Gregory Bateson delineates the subjective nature of all knowledge, due to the limitations and particularities of our perceptual activities. This interdependency between perception and what can be known of reality is, according to Bateson, "what every schoolboy should know." Such ideas, which began to break upon the world of empirical science with relativity theory and the uncertainty principle, are now often dismissed as truisms. Unfortunately, however, this is happening before we have been able to incorporate the new concept of the interdependency of perceiver and perceived into an active discipline and technique of thought.

I have already proposed one interdependency between time and the perception of time. Now I would like to examine a perceptual model given in Ulric Neisser's book *Cognition and Reality*, which is, as may be seen from the diagram, related to the model we have just used to conceptualize Mythic Time.

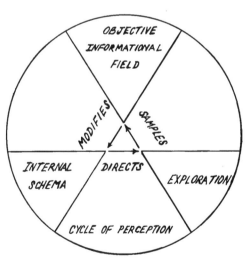

In his book, Neisser refutes the conventional linear model of perception and replaces it with a circular model in which the perceptual process takes place not instantaneously but in time, through constant accumulation. The perceiver is seen as engaged in a modifying exchange with a field of informational stimuli, that is, with information reaching him as vibratory variations carried by light, sound, etc. These patterns of varied vibrational intensity interact with a previously established anticipatory "schema" which is the coagulation of unavoidable linguistic and cultural biases subjectively maintained by the observer, the sum of his experientially acquired and internally stored cognitive perceptions. This interaction of an external object or informational field with internal "schema" will naturally tend to evoke direct exploration by the perceiver, which may then yield new information that may, in turn, modify, to some degree, the initial "schema," which may then perpetuate the cycle by directing further exploration, and so forth.

The processes of perception are thus visualized by Neisser as dynamic, cyclic triads, in which a constantly flowing circulation of interfused activity between perceiver and perceived, interiority and exteriority, subject and object, is dominated by an inherently selective schematic organization maintained within the consciousness of the perceiver in the form of patterned neural systems in the brain.

This unbroken circularity of the perceptual activity demands an image of reality which must always incorporate the sensing and cognizing organism as an inseparable aspect of perceived stimuli or events. Hence only a status of mind which simultaneously perceives not only the object field but also the structure and limitation of its own instrument in the act of perceiving can glimpse the Real. Such a status of mind appears to be achievable only through deep introspection and self-knowledge, of both a psychological and a physiological character, in combination with empirical methods of observation.

Although from a limited perspective along the continuous curve of the perceptual cycle the perceiver and the perceived, or the internal and the external, can and must be distinguished from one another, it is the continuous circular integration of perceiver and perceived that I shall be referring to as our definition of objective reality. For this reason the subject-object integration of mythology and sacred architecture appears to me to be an effective language for scientific formulation. Indeed, when we relate research from Cognitive Psychology to the implications of Heisenberg's uncertainty principle and aspects of Einstein's relativity theory, we are already carefully beginning to free ourselves from the nineteenth-century conviction that reason and experimental epistemologies have an exclusive access to the factuality of the empirical world.

In terms of Cognitive Psychology, if we tend to believe what we see, we also to a great degree see only what we have been taught to believe; and all perception is a process which provides information about the perceiver, as well as the thing perceived. This same idea was stated very clearly in ancient Hindu metaphysics:

Whether we know it or not, all things take on their reality from that which perceives them.

An Egyptian papyrus similarly speaks of three men walking together:

To one of them there are only two

—thus pointing out very simply how we forget that we are part of our own observations.

It follows, then, that perceptions, along with the mode of symbolization used to communicate them, are an inseparable aspect of universal creation. Nothing is a thing by itself. It takes its meaning and indeed its existence only in interaction with something else. From this point of view, the original and creative force, whether we call it the ultimate naked singularity, or non-polarized energy, or God, exists only insofar as creation is in interdependent relation with the perceiving consciousness. No creation comes into existence without perception. This philosophy, which leads us out of strict empiricism, need not drag us into solipsism where the observer is the only reality, if we keep in mind that the circle of perception does include actual vibrational variations of light and sound.

The Egyptians very succinctly formulated this subtle concept linguistically. In Egypt the symbol of the Eye was used to designate both the verb "to see" and the verb "to make" or "to create." We have a similar linguistic overlap in our Indo-European languages between the words "fact" and "manufacture." In summary, we may say that the factual sense of the universe is manufactured within the intelligence of the Eye.

In *Thematic Origins of Science from Kepler to Einstein,* Gerald Holton shows how pre-established cognitive "schemata" are active in the history and development of the sciences. He proposes that all communicable thoughts, no matter how empirical or mystic they may purport to be, contain intrinsic substrata of very basic assumptions such as underlie any formulated endeavor. These hidden criteria cause a pre-selection of beliefs, facts, hypotheses, explanatory and experimental methods, disciplines, life directives and goals—and no communicative teaching can escape this conceptual substratum. Thus ever-varying combinations of these thematic notions move through history, vacillating gradually, then stabilizing for a period, gaining a pervasiveness among a population and establishing the broad outlines of a culture's spiritual, aesthetic and intellectual style.

Holton points out that thematic notions tend to exist in couplet or triplet form. For instance, before a philosopher or scientist can approach the universe, he must ask, or have conscious or unconscious assumptions about, the following questions: Is the universe spatially finite, or is it infinite? Does it have a beginning and an end, or is it eternal? Is it basically a wave continuum, or is it made of distinct particles? Are the laws of development probabilistic or deterministic or predeterministic? Are these universal laws absolute or relative? Is the universe driven by an ultimate teleological goal, or is it an open ended, indeterminate eventfulness? Any formulation, any language, philosophy or teaching, Holton claims, whether scientific, religious or aesthetic, will be either overtly or unconsciously built upon assumptions falling on or between these basic polarized positions concerning the nature of reality. Our twentieth century, for instance, has witnessed a victory for the particle theory of reality, but only after a struggle which, in the course of history, has involved such thinkers as Heraclitus, Democritus, Aristotle, Einstein, de Broglie, Heisenberg, and many others.

In response to this recurring debate, Niels Bohr in 1927 offered Western scientific theory and method a profound and far-reaching conclusion. Bohr said that science should not attempt to reduce its understanding of radiation to a single, directly comprehensible mode but should accept instead the paradox that one cannot construct an experiment that simultaneously exhibits the wave and the particle aspects of matter. Each experiment at this level of penetration shows only one view. The observer's attempt should therefore be to incorporate apparently contradictory descriptions into an exhaustive overlay of the multiple aspects of a single reality. I will not go any further here into Bohr's well-known theory of complementarity, but will expand it rather into a broad, philosophical premise which relates directly to the approach to knowledge demonstrated by Temple Architecture. This is that the universe in reality always contains both polarities of all fundamental thematic notions which emerge from man's attempt to fathom its basic nature.

From this point of view we may assume that Universal Nature is a positively ambiguous passive field, which is somehow in structural or vibratory correspondence with the evolution of Mind, and which takes on and reflects certain characteristics projected onto it by the embodied intellect. Thus it has been said that man always discovers outside himself—in his cosmologies or natural science—what he is about to become.

I do not, however, intend this image of a multiple or ambiguous universe to be taken in any theoretical sense, such as is found in relativity theory, which sees events as determinable only by the positional relationships of the observer in space-time. The picture of the universe that I wish to approach is more nearly related to certain ideas presently emerging from probability equations in Quantum Mechanics. Here we find the proposition that, if an atom of, say, uranium is to decay or not to decay within a given number of seconds—and if it is not forced to decay—then it can only be determined probabilistically whether it will decay or not. This being the case, it should then be equally possible for the atom to do either one or the other. If it does not have both possibilities, then we are faced with the implication of an event that is predetermined, which is a disagreeable concept in modern physics, especially in view of the fact that, thanks to general relativity theory, every event is connected to every other event.

Paradoxically enough, then, probability theory brings up anew the whole question of predetermination and, in order to avoid it, finds it necessary to postulate at each "either/or" intersection in the life of an atom, an actual universe which expresses the extended ramifications of both possibilities evoked at that intersection. This leads to the question of whether it is possible to conceptualize a universe such that all different possible futures are not just theoretical but real possibilities. This, in turn, has led physicists to a multi-branching model, in which all possible universes are conceived of as lying in an interwoven or overlaid simultaneity, awaiting their awakening from a potential state into a manifested state as a result of the effect of events. In other words, we have a universal expression, which contains in an actual way all possibilities, but which moves and grows one way or another, due to the selected branching out of the possibilities contained in every atomic moment. Certainly, it is only in a multi-branching, simultaneously interwoven or overlaid universe that free will could exist. If an actual universe did not somewhere potentially exist containing the consequences of the choice we did not make, if only the universe resulting from the choice we did make existed, then there would be no free will or choice at all. But of course to conceive of, and respond to, such a multilevelled, simultaneous world-model would require a supra-rational conceptual level quite different from our own—one perhaps similar to the level of Higher Mind described by the Indian philosopher Sri Aurobindo:

> A universe where each God knows all the Gods and their places in existence, where each idea admits all other ideas and their right to be, each force concedes a place to all other forces and their truth and consequences; no delight of separate fulfilled existence or separate experience denies or condemns the delight of other existences and their experiences.

Let us leave here the ponderable question of perception and turn our attention to those fields of resonant and vibratory variations which we agree by consensus surround us in the form of an external world.


. 3 .

Two very important concepts arise out of the laws of resonance: resonance at a distance and the phenomenalization of tones through angulation.

Let us look at the first concept. When a piano tuner strikes his A-pitched tuning fork, it vibrates at 440 cycles per second (cps). If a nearby piano is tuned to this A above middle C, then the A string in that piano will start vibrating by itself at the same 440 cps frequency in response to the waves emitted by the fork—due to the right combination of the string's thickness, length and tension. Even the A string in a piano in the next room will start to vibrate.

From this observation, it is important to take note of several ideas. First, similar or corresponding resonant potentials in separate bodies (i.e., a tuning fork and a string) allow for a direct transfer of patterned activity; that is to say, when two elements are in a state of vibrational affinity, identical or similar patterns can pass between them across distances. Second, not only is this transfer of patterned activity possible on a basis of one-to-one equality (that is, 440 cps in one element to 440 cps in another) but also, if the sounding is forceful enough, a string tuned to 880 cps (the tone an octave above 440 cps) and a string tuned to 220 cps (one octave below) will both vibrate in response to our tuning fork at 440 cps.

In other words, there is an almost magical transfer of resonance, not only over distances but also between different octaves which—since Pythagorean thought allows us to use the characteristic laws of audible sound as a metaphor for all other periodic or oscillatory phenomena— we may think of as parallel to different definable levels of existence, such as the octave of the spirit, the octave of the mind and the octave of the body.

In order to better conceive of bodily existence as a vibratory condition, let us recall that all metabolic processes demonstrate oscillatory properties. Indeed, every living creature, from one point of view, is an electromagnetic system, and ultimately every activity is governed to some degree by electromagnetic laws. For example, our bodies are made up of molecules containing roughly the same number of positive and negative electrical charges; we have nerve impulses in the form of bio-electric waves which travel at thirty-five meters per second; our brain and its varied activity levels generate electromagnetic fields which extend outside the head; electricity is used by the brain to store and compute information; our nervous system is a compact, efficient, self-repairing bio-electromagnetic structure, containing three distinguishable neural systems (the sympathetic, parasympathetic and the voluntary) constructed of what is estimated to be over twenty billion cells, all carefully routed and intertwined; cells themselves use minute electromagnetic messages in conjunction with chemical compounds to react and to communicate with each other; and the eye-brain converts sunlight in the visible electromagnetic spectrum into photochemical and biochemical messages which are carried along to higher centers in the brain for more neuro-electrical processing and transmission. Our bodies, finally, from an electromagnetic point of view, fall about midway on the scale of electrical conductivity, being very poor conductors when compared with metals, but very good conductors when compared with the atmosphere which surrounds us. (The body, though it is hardly more than a leathery, membranous sack of water, does contain minute mineral compounds obtained mostly through digestion, which in ionized states in the cells, set up a charge differential enabling neuro-electrical currents to flow. As we shall see further on, these minerals in bondage with organic compounds cause bodily tissue to be responsive to electrical conditions in the environment.)

What I am trying to establish with all these bits of information is a model of man as "Homo Electromagneticus." That is, the body conceived of as a receptor, an independent transmitter and transducer, and a broadcaster of electromagnetic fields and impulses.

Now, from this point of view, the cosmos also appears to be an electromagnetic system, which means that it too may therefore fall metaphorically under the laws of resonance and harmonic affinity. Indeed, since Kepler's time there have been numerous mathematical models based upon the periodic movements of the solar system, all of which indicate that the solar system is a resonant structure—in the orbital and rotational periods of the planets, in their mean distances and rotational speeds, in the perihelion to aphelion ratios of their elliptical orbits, and even in the eight simultaneous quantum mechanic equations of the physicist Molchanov. All these models say the same thing: the planets musically resonate with each other and with their moons in what may be called an extremely low, inaudible yet acoustical, wave frequency. Resonance affects the planetary eddies which sweep across and between each of the planets like winds, and also the vast electromagnetic plasmic field which envelops the entire solar system. Planetary resonance on the interplanetary field can also affect the electromagnetic radiation cycles of the sun and thereby indirectly the earth's atmosphere. Thus even from these brief comments one can glimpse the vast implications of this idea of resonance at a distance.

The second characteristics of acoustical or resonant fields, called the phenomenalization of the partial or overtones, is another vibrational principle which can, in the Pythagorean spirit, be expanded into a cosmological model.

When we sound a fundamental tone, say A at 440 cps, and we wish to generate its octave at 880 cps, we can do this in one of two ways. We can either divide the string length (A) in half immediately, or we can sound all the "partial" tones or divisions in between 440 and 880 cps by sounding, for example, one ninth of the string, or a fifth, or a quarter, or third, etc., all the way up to the division by two into halves. This is similar to obtaining the note A either as a whole dollar bill or in the form of nickels, dimes, quarters, etc. In other words, every tone that we hear as a single note is actually a composite of many partials and sub-partials, all merged together.

In order to hear a particular partial which is normally blended into the whole or "fundamental" tone, Hermann Helmholtz designed small cup-like resonators. These, when held to the ear, at somewhere between a forty and a forty-five degree angle to the eardrum, allow one to hear separately—to "phenomenalize"—these partial tones, the particular partial heard depending upon the shape and size of the little cup. Another method is simply to take an ordinary drinking tumbler and to hold it next to the ear while sounding a fundamental tone. By slightly shifting the angle of the tumbler while the tone is sounding, one can hear in progression a series of partials resulting from the change in the angle. It follows from this, not only that every whole tone is a simultaneous combination of all its partials, such that the shift in the angulation of the resonator allows one to hear the different partials contained in it, but also that there is a relationship between the structure of audible sound and geometry, in which the geometric angles act as a controlling device to release certain potential qualities locked within a holistic sound pattern.

If we consider angles as whole number ratios or proportions, as did the ancients—so that two to three (2:3) forms an angle—then this phenomenalization of tones has wide implications and applications to architectural design. And if we apply this model on a cosmic level, then the effect of angulation on resonant patterns could be a key to understanding how angles of planetary configuration might affect or modify the electromagnetic atmosphere of the solar system and thus affect the dispersal of radiation from the sun.

In any case, if we begin to consider ourselves, our architecture and our solar system as interpenetrating resonant fields, we would undoubtedly have a much different set of personal, cultural and scientific concepts, methods and goals than we presently have. For example, both the scientific and the science-fiction search for life on other planets would cease immediately, because we would clearly conceive that all the planets are part of a resonating system of harmonies which allows energy to manifest itself as life on earth. From this point of view, all the planets would partake of this "earth" process, and "earth" would be considered the locus at which the combination of factors allowing vibratory resonance to embody itself intersect. It would be realized that the geometry of life is the geometry of earth—that the slightest change in the rate of rotation or in the tilt of the axis or in the moon's gravitational pull, or the slightest shift in the distance from the sun—any one of these—would destroy life as we know it. "Earth," then, is a terribly precise geometric and rhythmic equation whose result is conscious life. Anywhere in the universe that this equation occurs is, in essence and in consciousness, "Earth," and is therefore not separate from us in distance.

It is for this reason that the ancient sages sought to find and retain the dimensions of the earth and its periodicities, considering it to be the module in the harmonic structure through which resonant energy must pass in order to become incarnate form. And today, contemporary research in the field of helio-biology is revealing the relationship between celestial resonance and life processes, and showing that man and many living creatures have a sensitivity to electromagnetic changes in the man-made and natural environments surpassing that of the most elaborate mechanical instruments. We live in a turbulent sea of electromagnetic fields, many of which are necessary for our biological maintenance and many of which can be debilitating or deadly. For the time being, however, let us look again more generally at what the laws of resonance tell us about the transmission of patterns from one field to another.

A periodic driving force will produce a maximum response from an adjacent system when the frequency of the applied system is equal to the natural vibratory frequency of the second system. Theoretically, therefore, there is no reason why the electromagnetic signals of our bodies should not be penetrated, disrupted or interfered with by other fields outside the body. It has, for instance, been shown in experiments with volunteers exposed to certain Very Low Frequency (VLF) ranges that the body suffers almost immediately from fainting, nausea or loss of control under such exposure. On the other hand, it has also been shown that if classical music is played during the experiment the ill-effects attributed to the VLF waves are nullified. So we are given here an idea of harmonious sounds forming a kind of interceding vibratory architecture around the body, protecting it, so to speak, from disruptive or imbalanced environmental radiation.

We have other means than music, however, by which we can organize the often chaotic fields that are contained in, and surround, the body. Strong fields of concentrated thought, or emotional patterns and images, can be focussed by our minds on the body rhythms and markedly alter them, in beneficial or non-beneficial ways. Words, particularly mantric forms, but all speech—including gesture and dance—act to organize the vibratory conditions around us, as do the emanations from colors and the fields set up by graphic and sculpted images.

All the methods of symbolization, then, are tools with which we mould and shape the oscillatory fields and patterns around us, and architecture is our most powerful symbolizing process for acting upon and forming the resonant environment. The architecture of the past, particularly Temple Architecture, generally acted as an electromagnetic insulator—that is, like a Faraday cage, screening out the environmental electricity, magnetism and noise. Such architecture, as we know, was conceived according to universal consonant proportion, thereby giving the inhabitant the opportunity of being "bio-entrained" to the patterns of the original cosmic harmony. (And, as we shall see, when the body is shielded from random electromagnetic activity, all the metabolic processes slow down.) Our recent architecture, on the other hand, has been constructed of materials which are not insulators but are instead good electrical or vibratory conductors—hollow blocks or hollow wooden frames, or iron beams and girders, or metal-reinforced concrete, etc. In addition, we surround these conductive structures with dense electromagnetic transmitters and appliances, and then submerge in turn all of this electromagnetic turmoil in a chaos of urban mechanical noise.

To conclude this section: We have bodily instruments which are consciously or unconsciously receptive to the terrestrial and celestial milieu on many levels of frequency; these external environmental patterns trigger and guide, and to some degree control, the internal functions which unfold the metabolic time capsule of the electromagnetic body. But this is not all, for we have at our disposal the processes of symbolization—of the Word or Logos—through which we can select, attune, harmonize and elevate our individual vibratory allotment towards that of the universal form of creation.

## . 4 .

All life-processes and all living organisms conform to one and the same pattern: a developmental growth which continues until attaining a genetically coded, predetermined form. Here is a well-known and mysterious example, from Kenneth Boulding's *The Image,* concerning the behavior of certain amoebas:

As long as the food supply is abundant they eat, grow, divide and so multiply. If, however, food becomes scarce, an extraordinary change in behavior occurs. Thousands of separate cells move together to form a worm-like object. By means of concerted movements along the cells, this object moves forward somewhat on the principle of the inchworm. After it has moved a certain distance, it begins to erect itself into a plant-like object. Differentiation takes place within the separate cells, depending on their position within the object. Those in the stalks become hard and rigid and die. Those in the flower-like portion eventually transform themselves into a seed-like spore, which is then scattered and may then remain dormant for a long time, until conditions become favorable again. Here is exhibited in most dramatic form the mystery of the plant, that is, the cell society. Can it be doubted that each single-celled amoeba possesses in some sense an image of its function in the social organization and that certain messages that it receives—for instance the frequency of food ingestion—are interpreted to mean that the drama must now begin.

Organisms grow much as do buildings. The genetic material acts both as blueprint and mason, compelling substance from the environment to adopt the required or imagined form. As long as such an intrinsic pattern of predetermination exists in living systems, it is possible that it also exists as a universal factor, since matter can be nothing more than a symbolic description of the unseen physical and metaphysical forces which form it. This universal biological theme—the passage from a seed-idea or genetic pattern into a form—was the metaphoric basis of the theology and cosmology of temple-building civilizations. Humankind and universe were considered to be growing towards a predetermined image contained in the seeding which initially caused pure cosmic space to contract or warp into galactic formation. The revelation of this cosmic seed, Word or plan was the subject and content of sacred architectural design. The explanation of exactly how genetic messages exercise control over the organization of the forms and behavior of living creatures is a persistent biological mystery, as is, philosophically, the question of how an initial teleological intention could preside over this universal evolution. In this, as in other areas, science seems to be a discipline that avoids dealing with the important questions which apparently cannot be answered, and tackles instead the unimportant questions which apparently can be answered.

The neo-Darwinian theory of evolution, for instance, relying as it does upon a concept of natural selection acting upon what is considered to be a random occurrence of genetic mutation, is unable to explain adequately a number of aspects of organismic evolution—such as incidents in nature where learned behavior in animal species converts into instinctual behavior. It appears that behavior, originally learned, may, after generations, become transferred and then fixed in the autonomic nervous system, there becoming an instinct which can apparently accelerate the selection of related bodily characteristics. This acceleration, due in animals to shifts from learned to autonomic neural patterns, appears to be reversed in human evolution. Here autonomic neural patterns—such as breathing, heartbeat, blood circulation, fear and pain reflexes, and sexual drive—can be transferred from autonomic to conscious levels of learning and control, and thereby act, according to ancient spiritual philosophies, as evolutionary accelerators for humanity.

(With the recent, widening acceptance of behavior and learning as evolutionary forces we are observing a major shift in contemporary evolutionary theory, away from the more mechanistic interpretation of Darwinism toward a more Lamarckian view. This older view maintained that changes in the environment will cause changes in behavior, which in turn could induce structural, physical changes that were called "acquired characteristics," and which Lamarck supposed could be transmitted genetically and so become "inherited" characteristics. In the 160 years since the appearance of Lamarck's theory, all attempts to demonstrate the inheritance of acquired characteristics have failed. Nevertheless, Lamarck's premonition of behavior and learning as evolutionary forces was remarkable.)

In those cases in which learned behavior in animal species is converted into instinctual behavior, it seems that gene combinations better suited to allow for an expression of the animal's learned habits may tend to be selected and to survive, in preference to those which do not. In this manner, learning and behavioral change may set up a new selective pressure and, in doing so, may play a decisive or modifying role in evolution. In other words, even though it appears that changed behavior and related morphological changes brought about by environmental interaction cannot imprint themselves directly on the genetic code, the organism nevertheless absorbs from this interaction non-genetic information in the form of increased knowledge. This knowledge becomes embedded in humankind, not in our genes or autonomic instinct, but in the structure of our perception, cognition, language, behavior and traditions; and in these modalities it is transmitted to future generations in the form of symbols.

This capacity for explicit linguistic reasoning through aural and visual symbols sharply demarcates human evolution from the rest of the animal world. Remember that a man is not better at learning to run in a maze than a rat, unless he is assisted by maps—either visually or verbally imaged in his memory, or drawn out as an accurate, proportional symbol. Baby rats immediately removed from their parents at birth generation after generation show no loss of their rat-like ways, whereas the entire structure of human behavior and society as we know it would crumble if the transmission of symbols and techniques were similarly interrupted. Language and symbolic processes have transformed learning and behavior into a biological instrument which, in humanity, challenges natural selection as the prime evolutionary mover and brings us to the threshold of a new potential in evolution—a survival mechanism based on the transmission of acquired knowledge, skills and experience, not through genetic inheritance, but through a structural system of essential symbols, and in which may well lie the key to the original function of Art, as well as of Science.

There are those who create and transmit symbols, and there are those who destroy them. Ancient Egypt is an example of a culture built solely on a system of psycho-spiritual symbolization. Herodotus was told by an Egyptian priest that Egypt had continued and endured undisturbed while "the sun had twice risen where it now sets, and twice set where it now rises"—a remark that can be interpreted to mean the passage of one and one-half precessional cycles, or approximately 36,000 years! However, we know that even during the three or four thousand years of Egypt's historical period there had been periods of great unrest and disruption. We must therefore interpret the priest's remark to refer, not to physical Egypt, but to the unbroken transmission of symbols which remained consistent from the first kings of the First Dynasty down to the closing of the Temples four thousand years later. So powerful indeed was this transmission that many of these same symbols remain with us today.

Among contemporary Western thinkers, it was Alfred Russel Wallace, co-author of the Darwinian theory of evolution, who realized the implications of the fundamental change that had taken place with the advent of human mental evolution—a fact that has been largely ignored in our social philosophies, but which seems, as I say, to have been a most basic consideration in ancient Temple-centered society. Wallace pointed out that the moment people clothe themselves and pass large portions of their life within constructed habitats, use fuel for thermo-regulation and apply agriculture and weaponry to regulate their food flow—the moment they partake, in other words, of structures of civilization—at that moment they escape the slow but inexorable laws of natural selection. Wallace speculated that to the degree that the body is protected from the changes brought about by selection due to environmental influences, to this same degree the mind becomes the recipient of, and must react to, those very influences from which the body escaped. At that point, human evolution becomes dominated by the unprecedented growth in particular areas of the brain and by particular types of mental activity; and the fossil evidence itself indicates that the surprising growth of brain size within a small fraction of evolutionary time is paralleled by the growth and development of verbal communication. In other words, those individuals and populations with better speech facilities, and with larger associational centers of reasoning in the cerebral cortex, must have had a selective advantage, thus allowing the path of human evolution to flow virtually unimpeded toward the production of the external structures of civilization.

The Egyptians acknowledged the unprecedented role of the symbol in human evolution by holding to the "Creative Word" as the explanation of their world. The world to them was a symbolic stage on which God played out his role as regulator and sustainer of all created things, the multitudinous attributes of the world that are in fact his Creative Word at work. The *Shebaka Text* says:

> The Company of the Gods [is]... the teeth and lips in the great mouth which gave all things their names... and thus happens every word of God from what his heart thought and his tongue commanded.

The primary act of symbolization for Humankind too is "spoken." Because of his controlled voice, he need not reach outside himself for the material to make his first conscious symbols. And in the universe as well, the primary acts in the formation of galaxies seem to be sonic booms which, in combination with gravity, organize clouds of intergalactic dust into nodes and eddies that begin to form vast clusters of stars. Thus Novalis said, "Sound is to the study of astronomy what God is to the study of metaphysics."

Hans Jenny's experiments have shown that sound frequencies do have the gravity-like propensity to call into arrangement random, suspended particles of substance, and thus to create formal periodic organizations. All of which is to say that sound may be conceived of as an instrument through which temporal patterns become formal spatial patterns.

On the biological level of organization, to quote Gregory Bateson:

> The shapes of plants and animals are transforms of messages. Anatomy must contain an analogue of grammar because all anatomy is a transform of contextually shaped message material.

That is, biology gives us the model of genetic, symbolic messages which call form and variation into existence, just as, in a parallel way, mental symbols precede and call into existence corresponding resonant forms and structures. From another level of causality, all forms of life and mind on earth, including the genetic message, must somehow be contained potentially in the messaged, patterned fields of light and energy which impact with the earth. To the Egyptian, the symbolic process was, like time and perception, cyclical. For the symbolic mind, not only do intellectual biological messages "inform" themselves by means of the grammar of the earth's geo-celestial geometry and rhythm, but also natural forms themselves can be considered symbolic messages revealing the potentials for the evolution of conscious mind and life. There is nothing new under the sun: all the potentials for light are manifest in one form or another for those who view them symbolically. Conceptual forms are released from their entrapment in matter by being transformed within the symbolic mind into metaphysical analogies. Symbols, then, are the intermediaries between time's messages and the appearance and disappearance of form.

Consider the intriguing case of the salamander—whose image, incidentally, in the center of a flame or radiant field is an ancient alchemical symbol. The salamander sheds and regrows its tail in a rhythm with the earth's orbit around the sun (or when it happens to lose its tail by accident). When it does so, it makes use of a peculiar process that humans no longer seem to have the capacity to perform: that is, a mass of primary cells gradually organizes itself into a complete, multi-tissued limb, with all the appropriate differentiation. We know that there are electromagnetic forces at work in this, as in all, cellular regrowth. Indeed, in general, there is a flow of bioelectric energy in the healing of a wound through the flow from the positively charged wound tissue toward the negatively charged surrounding area. In such a healing process, humans presently only regrow a crude, non-differentiated cellular structure called scar-tissue. The salamander, however, like other reptiles sets up a bioelectric field where its tail used to be, which allows for refined, organized, differentiated tissue to reappear.

The Egyptian, then, would see the salamander as a symbol of a general potential for self-formation. To such a symbolic mentality, the physical body is only a tail in a concentric organization of interwoven resonant fields—which the Egyptian symbolized in the royal burial practice in which the mummy is surrounded by eight enveloping coffins of wood, stone or gold. The salamander in its projection of its own tail, provides the symbolic mind with a model for the shedding of our physical form, together with the direct re-projection of another. Such, in fact, it has been proposed, was one of the developmental goals of the initiatic kings: to establish their consciousness completely in the resonant message-configuration from which it would be possible to evoke the precise form or level of the succeeding incarnation.

For those reasons, the Egyptians carved their essential symbols in stone. But the most important mode of transmitting this immutable knowledge was architecture, in which the simultaneity of dimensional volume permitted the greatest impact and accuracy for the representation of those metaphysical concepts which constitute humanity's hope of continuation and evolutionary flowering. It becomes apparent, indeed, from the study of Temple Architecture, that the Sages who created the structures were well aware that with the attainment of symbolic language— "the gift of the word"—especially the language of architecture, the responsibility for human evolution had shifted to a large degree to humanity itself. The Temple for them was a center of the learning and dissemination of a psycho-physical and spiritual science whose purpose was to reveal and develop symbolic, intellectual and physical techniques which might effect perceptual, behavioral and physiological changes in the human organism—a science having the purpose of gradually leading towards humanity's highest conceivable evolutionary potential, towards the appearance, that is, of a Divine or Supra-Human, an organismic being who had mastered the contingencies and dualities of mortal existence.

This image of the perfectibility of Humanity was maintained in Egyptian culture by the presence of the King, while the initiatic Temple at the nucleus of the society is an indicator that the population was collectively and actively engaged in a self-creative phase of evolutionary unfolding. Here we may cite as symbol the Great *Neter* as *Ka-mut-f* (Bull of his Mother) in which the phallus is figured on the body at the level of the naval.

The inscription reads, "He who gives birth to himself."—which is the biological principle of parthenogenesis raised to metaphysical expression.

From the viewpoint of the Temple, then, all aspects of civilization—buildings, arts, agriculture, metallurgy, etc.—are to be considered as sacred techniques, intended not simply to provide physical protection and comfort, but as specific instruments in the universal process of humanity's spiritual self-manifestation. I mean by "spiritual" what we are in essential origin and evolutionary potential. Temple wisdom considered civilization as only a temporary capsule, lodged in the aeons of evolutionary time, within which humanity, momentarily alleviated from the pressures and restraints of the vast cyclic fluctuations (represented by Osiris in the Egyptian myth), might in the light of aware self-consciousness (symbolized by Re) participate in the enactment of the birth of its own next form. Egypt summarized its commitment to a philosophy of evolution through consciousness thus:

> Yesterday belongs to Osiris; tomorrow belongs to Re.

One of the major causes of the interruption in this envisioning of conscious evolution has been the confusing problem of mind-body dualism, which has haunted Western philosophers at least since Aristotle, and which seems to arise out of several "symbolizing" misconceptions. The first is that we no longer possess the linguistic terms with which we can, without separating them, define both reality and our experience of it. We have no linguistic models such as those exemplified in ancient mythology, through which we can experience mind and body, consciousness and matter, subject and object, as integral, interpenetrating or simultaneous parallels. Secondly, we no longer possess a multi-levelled language structure with which we can describe a spatial experience apprehended non-visually. For example, we do not know how to experience or communicate about a space generated solely by audition, or any other sensorial modality apart from sight. This means that we cannot accurately conceive the subtle, non-visual resonance which occurs between our thoughts about things and the things themselves; and thus we create an imaginary space in which our webs of mental images exist, so we think, separately from the real world of material objects.

Benjamin Whorf has shown, however, that this separation of the thought world from the object world—the world of mind from the world of body—did not exist for the Hopi. Nor, as we shall see, did it exist for Egyptian thought. Whorf argues that many ancient peoples conceived of thought as an active, all-pervasive energy in the physical world, much as we think of light or electromagnetism.

It is not unnatural to suppose that thought, like any other force, leaves everywhere its traces or effects. We think of our thought as dealing with mental images alone, which is not the thing itself, but a mental surrogate.

And around this accumulation of linguistic surrogates we construct an imaginary space.

The Hopi thought world has no imaginary space. The corollary to this is that it may not locate thought dealing with real space anywhere but in real space itself, nor can it insulate real space from the effects of thought.

But of course there is another side to this. Our complex fabric of surrogate images, located in an imagined, separate, mental field, is the dark edge of the sword of symbolism which appeared to humanity as a gift so that it might cleave through the layers of evolutionary time. Humans have the capacity, through symbolism, to create totally imaginary mental worlds—such as egoism on one level, mechanism on another, or Nazism on still another—worlds having a very limited relationship to the fullness of an integrated sense of reality. Humanity alone seems capable of creating vast, symbolic forms inconsistent with the deeper rhythmic wholes of universal expression. In spite of this, it is neither necessary nor possible to destroy this *Maya*, because the perceptual mode is intrinsic and necessary to Creation, and with the advent of language and architecture we have come to rely on the ambiguous power of the Image as a light to guide us. But we must endeavor to make this veil coincide accurately with the vision of the integrally real. Indeed, a precise, integral and manifold system of symbolization in resonance with both objective fields and metaphysical realities is the instrument by which thought and conscious vibration can be focussed so as to act formatively on matter and physiology.

The Greeks gave the name of "Gymnosophism" to the mind-body educative practices that they observed in Egyptian Temples. These proposed a system of physio-respiratory mastery and purification as the trigger that would allow an ascent through various levels of philosophic perception, comprehension and vision. Indeed, Greek historians marvelled at the impeccably hygienic standards and the moral, intellectual and religious character of the Egyptians—it was as if a whole segment of the culture were involved in an elaborate collective system of purification and development. This in fact was the case, and, in this sense, the initiatic process was nothing other than the application of an evolutionary theory. In Egypt, every capable male was periodically recruited to spend several months within the Temple. Naturally, only a few of these recruits would find Temple life appropriate and remain to become priests; most would return to ordinary society with the enrichment brought about by this exposure to spiritual life. In this way, spiritual directives could penetrate many reaches of society and influence the entire structure of living.

All of civilization was thus an alchemical act, attempting to transmute time, by elevating the body, whose development is still phased to the greater rhythms of macro-evolution and placing its development in a pulsation corresponding to the evolution of consciousness and mind. Social and individual activity thus became a living ritual, evoking and symbolizing the drama of personal and collective self-evolution.

The entire social philosophy of Egypt is summarized in a wall-relief in the tomb of Ptahhotep at Meir. Three figures are shown—one standing, one seated and one kneeling. If one measures these figures, it may be seen that the height of the seated figure gives the exact geometric mean term between the two extremes. Here, in other words, we have the three postures of the Human Being, each with its separate dimensions, joined in the continuous connectivity of a proportional relationship. First, we have the standing, active, doing, fabricating, warring, trading, building man, called *rajasic* in Sanskrit; next the seated, thinking, symbol making and transmitting scientist, poet, sage, teacher, called *sattvic* in Sanskrit; and finally the kneeling, mystic, visionary yogi, the *tamasic* man in Sanskrit. There is no exclusion of one level of experience in favor of another: non-conceptual experience, *extase*, does not eliminate *entase*, the spiritual does not eliminate or devalue the intellectual or physical. From the point of view of Egyptian wisdom, no society could long endure without a constant flow of communication between these three postures. Indeed, the Pharaoh contained in himself all three of them.

Without such a spiritually self-aware, self-perfecting core, guided by the pinnacle of an institution like the Temple, civilization loses sight of its evolutionary purpose and falls inevitably into imbalance and decay. Humanity needs the Supra-Human, the Royal Person, the Anthropocosm towards which it may draw itself. Without this image of the future Human form, Humanity will have no future form; without an image of the universe there can be no universe. The image of the future Human and the image of the universe are one and, as we shall see, comprise the geometry of Temple architecture.

## I. The Geometry of Time and Transformation

Perhaps time does not pass, perhaps every instant of one's life exists always—the event and one's consciousness at the moment of the event being unalterable points located eternally in space-time. From this point of view, memory traces of an event do not disappear but always have time co-ordinates with greater values than those that mark the moment of its occurrence in one's consciousness. That is, memories of thoughts or events occur at a "later" time than the time the thoughts or events happen.

The concept of time summarized here in the jargon of relativity physics' space-time diagrams also emerges out of an ancient geometric diagram which was fundamental to the architecture and mathematics of several Temple-building cultures. This geometric figure, called the *gnomon* by the Greeks, has fascinated people for thousands of years. There is every indication that the Ancients held to a philosophical position regarding Time which is made evident through the contemplation of this figure.

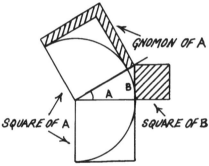

In the figure above, the square of B is equal to the gnomon of A. The width of this gnomon is the difference between the hypotenuse and the base of the triangle, that is, between the reading in sine and in tangent.

Before we can begin to explain the attributes of the gnomon, however, it will be necessary first to show its relation to the figures of the square, the circle and the spiral, noting how all of these relate to our theme of Cosmic Time, which Temple Architecture sought to represent, and remembering that it is only through an image of Time that the experience of time becomes comprehensible to us.

The earth is spherical. Brahmanic texts say this repeatedly, and it is unquestionably implied in certain Egyptian texts, measurements and representations. But, in the Temple, in India and China, the earth is symbolized by the square. This is because a whirling sphere in space evokes an abstract, invisible line through its center, which we call the axis. By means of this axis, the earth becomes aligned with a fixed position in the universe, from which the four cardinal points or orientations may be established: up-down or north-south and east-west. These cardinal points are where heaven and earth seem to meet or intersect. From the observer's point of view, the sun rises in the east and sets in the west; the other cardinal points, north and south or noon and midnight, complete the fourfold orientation of the square.

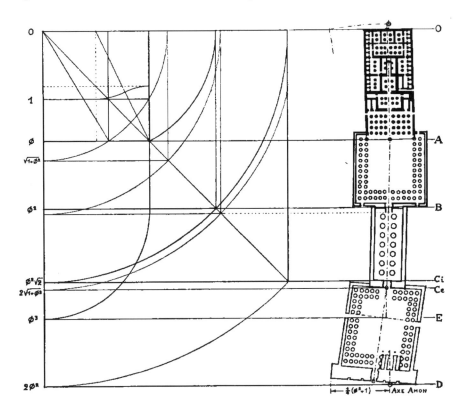

The Temple of Luxor was built in stages which correspond to the growth by gnomonic expansion of an initial cube the size of the first stage, the secret sanctuaries. (R. A. Schwaller de Lubicz, *Le Temple de l'Homme*, Paris, Caracteres, 1957.)

In this way, through the fixation of its axis as a contact point with the heavens, so to speak, the earth comes into being. Its position is maintained and regulated by this contact, and by the regular appearance and disappearance of the sun, moon and stars; and so these points become the seal of a marriage between the heavens and the earth. The four cardinal points—the four orientations—are beheld periodically and become known as perpetual recurrences. They become permanent in a cyclic sense by which the passage of day is measured as time. Thus the square, associated with the number four, and its expansion into a cube, associated with the number six, and their multiples, are the numbers which measure time.

In order to understand why Temple Architecture from many cultures is almost wholly preoccupied with the four cardinal orientations which mark the daily and seasonal cycles, and with the geometric plan of the simple square which ideally represents them, let us review some material from the much-discussed research into biological clocks. Over twenty years of research in this field continues to demonstrate that metabolic processes in living organisms are geared to astronomical periodicities, such as the rotation of the earth upon its axis, the earth's revolution around the sun, and the moon's encircling of the earth. Indeed, it is presently believed there is no physiological process which does not exhibit cyclic variations, and that all organisms on earth contain metabolic clocks which trigger essential internal biological activities, at apportioned intervals related to geo-celestial cycles.

This all-pervasiveness of bioclocks gives us a sturdy empirical metaphor upon which to expand a philosophy of evolution based on the interrelatedness of our interiority with the phenomenal universe. Literally thousands of interrelated rhythms in body chemistry are cyclically orchestrated with geophysical and celestial periodicities—such as the blood and the urine, the levels of sugar, iron, calcium, sodium, potassium, corticosterone and adrenocortical outputs (which affect both our physical and psychological well-being), fibrialytic activity in the plasm, deep body temperature, blood pressure, cellular division, and the hormonal patterns of growth and maturation, as well as many neural patterns.

In one experiment with a single-celled plant, algae, whose photosynthetic processes and secretions are known to be controlled by intervals in the daily cycle, it was found that even after removing the cell's nucleus by severing the basal rhyzoid, a number of cyclic rhythms continued undisturbed over a significant period of time. It appears, then, that periodicity is deep-seated even in structured cells, but also that the time-keeping power of life resides in the cytoplasmic substance itself.

Another experiment offers a wonderful example of integrated time-space perception, based upon the four spatial orientations. Birds were placed in coops on the northern side of a circular arena, and were trained always to fly to the southern corner at a certain time to pick up a food reward. They were then placed in an enclosed room for a week, and by means of artificial light were phased to a different light cycle—

lights were turned on at midnight and off at noon, so as to effect a six-hour phase-change from normal. When the birds were returned to the arena, they immediately flew to the east rather than to the south side to look for their food reward—an error of exactly ninety degrees. But since the sun moves fifteen degrees of arc every hour, this ninety-degree error coincides exactly with the six-hour phase-change in the birds' light-dark cycle. This and other similar experiments have shown that a bird's directional sense is related to its light-dark bioclock cycle (related to east-west orientation), and furthermore that its instinctive ability to navigate during migration depends upon an innate awareness of what hemisphere it is in, plus the ability to site and interpret the sun's position as a time-space coordinate (which is related to north-south orientation). How refined this living time-space relationship seems compared to the erudite mathematical formulae of our present relativity theory! Such innate capacities for a time-space cognition are found among people of primitive societies and are based upon the simple division of the solar cycle by the four natural orientations.

Not unexpectedly then, just as our bodily organization originates from the periodicity based upon the fourfold interrelatedness of earth and sky, so also it seems does the life of the intellect. Archeological remains show us the great effort that Neolithic humans made to divine, consecrate and retain, through stone sitings and interval markings on bones, the essential temporal patterns. These allowed them to envision an order out of the inexplicable, vast surroundings in which they found themselves. Initially, humans may have become intuitively aware of the structure of time by means of their internal biological clocks; but thereafter they created a continual stream of measuring devices to record the passage of cyclic and geophysical events—from monoliths, pyramids and obelisks, on up to ultra-refined atomic clocks—only to return to the beginning and discover once again that, through adaptive response to external cyclic changes, they had already absorbed and, let us say, incarnated, the very geophysical rhythmicity they sought.

This same idea of life as a process of absorbing and miniaturizing the periodicity of cosmic movement recurs in a different way in contemporary brain research in which it has been shown that over eight percent of the neural synapses of the cerebral cortex in infants form and develop only in response to external stimuli received from the environment. Without this pulse-carrying activity many of the neurons would not form. In other words, the neural structure of the brain is also a result of the transformation of external perception and experience into physiological form and process.

This vision of neurobiological processes as digestion of the laws of universal movement in the form of rhythmic time patterns touches upon the dominant evolutionary theory of ancient Temple philosophy. According to this, the metaphysical vocation of physical humanity was, through evolutionary time, to embody and express the vibratory, rhythmic life of Cosmic Humanity, which was felt to exist abstractly, like an inaudible music, in the proportional combinations and intervals of universal movement.

To arrive at a more concrete image of how celestial radiation becomes a cellular part of the human being, I would like to cite briefly the work of Dr. Stuart Hameroff, an American medical researcher, and Dr. Fritz Popp, a German biophysicist, concerning the microtubules of the human cell. Microtubules are tiny, hollow, cylindrical bodies, less than 270 angstroms in diameter, which move in mysterious, rhythmic ways within the cell, dissolving and reappearing, yet structurally active in the contractile mechanism of the cell membrane. Hameroff has suggested that these small tubes should be considered as bio-resonators, because he has calculated that they may resonate at close to the ultraviolet light frequency of ten to the sixteenth hertz. He points out that their outer layer of skin is translucent and light refractive, admitting ultraviolet light into the tube, and suggests that, once inside, this light could be resonantly amplified by the microtubule and so be transmitted as an active force in the body. It has even been proposed that the ultraviolet light communication may be a primary regulator in all cellular processes and may even act to guide the DNA molecules to the right place in the double helix structure.

It seems also that the instructions which regulate cellular mitosis and the body's replacement of millions of old cells with new cells each second may be carried into the body by electromagnetic waves through the affinity of bio-resonators just such as these microtubule. Cellular abnormalities, such as unchecked growth of cells in cancer, would in this model be a result not only of the resonant factors in the cell's organization, but also of the disruption in the earth's atmosphere, that is, in its functioning as a filter and transmitter of the precise life-favoring frequencies of celestial radiation. It seems that without the messages from the sky, life's essential organization is impossible.

Biological processes thus appear not simply as reflections, but more as absorptions—one might even say "digestion"—of the rhythmic yet abstract life of the universe. Metabolic life, being dependent upon cosmic rhythms in order to maintain its functions and processes, becomes actually a transcription of the temporal intervals created by the celestial movements of the solar system and the effects these movements have upon the light, heat, electricity, magnetism, gravity and atmosphere of the earth.

The theme of evolution as metaphysical digestion was primary to a universe considered as a vast organism, and fostered a mytho-scientific-symbolic structure which integrated psychological and spiritual viewpoints to a greater degree than can the more mechanical Darwinian view of adaptation. In the Upanishads we find the following statement made by the conscious energy of the celestial macrocosm to Manifesting Life, which is meant to embody universal harmonic laws:

> He who recreates me protects me. I am food. He who refuses to recreate me I eat as food. I am these worlds and I eat these worlds. He who knows this knows Upanishad.

Using such an image of digestion to describe the dynamics of change in evolution—that is, a gradual digestion by earthly existence of the pre-existent, ever-moving patterns contained in the rhythms of the celestial bodies—would in ancient thought be considered to be at a similar level of causality as using our present concept of statistical randomness in the appearance and disappearance of genetic mutation to explain the continuous modification and change in organismic evolution.

That life embodies and expresses on physical and psychological levels the abstract, energetic impulses of the heavens is of course a basic assumption of Astrology, but we do not need to evaluate the relevance of this model of cosmic digestion from an astrological point of view. Modern science itself, as we shall see, provides a number of concepts which lend support to the view of an interdependent earth-sky interaction. To the Ancients, this knowledge was conceived of as a digestion and assimilation taking place between two essential symbols. For them digestion was a biological metaphor which effectively clarified the process of the transmutation of substance from any one level of conscious existence to another—from mineral to plant, from plant to animal, and from animal to human—a domain of transmutation involving a qualitative change in both substance and consciousness, which was the essential mystery and focus of ancient science, including medieval alchemy.

Similarly, for modern science, all of matter in its essence and origin is light, beginning in the thermonuclear heat, deep in the burning hearts of massive stars, where the vital elements of life, as well as the heavy metals, are cosmically manufactured. Upon the death of these stars in supernova explosions, ninety percent of the stellar material is blasted outwards and distributed through interstellar space, before being recycled into suns, moons and planets. You and I, and indeed all life on earth, were made possible by the carbon and mineral formations forged in the light and energy of stars which died in explosions tens of billions of years ago. The entire animal kingdom, including humans, is only an elaboration, via the food chain, of an initial botanical transformation of solar radiation. Plants, through photosynthesis, transmute minerals and sunlight into hydrocarbons, and when we burn wood or oil, or when internally we burn food, we release the light locked up in the form of heat in the chemical bonds of these organic compounds.

The final stage in this continuous transformation of light into heat, substance and life is the transformation occurring in the eyes and brains of human beings. Here the raw photons of physical light are transmuted into the light of the intelligence. This redemption of light from a mechanical, energetic status into a perceiving, acting, feeling, willing, self-conscious, self-transforming intelligence was considered by ancient evolutionary theory to be the product towards which the great universal digestion yearns.

There is one more point of view from which this theme of digestion and transmutation may profitably be illuminated. The Ancients saw in the human body a synthetic image through which to gain access to the processes and purposes of universal creation. For them the body depicted the interrelationship of two distinguishable yet inseparable processes—consciousness and matter, mind and body, sky and earth— whose increased harmonization and integration was the key to humanity's future evolution.

The diagram on the following page shows the simultaneous development of the two long, hollow tubular tracts which form very early within the ball-shaped cluster of cells in the human zygote. The closed tube on the top will become the brain and spinal cord, an enclosure in which indirectly received information is retained; while the tube at the bottom, open at both ends, will become the digestive tract. Embryologically, it is as if the entire body begins to materialize around these two hollow, tubular passages of transmutation.

The activity of the lower transmutation—the digestive tract—is a separation of the pure from the impure, a heat generating process fueled by externally procured substantial nourishment. In ancient cosmology this was the image of the Earth, called Geb in Egypt. The activity of higher transmutation, the enclosed tract of the brain and spinal cord, uses the energies assimilated by the lower as support for the further transformation of light into the subtle expression of mind and psyche. Here, as with body heat, the heat of concentration produces a tangible field of creative energy; and this energy, plus the refinement of substance derived from the lower digestion, feeds into the secretions of the cranial glands which control the body's rhythmic maturations, as well as the manufacture of the reproductive fluids. All these processes in ancient cosmology are related to the image of the Sky, called Nut in Egypt.

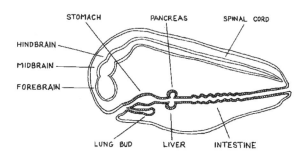

We find this parallelism continued in the metaphysical image of the *Dwat*, the "inversed" or "under" world. On the physical plane the *Dwat* is the region traversed by the solar globe when it has sunk beneath the western horizon. On the psychic plane, the *Dwat* is the locus of transformation. The Great *Neter* Re, as the solar deity, descends, as the texts say, into the *Dwat* in order to gain knowledge of his self-embodiment. He must, therefore, as he proceeds through the hours of the night, go through all the phases of incarnation from nutrition through metabolism and the transmutation of substance into vital energy and finally into the subtle forces of intelligence.

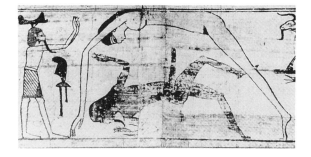

These transformations are symbolized by the metamorphoses of the scarab. After the egg-phase, the scarab exists as a worm or larva, which does little other than absorb and digest food. It is the digestive tract. Then comes the pupal phase, during which a cocoon is woven in which the creature exists without food or movement. This recalls the cerebro-spinal tract. (Note here that the cocoon may also serve as an image for the woven world of cerebral, conceptual symbols which provides an arresting enclosure surrounding the life and mind—just as do the civilizational structures built up through the use of such symbols. These body-mind enclosures seem to mark a definitive stage in humanity's continuing evolution. The dense web of artificial electromagnetic radiation, generated by industrial civilization, that presently surrounds the earth suggests the final encrustation of the light-obscuring cocoon, the same cocoon of civilization which suddenly enveloped nearly the entire inhabited portion of the earth, spreading out from three centers—the Middle East, the Indus River and China—in the last millennium before Christ.) This pupal phase, however, is finally followed by the release into a winged, sky-born creature, Khepri, the scarab-deity of the rising sun, symbol of transformation.

With this in mind, we will perhaps be able to understand better how ancient peoples, such as the Egyptian and Hindu Temple-sages, with a deep, vitally intuitive, metaphysical cosmology might metaphorically invest elaborate arrays of related concepts in simple, natural, geometric images—to which we must now return.

The square, as we have seen, is the essential and perfect form in ancient thought. It both presupposes the circle and results from it: it is the cosmic ideation of the perfect equilibrium achievable between pairs of diametrically opposed forces. The eternally moving, ever-expansive energy of the cosmos expresses itself as a curvature, and the ideality of curvature is the circle. But when this incessant movement yields to a comprehensive order, one finds the square. Even today, the formulations through which we measure the effect of intensities of light radiation, sound and gravity all contain squares, inverse square ratios or square roots.

The earth held in fourfold relationship, or in the sky's embrace, subject to its laws of time, was called in Egypt *Ta-Meri*—the cultivated or established earth as the attractor or magnet of heaven. And in the Hindu system, the square as helio-planetary cosmogram was called the *Prthiva mandala,* and it was this that gave the floor plan of the Temple. It allowed for the contemplation of the elliptical structure of the equinoctial and solstitial points in an eternal cycle. Hence the continual birth and death of the day and of the year became the metaphor for understanding the becoming and return of vaster cosmic cycles.

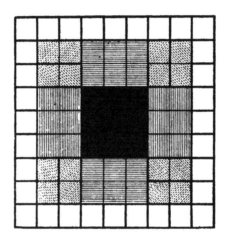

The floor of the Temple was begun by placing together four bricks, each one foot square, forming the square of two, and then expanding this platform to the square of three. Each sequential expansion was considered as an expanding altar of sacrifice. And it is this expansion of the platform by squares of two, four, nine, sixteen, twenty-five and on up to eight-one, which leads us at last to the central topic of this talk, the traditional Pythagorean mathematical problem of the square gnomon, defined by the Greek mathematician Hero of Alexandria as follows: "A Gnomon is any figure which, when added to an original figure, leaves the resultant figure similar to the original." Or as Aristotle said of it: "There are certain things which suffer no alteration save in magnitude when they grow."

There are interesting implications concerning growth and number-pattern through gnomonic expansion. One mathematical characteristic, for instance, is that all figures which grow by gnomonic expansion create intersections upon which logarithmic spirals can be drawn—such as those found so ubiquitously in nature: in the spiralling trunks of huge eucalyptus trees, the horns of rams and reindeer, our skeletal bones, mollusc shells (particularly the *Nautilus pompilius,* which follows the spiral derived from the Golden Proportion). Similar spirals can be found in the successive florets of the sunflower, in the outline of the cordiform leaf, in a lock of hair, or a snake coil, or an elephant trunk, an umbilical cord, or in the cochlea of the inner ear.

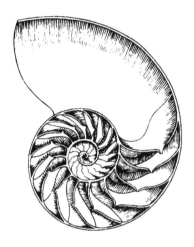

All these spirals are a result of the process of gnomonic growth, of which the square and the *gnomon* may be considered the archetypal form. That is to say, although each logarithmic spiral is derived from a different rectangle or other geometric figure, one always needs an intersection of four radii separated by a right angle in order to set up the construction. The logarithmic spiral is so rich in geometric and algebraic harmonies that the traditional geometers named it *Spira Mirabilis,* the Miraculous Spiral. For instance, while the radius of the spiral, through geometric growth, increases in geometric progression, the angle increases in an arithmetic progression. These are, of course, as we shall see, the two numerical progressions which yield all the ratios from which the musical scales are constructed. In other words, we may find in the miraculous spiralling of gnomonic figures a close association between the temporal laws of sound and the proportional laws of space.

# GNOMONS

1) If we add to a square an L-shaped portion, shaped like a carpenter's square, the resulting figure is still a square; and the portion which we have so added, with this singular result, is called in Greek a 'gnomon'....

2) For example, if we make a rectangle such that the two sides are in the ratio of 1 to the square root of 2, it is obvious that, on doubling it, we obtain a similar figure; for 1 is to the square root of 2, as the square root of 2 is to 2; and each half of the figure, accordingly, is now a gnomon to the other....

3) For another elegant example, let us start with a rectangle (A) whose sides are in the proportion of the 'divine' or 'golden section'...The gnomon to this rectangle is the square (B) erected on its longer side, and so on....

4) In any triangle, as Hero of Alexandria tells us, one part is always a gnomon to the other part. For instance, in the triangle ABC, let us draw BD, so as to make the angle CBD equal to the angle A. Then the part BCD is a triangle similar to the whole triangle ABC, and ABC is a gnomon to BCD. A very elegant case is when the original triangle ABC is an isosceles triangle having one angle of 36°, and the other two angles, therefore, equal to 72°. Then by bisecting one of the angles of the base, we subdivide the large isosceles triangle into two triangles, one similar to the whole and the other its gnomon....

5) If we take any one of these figures, for instance the isosceles triangle, and add to it (or subtract from it) in succession a series of gnomons, so converting it into larger and larger (or smaller and smaller) triangles all similar to the first, we find that the apices (or other corresponding points) of all these triangles have their locus upon an equilateral spiral....

6) Lastly, whensoever we fill up space with a collection of equal and similar figures, there we can always discover a series of equiangular spirals in their successive multiples....

From *On Growth and Form* by D'Arcy Thompson, pp. 181-185.

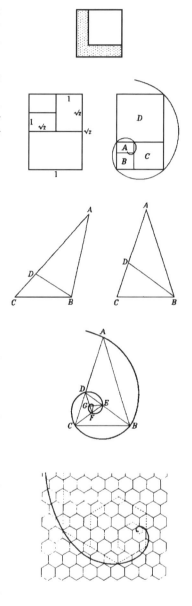

Why, we may ask ourselves, does the logarithmic spiral appear in some natural forms but not others? Living tissue grows basically in two distinct ways. The first is exemplified in the growth of softer, fleshier tissue in which, throughout nature, there is a constant sloughing off of old cells and replacement by newly created ones. But it is the second, the process of organic growth, by accretion, that is, by accumulative increase, which displays the logarithmic spiral. This type of growth commingles the old form with the new: the existing structure remains intact, while another of the same shape emerges as an incremental expansion of what already exists, as in the pattern of growth exhibited in the simple diagram of the square and its gnomon. This is the way the more permanent tissues of the body—such as bones, teeth, horns—accomplish their cellular addition.

The growth of the human brain itself seems to have evolved through such a process of gnomonic expansion. The same bulb (the inner or hind-brain) which dominated during the reptilian phase of evolution is still present within us. Added on top of this is the mid-brain limbic area, which was the dominant mental apparatus during the mammalian phase of evolution; and finally there is a logarithmic emergence of the cerebral cortex in the evolution of the higher human being.

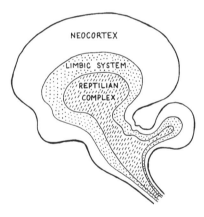

Lastly, remembering that the spiral, as we have seen, is formed by an arrangement of separate units (squares, rectangles) in the comodulated harmonic expansion called gnomonic growth, we may note that there is a teleological message contained in the image of the spiral itself; for it moves in successively opposite directions towards the ultimate expression of both the infinitely expanded and the infinitely contracted. The spiral is constantly approaching these two incomprehensible aspects of the ultimate reality, and therefore symbolizes a universe moving toward the perfect singularity from which it arose.

Thus the spiral-like solar influences caused by the arms of our galaxy constitute an image of the continuous connectivity between fundamental polarity—infinite and finite, macrocosm and microcosm.

With such images of the gnomon in mind, let us resume our attempt to find in this figure an image of Time.

We believe that time is passing only because our ordinary consciousness, absorbed in the transiency of material forms, is capable of "illuminating" only one particular moving cross section of space-time at each instant. In other words, form and substance, including the brain and body through which we perceive, are continually changing, and we experience time as passing because each instant of consciousness is different. This is because we are always thinking new thoughts, experiencing and noticing new things, metabolizing new substances; and it is this constant sequential difference of one instant from the last or the next that gives the experience of time passing—the mind-body relationship drives time into its appearing and disappearing movement. But through meditation techniques, in which perceptions and thoughts are trained to subside, or through Mantra, by which each instant is made, through repetition, to appear the same as every other instant, the sense of the irrevocable movement of time can be arrested, and a "timeless" status of consciousness experienced.

This is, of course, only a very external view of the mechanics of meditation, such as is proposed by the physicist R. B. Rucker in his book *Geometry, Relativity and the Fourth Dimension,* but it does lead us to several exciting implications concerning the experience of time. Clearly, variations in temporal perception are a factor separating one individual consciousness from another within a species and, to an even greater degree, separating the conscious awareness of different species. It may be said, indeed, that each distinct variation in the pattern of temporal recognition constitutes an entirely different universe of perception. For example, birds have a capacity for temporal recognition eight to ten times more rapid than we do. For them, pictures flashing at twenty-four frames per second, which appear to us as a continuous, moving picture, remain still photos until the velocity of 240 frames per second is reached. Likewise, sounds which are to us a continuous whistle are to birds separate and distinct peeps. In other words, birds are able to record ten times as many granulated perceptions as we can in any given temporal interval, which accounts for the acute rapidity of their reflex responses. It is even possible to say this perceptual rapidity was not developed in birds to enhance flight ability, but rather that birds fly only because it is a movement which suitably embodies and expresses this perceptual rapidity.

The sense of time, then, is related to the rate of change in phenomenal experience. This, in turn, leads to an idea with much experimental veri- fication, namely that time-sense is inversely related to metabolism. Children, for instance, who have faster metabolic rates than adults, experience time passing more slowly than do adults who, with their slower metabolism, sense time passing more rapidly. It is also known that consciousness altering drugs such as alcohol, heroin, cannabis and the hallucinogens directly affect time-perception, each in quite different ways. Related to these more extreme time-bending stimulants is, of course, the question of a society's diet. Nutritionists have observed that in the industrial societies of the Western world over the last twenty-five to fifty years a severe dietary increase has occurred in the use of high protein animal products, fat, refined sugar and high acid foods, particularly tropical fruit preparations. It may be noted that excess citric acid in the system may accelerate the availability of energy for consumption in activity, while it is also known that acids play a role in the breakdown of protein. Thus excesses of both protein and acid in the diet could allow for a manifold increase in the metabolic turnover of energy and tissue. Sugar, also a powerful metabolic stimulant, can in addition affect the entire timing of the endocrinal and hormonal system, causing the individual to phase through each stage of maturation more quickly: children enter adolescence younger, as do adolescents adulthood, and the adult begins the process of aging and decline sooner, in populations where white sugar consumption has been severely proportionately increased.

It may be assumed that such an acceleration in rates of metabolism and maturation allows for more segments of phenomenal time to be raced through, or crowded into, each phase or life-span, thereby biochemically altering and dominating the entire experience and perception of time—the vast majority of the population experiencing it without any objective reference, and so remaining unaware of the nature and implications of the perceptual shift that has occurred. In other words, this induced rapid-phasing may place physiological maturation out of synchronization with maturation in psychological and other levels which are dependent upon a slower absorption of, and reflection upon, phenomenal experience, and in this way the organism may feed disproportionately upon phenomenal, eventful time rather than on contemplative or symbolic time.

It appears, then, that people's amazing capacities to architecturalize their physical, chemical and vibrational environment are a profoundly subtle and complex process. Indeed, we can see that to the degree that we modify our environment, it in turn modifies us.

These ideas suggest and bring into focus perhaps the most important means at our disposal for altering temporal perception (and therefore environment), but one which has as yet no determinable relationship to biochemical fluctuations. This is the process of creating and using symbols. This process allows human individuals and populations to communicate over vast spans of time and space, regardless of mortality and destruction—giving the human mind the opportunity to flow backwards and forward in time through the retention or projection of symbols contained within its own memory and imagination. For humanity, symbols have become an inseparable aspect of temporal perception, and we may note that the more synthetic the symbol the greater the expanse of time that it will encompass.

For these reasons, the many considerations and techniques which affect the perception of time were held to be of great importance in ancient Temple civilizations, all of which maintained a vision of Transcendental Time as the essential universal Cause, containing, like a DNA code, all the intervals and number patterns—triggers of rhythmic release, signals—for the entire universal unfolding. A Hindu architectural sutra sums up this vision:

> Time is awake when all things sleep.
> Time stands straight when all things fall,
> Time shuts in and will not be shut.
> 'Is', 'was' and 'shall be' are only Time's children:
> O reasoning, be witness and be stable.

To these two characteristics of Time—Passing Time, or the perception of a fleeting directional movement from a dissolving past through an imperceptible present to an imaginary future, and Static Time, which is an all-containing eternal fullness—the Gnomonic Principle adds a further description. This is Time as Growth: an eternal expansion of growth upon growth, an evolution, one might say, belonging to the conscious energies which transcend the forms and energies through which they manifest, a growth whose eternally enduring continuation is at once mimicked and yet attested to in the growth of the cells, fibers and tissues of living nature.

In this way, through the Gnomonic Principle, past time remains present in form, and the form develops through the pulsating rhythmic expansion of gnomonic growth. To remove the most recently accreted layer or compartment from a nautilus shell is actually to move backwards in the lifetime of the object. Logarithmically developed forms always carry this element of retention of past time. Indeed, it may be said that all phases of Time exist in ever-present gnomonic layers, like the light-year structure of galactic space that makes every glance into the starry night sky a view into both the past of distant bodies and the future energy waves which will strike and influence the earth. This is perhaps an uncomfortable idea to accept, since from this point of view all aspects of the material world, including our own bodies, are in the past tense, existing in a gnomonic layer already bypassed by inflowing energies. Nevertheless, this is the concept which Temple builders derived from the symbol of the gnomon. The *Atharva Veda* says,

> Name and Form are in the Residue. The world is in the Residue. Indra and Agni are in the Residue. The Universe is in the Residue. Heaven and Earth, all Existence is in the Residue. The water, the ocean, the moon and the wind are in the Residue.

And let us remember that it is the residual, inorganic minerals in the body which transmit the bio-electric energy that makes conscious, incarnate life possible.

To the Temple architect-seer, observations of Nature were transparent metaphors revealing the metaphysical reality of his universe. In observing Nature, he saw two processes of growth and form, each related to a different characteristic of Time. One was transient creation and dissolution, relating to a particular sense of Time marked by cyclic appearance and disappearance—the lunar, Osirian pattern. The other was growth by accumulative, gnomonic increase, relating to a sense of the endless, all-containing fullness of Time, revealing a continuous evolution and having, at every given moment, a past with its fundamental results still in evidence, a present in which the results are still in the process of becoming, and a future in which yet unevolved powers and forms of being are implied and must appear for there to be a full and perfect manifestation. This was associated with the solar pattern, that totality of Time contained in a radiant sphere of Light, in which there is an eternal element, Re, in whose unbroken gnomonic expansion the Temple architect saw the rhythmic laws governing the evolution of the universal consciousness standing behind all manifestation. Indeed, in Egyptian the word Temple means "house of the utterance," that is, the Divine Word, Re, which pulsated through its spirit-space, setting up the harmonic periodicities of eternal cosmic Time.

This vision is precisely stated in Egyptian iconography: the geometric figure of a square with its gnomon demonstrates the passage from four to five, that is, from the elemental world to the realm of life, and this same geometry underlies the "Throne of Osiris" on which the King sits. This royal throne was called "The Throne of the World," and it was the proportions and angles extracted from this figure that the ancient builders used to determine many of the shapes and orientations of the Temple. The original unity within the four squares of the square of two is projected outwards to form the gnomon, the fifth part, which is approximately equal in area to each of the other four squares. The King, as representative of the solar power on earth, is thus appropriately associated with the fixed element, the gnomon, intrinsic to all logarithmic expansion. Yet this throne is also the throne of Osiris in his otherworldly kingdom of potentiality. As such, the throne is the fixed support on which the Osirian cycles of flux must rest.

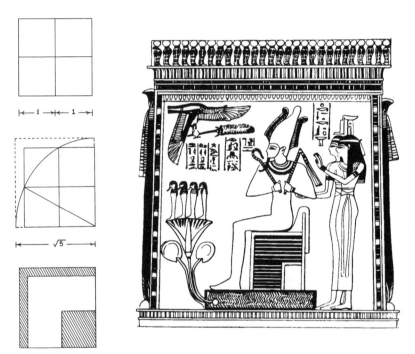

The living king, however, is not only the earthly embodiment of the eternal solar power, he is also Horus, the son of Osiris, who receives and brings his father's essence-force into the world again. This relationship of father to son, or of dead king to living king, as an image of the pulsation of the gnomonic essence of the past into the present and future, was greatly stressed in Egyptian culture. If the power and influence of the dead king, the father, are related to the original square, and the energies and activities of the living king, the son, to its gnomonic expansion, we can see how the entire social order relates the living individual to an ancestral community through this principle. Thus, the continuity of Egyptian culture demonstrated a continual innovation in which nothing of the essence was ever lost.

From the Egyptian point of view, then, Time can and does take many forms. Working sometimes separately and sequentially, and sometimes simultaneously to produce the varied levels of conscious existence and the various modes of perceptual awareness, these are all held, as we have hinted, in the myth of Isis, Osiris, Seth and Horus. With myth we do not commit the error of materializing Time and Space, but rather we are presented with the images that give shape and meaning to them.

We have seen Time in the form of a circle, Osirian Time, in which every thing or every event is an eternal recurrence of things and events that have always been. This is a time sense that is appropriate for the physical development of organic life, in which large and repetitive cycles are needed to inscribe and develop the behavioral expression of consciousness into the cellular organization. This Osirian form of consciousness is close to the earth and sky and open to their influences, close to the mechanism of nature which develops incarnate form.

Besides this form of Time, there is also Time which appears to us as linear, as a succession of material units strung out on a thread that points progressively from past to future. This is objectified Time and is represented in the Egyptian myth by Seth, the brother and murderer of Osiris. Between these—the linear, segmented, Sethian experience of Time which now dominates Western mentality, and the endless cyclical, Osirian wheels of Time associated with Oriental thinking—there intervenes the third image of Time, that of the Spiral and the Gnomon, which may be related to Horus in the myth.

The struggle of Seth and Horus, as related in the myth, is on one level a depiction of these two forms of temporal perception. Seth characterizes the *lila* of an endless, universal play, the apparent enumeration of all forms and possibilities. His power lies in his testicles, the procreative organ of endless multiplicities and varieties. He is the square root of two; and of senses he is taste. Horus, on the other hand, characterizes the instantaneously all-seeing consciousness, the continuous, unbroken expansiveness that lies behind the forms and makes possible an aimed universe having the single goal of drawing out of the chaos of all possibilities an incarnation of the image of the ultimate, universal Consciousness which has pre-figured its birth in the mirror of the heavens.

In this same myth, Isis, the Egyptian symbol of the Transcendent Mother, tilts the scales in the great trial before the Council of *Neters* authorized by Re, the Supreme Judge, to judge and select Seth or Osiris to succeed to the Throne of Osiris. Due to her influence, the *Neters* finally judge against Seth's irrepressible request for a universe of endless, purposeless play of forms and energies. Isis, in the role of the Great Mother, demands that the labor and sacrifice of cosmic creation and procreation bring forth a child—that is, a universal and divine Human—Horus, in the image of Re.

It is for this reason that the bird symbol, and particularly the eye of Horus, the falcon-headed son of Isis and Osiris, is conceived in Egypt as the redemption of human perceptual consciousness which, in the course of human evolution, had become trapped, as it were, by Seth, with the head of a desert animal, the symbol of the slow, separative, enumerating, specifying consciousness. It is Seth who murdered and cut into pieces the body of Osiris, symbol of the cyclic, ever-flowing, eternally recurring bio-and-macro-evolutionary cycles of Time. As the myth relates, Horus accomplished the reconstitution and ascension of the innate, vegetal, cyclic energy belonging to his deceased father, Osiris, in order that these two influences, that of the Osirian cycles of reincarnation and that of the spiral ascension of the resurrectional or Christic force, would work in complement with each other.

From the Egyptians we may learn that if we do not grow in continuous, gnomonic expansion out of our own past symbols and consciousness, that is, if we are unable to read the coded message of our own history, we are in danger of severing the destiny of a spiralling evolution. If we do not extend ourselves to include the full and conscious growth in time of a future vision that is not other than, but never the same as, the past, then we are faced with the ordeal of looking back at India and Egypt as the highest peak of human development for this cycle, and we would have to accept the view of Albert Champdor who wrote thus about the final destruction of Egypt by the Assyrian invaders:

> Disasters always follow one after another like a vision. Evil is always the same. Over this land of Egypt, which was for so long the soul of human civilization, was heard a dreadful sound, one which continues to be heard unto this day—the noise of crumbling Temples and the Obliteration of God's face. Thirty-five centuries later, Egypt of the ancients must be viewed as the most astonishing attainment ever among civilized peoples on both material and spiritual planes. And so doubtless it will remain until this universe is cold in space and nothing more than a cinder in the tumultuous cosmic flames of Time's memory.

## II. Cosmic Numbers and Temple Architecture:
## The Number Nineteen

An old Sufi aphorism says,

> As a sword cannot cut itself, nor a finger touch its own tip, so mind cannot see itself.

Yet mind has the possibility of seeing itself reflected in the forms and symbols to which it gives birth. Its words and numbers, forms and images, are metaphors describing itself, and so are our most powerful tools for penetrating into its actions and modes.

It is in this way, I believe, that the Ancients looked upon the primary symbols of Numbers.

> Numbers are the sources of Form and Energy in the world; they are dynamic and active even among themselves. Hence, they convey in relationship to one another specific qualities which take on an almost human characteristic in their capacity for mutual influence.

This quotation from the writings of Theon of Smyrna, a second-century Greek mathematician, expresses a view of Numbers traditionally held by centuries of Pythagorean philosophers, whose tradition of cosmological geometry originated in the Temples of Egypt. Indeed, in *Le Temple de L'Homme*, R. A. Schwaller de Lubicz voluminously verifies that the Temple of Luxor contains an inexhaustible amount of numerical and geometric relationships used metaphorically, as in the true Pythagorean tradition, to reveal dynamic relationships between the forms and energies of a living Universe.

Using a major geometric division found in the floor-plan of the Temple of Luxor as a starting point, I want now to do an exercise in the old method of number allegory to attempt to unravel an intricate array of facts, concepts, observations and intuitions which the ancient philosophers built up around a single number symbol. We will take only one number, the number nineteen, and follow its meanings and implications as these must have been embedded in the Temple.

Before we begin, however, let us try to envisage this material not merely as a compilation of numerological coincidences, but as a method for the utilization and education of memory—only a much different utilization of it from our own.

Memory is perhaps the least understood of our cognitive faculties. Appearing in some recent experiments as simply an aspect of the neuro-electric activity of the neo-cortex, in others as related to substances secreted in the brain's chemistry, in still others it is linked to actual cellular storage centers in the brain. In other words, it is not yet decided experimentally whether memory storage is neuro-electric, neuro-chemical or somatic—or even perhaps ultimately multi-aspected like the universe it records. What is evident, nevertheless, is that the systematic use of written letters or symbols, a relatively recent innovation in evolution, has provoked a new memory structure—one in which those words with closely related meanings are stored near each other in the brain, so that one word stimulates the retrieval of related words, as in a dictionary or thesaurus. This emergence of a new, long-term, memory apparatus, bound to the logic, semantics and meanings of the vocabulary of an inherited language, which has occurred since the invention of alphabetic writing, again recalls the ancient image of the brain as a constantly mutating, receptive organ, digesting and embodying the various experiences of consciousness as they appear in evolution.

With this more recent form of memory, the mind does not seem to remember thoughts or formulations very well unless they are written down, or at least spoken aloud. It is thus a dialectical memory, whose operation while appearing instantaneous, actually goes through a series of steps, starting with an encoding process which converts the names and categories in a sentence into an internal representation. For example, visual images of the words, in the case of written materials, are transformed into phonetic elements, that is, into an aural medium; next the location of the category of these names is found within the structure of long-term memory, just as words are found in the dictionary; then the stored information about each category is checked to determine what set or relations exists between the categories, an operation that could rely upon some type of cross-reference within the memory structure itself. Based upon the outcome of these three states of the memory process, a recognition and response is then achieved.

But there is also an older form of memory which responds directly to sounds, smells and images. These responses are particularly related to the recall experiences of the deeper, emotional, intuitive and dream nature. Now, while the newer, sophisticated, long-term human memory is located in the neo-cortex, the older, sensation-triggered memory seems to be located in the hippocampus of the mid-brain, which is associated with the primitive olfactory responses and is also in communication with the frontal lobe, the seat of abstract reason.

This binary quality of memory recalls the oft-quoted passage from Plato's *Phaedrus* in which the great King Thamus refuses the gift of the alphabet when it is presented to him by the Egyptian god Thoth. The King says,

> If men learn this, it will implant forgetfulness in their souls; they will cease to exercise memory because they will rely on that which is written, calling things to remembrance no longer from within themselves, but by means of external marks. What you have discovered is a recipe not for memory, but for reminder. And it is no true wisdom that you offer your disciples, but only its semblance, for by telling them of many things without teaching them you will make them seem to know much, while for the most part they know nothing, and as men filled, not with wisdom, but with the conceit of wisdom, they will be a burden to their fellows. (*Phaedrus* 275 a, b)

Bearing in mind Plato's concept of knowledge as "remembrance," we may visualize gnomonic growth as the model by which this newer, linguistic, sequential memory is simply superimposed over the ancient, immediate and simultaneous memory mode, and may imagine, as perhaps Plato did, that the newer memory draws up fragments from the older, holistic memory, and then reformulates them in contexts suitable for the thoughts of the rational mind. Because the structure of our language is sequential, we have developed thought patterns that cognize one thing after another, whereas in reality everything is a simultaneity of interconnected relationships, a psycho-physical perceptual experience that hieroglyphic images and Numbers support. With Temple proportion and Number, then, we are returning to a form of preliterate mind for which arrangements of numbers and images are symbols, or metaphysical codes, corresponding to the interaction of energies and forces at work behind phenomena and their perception, a concentrated penetration into which releases in the perceiver a sudden flood of interrelated patterns.

With this understanding of the ancient, symbolic mind as a guide, let us begin our discussion of the number nineteen.

In Plato's *Timaeus* the interwoven progressions of the squares and cubes of the numbers two and three provide all that is necessary for the formation of the World Soul. Multiples of these two series—one, two, four, eight and one, three, nine, twenty-seven—give sufficient scalar divisions to provide all the tonal material necessary to create a universe of Music, on both audible and supra-audible levels. Now, the gnomon between the square of two (the primal female number) and the square of three (the primal male number) is five. And in traditional numerology five is the number of the incarnate Human Being, in that the human being is a being of five senses, five extensions, five breaths, etc., while the gnomon between the cube of two (which is eight) and the cube of three (which is twenty-seven) is nineteen. This number nineteen leads us to the Egyptian canon of proportion which provides the ground plan for the Temple of Luxor.

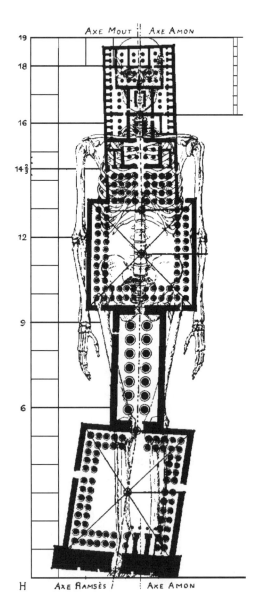

A canon of the human body is generally conceived in the form of a vertical and horizontal grid, established by the repetition of some fixed size or module, which identifies the position and scale of members and parts of the body. For instance, in the art academies of recent times a human canon was established by determining a desirable size for the head of the figure to be drawn, and this head-size was then used to construct a grid upon which all the major proportions of the body could be found. The Greeks used seven, seven-and-a-half or eight head-lengths to determine the proper height for the entire figure, depending upon the individual's body type. This technique of a canon was employed in various forms in many ancient cultures in the cartoons for planning sculptures, wall-reliefs and paintings, and it continued to dominate aesthetic composition through the Renaissance. Slightly different subdivisions of the body, however, are found in different cultures. In the paintings of the Japanese artist Hokusai, for instance, the total height of the ideal human was divided into sixteen units. Other human canons divide the height into eight units—a division related to the musical octave—or twenty-two units, related to the Hebrew alphabet or the number of years in the sunspot cycle, while the Greeks, whose sculptural emphasis was founded on the aesthetic, or even athletic, beauty of external, sensible man, used a canon of eighteen units, which provides a proportional standard for achieving this effect according to the Golden Mean.

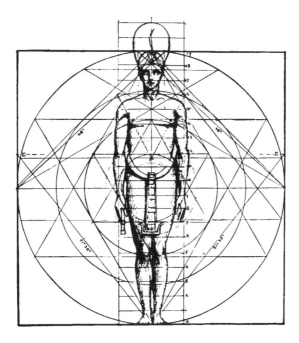

In Egypt the canon of human proportion was based upon the division of the Cosmic Human into nineteen units and served as a metaphysical cryptogram of wordless transmission of universal geometric relationships contained in an idealization of a perfected human form, the Pharaoh. The human body was thus conceived as a sort of cognitive map containing the essential universal laws expressed in terms of proportional relationships—for the geometrical, proportional relationships, such as Phi (the Golden Section), Pi (the measure of the circle), and the so-called sacred square roots of two, three and five, which the Egyptians revealed as aspects of the proportions of the body, are the same geometric constants that underlie the diversities of form, speciation, shape and process in all of phenomenal nature. We find a similar idea expressed in the Hindu architectural sutras thus:

The Universal Being is present in the Temple by means of proportion.

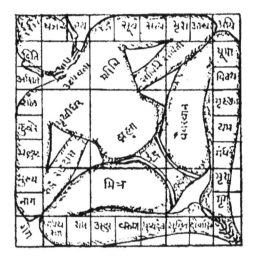

This universalization of the incarnate form had not only a philosophical and symbolic importance, but also a physiological one. We shall find that these geometric, proportional intersections coincide with the organs and neuro-vital centers that were prominent in the ancient, physiological, yogic science by which mind-body processes were elevated from a limited, individual consciousness to a holistic and universal one.

For these reasons the Egyptian canon, as R. A. Schwaller de Lubicz points out, used the number nineteen, primarily because it lends itself to a particular construction of Phi, the Golden Number.

One unit of this canon of nineteen corresponds, not to the full head-size, as in the canons of seven, seven-and-a-half, and eight, but instead only to the crown of the skull. In removing the skull-crown—which, as we shall see, has mathematical, physiological and cosmo-symbolic importance—the remaining eighteen units constitute the height of the human being up to the diadem or headband that encircles the forehead of the King. This causes the navel to fall at exactly eleven units, and eighteen elevenths is a proportional relationship which closely approximates the irrational Golden Section, Phi.

The Golden Section, the first and archetypal form for all divisions of a unity into extreme and mean terms, results from a proportional division and creates what is called "geometric proportion," which can then generate "geometric progressions." A geometric proportion occurs when a is to b as b is to c, or in numbers, when two is to four as four is to eight. In other words, a relation is drawn between two extreme terms a and c, through the mean which is b. The Golden Section results from the unique case in which the geometric proportion is stated with only two terms: i. e., a is to be as b is to a plus b—that is, the smaller is to the mean as the mean is to the smaller plus the mean.

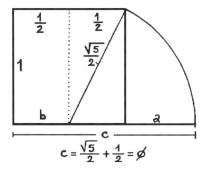

$$c = \frac{\sqrt{5}}{2} + \frac{1}{2} = \emptyset$$

Because of this perfect simplicity and tightness, the Golden Section represents the most reduced relationship through which a unity may be expressed in proportional form. Thus it became known in ancient geometric symbolism as the source of all geometric proportions. In a cosmology which considers the Universe as a symphonic arrangement of interpenetrating, resonating, proportional frequencies or fields, the Golden Section remains the field of proportionality closest to the Original Unity: so that it might even be called the "Son of God." In Greece it was called the *Logos* the "one true proportion," and it was considered the origin of knowledge as well as of beauty, because it is proportional thought which makes possible the intellect, that is, the consciousness capable of comparison. Proportionality was to the ancient epistemologist the basic process underlying all creation, as well as all knowledge of that creation. We only establish knowledge about something through its relation to something else. Language, images, symbols, formulae, measurement, observation are all products of *analogos*, for the human mind has the tendency to register, understand, and recall events in terms of the similarities to, and differences from, other events. The mind is, from this point of view, an instrument for making analogical models; that is to say it is an instrument whereby one thing may see itself reflected in another—which is, in a certain sense, a way to describe love. Many spiritual cultures of the past thus held this unique division in high esteem.

In the Egyptian canonical body, the Golden Section was established between the soles of the feet and the head, figured, as we have said, with the skull cap, containing the cerebral or neo-cortex, removed. The Golden Mean point was thereby determined by the navel, the psychophysical center of the body. This is the place of the *Samana prana* in the Hindu system, the area called the "seed-pod," where the male spermatic essence is ripened. As Matila Ghyka has shown in his classic work on the Golden Section, *Le Nombre d'Or*, the navel oscillates biometrically during growth above and below the exact division of the body's height by the golden proportion. It is a little below in childhood, a little above in adolescence, and ideally arrives at the true proportional position upon the achievement of adulthood or perfection. Below this point are the *hara*, the point of inwardly centered equilibrium in Buddhist meditational practice, and the *Svadhisthana Chakra* (the hypo-gastric plexus), while above it is the *Manipura Chakra*, at the solar plexus.

Thus the navel-point may be considered the interface between the higher and lower energy principles contained in the body, and we may recall in this light the following lines from the Upanishads:

> I am that which binds
> I am that which binds
> I am the golden navel of the Universe
> He who knows this
>         knows Upanishad

(The word *upanishad*, by the way, means, from one point of view, "near approach.")

In the Egyptian canon, then, the nineteenth unit locates the diadem or headband, and so evokes the idea of the crowning of the King. This in turn carries the idea of separating off the top of the head, that is the crown or cranial cap containing the two divided lobes of the neo-cortex. These lobes, because of the bilateral functioning, allow comparative perception, cerebral discernment and judgment, visual and verbal objectification of perceptions, and separate self-awareness—in other words, the entire sense of ourselves as separate psychological entities.

According to ancient, symbolic thought, the growth of this grey-white cerebral matter is lunar in character, both because it eclipses the solar mind—the heart-and-blood-driven mind of the autonomic system governed by the hypothalamic and cranial glands which, as we shall see, respond to the celestial rhythms contained in the solar day and the seasonal changes of the year—and because it functions in terms of reflected light. Thus Thoth, the *Neter* of intelligence and mind, is a lunar deity.

Physiologically this means that the external eyes, in carrying images to the cortex, receive only a varied array of photons from our source of light, the sun, which the retina must decelerate into such frequencies as can be transmitted by the optic and cerebral nerves. These arrays or patterns of light, received and modified by the eye, are then spread across the images, memories, hypotheses and schematic prejudgments that we have stored in our conscious and semi-conscious minds in the form of neural patterns. Our minds then project or reflect back onto the outer world the formal, objective, specifying characteristics that we maintain as images in our perceptual schema. We thus obtain the impression that these ever-shifting patterns and arrays of light are a world of fixed, separate objects, but in fact it is our eyes which have transformed a particularized light-energy resonant field into apples, tables and chairs.

This reflective, projecting, moon-like activity of the retina and cerebral cortex gives all our sense organs, especially the eyes and ears, a dual function. They are both receptors of external stimuli and also projectors of our internally held cognitive, reactive image of the objective world. This means that objects are themselves objects only insofar as they exist within ourselves, functionally inscribed, either innately or through learning, within the sensory or cognitive apparatus that we use to specify them. The world experienced through the senses is a reflected projection of our physiological and intellectual nature, and so is only relatively real, as is our own image reflected in a mirror and then returned back to us again. Indeed, in Egyptian, the word for "mirror" and the word for "life" have the same phonetic spelling, *ankh*, and Egyptian craftsmen often made mirrors in the shape of the *ankh* symbol, thus making even such a mundane article as this into a reminder of the drama of consciousness involved in a self-perceptive evolution.

There are other characteristics which make the moon an effective metaphor for the dual lobes of the cerebral cortex. We may note first that in the cerebral cortex, although the full number of cells is attained and fixed in early infancy, these cells are destroyed and replenished every month in cycle with the moon. A more important symbolic function, through which the moon and the cerebral cortex coincide, is contained in the following: metabolism, as we shall see, is controlled by the endocrinal glands which secrete hormones—"exciters"—directly into the bloodstream, which is, of course, traditionally the bearer of solar intelligence, and whose hormonal, procreative, regulating intelligence the lunar neo-cortex then comes to obscure, eclipse or reflect. The master regulators of this hormonal system are the pineal and pituitary glands, and the activation of these is, in turn, often regulated and coordinated by the hypothalamus, sometimes symbolized by the androgynous *Neter*, Hapi, the Nile God.

In one instance Hapi is shown seated in a cave or ventricle, cut off, that is, eclipsed, by the outline of a serpent, which in Egypt represents the dualized consciousness of the cerebro-spinal system, here pictured in the shape of the neo-cortex. Hapi pours from two urns, which perhaps represent the pineal and pituitary glands, the fluids which initiate the cyclic flow of the Nile's fertility, just as in the cave of the brain the androgynous or anatomically undifferentiated area of the hypothalamus stimulates the two glands which determine and bring forth sexual differentiation, maturity and fertility in an organism.

One of the effects of the eclipsing by the neo-cortex of this solar, hormonal intelligence which circulates directly through the blood and heart is the progressive decline during evolution of the hormonal control of behavior. For example, looking back in evolution we find that sexual behavior in most animals is phased to the light cycle of the solar year, allowing, like the Nile, only a seasonal fertility. With human sexuality, on the other hand, we find fertility phased to the briefer lunation cycle, creating a condition of continuous sexuality. The lunar nature of this condition has a living symbol in the shape of the dual lobes of the neo-cortex whose development brought it about, for it is this brain which has sexualized or dualized our perception of the world into self and other, either/or, left and right, subject and object, right and wrong.

Clinically speaking, this neo-cortex or lunar crown may, like a satellite, be completely removed without the disruption of organic life processes—the bio-rhythmic autonomic controls in the mid-brain will continue to operate. In Egypt, the whole ritual of the crowning of the King is related to this physiological, symbolic insight, which is expressed in the canon of nineteen. The King, upon coronation, assumes the crown or diadem marking the removal of the upper portion of the head and wears on his forehead the solar or inner eye symbolized by the bird and the reptile, but this instinctual, hormonal eye is, in the King's case, transformed into a deep, intuitive, symbolic and innate knowledge by virtue of now being in harmony with the reasoning, conceptual centers of the frontal lobes and the neo-cortex. This harmonious knowledge, symbolized by the serpent coming over the top of the head to the forehead, connects the old brain with the new. When aligned with the profound structure of symbolic reasoning, the instantaneous, innate flashes of intuitive temporal recognition become expanded into encompassing patterns of insight and, thus joined, the two brains are raised to the crown above the head.

Underneath the golden mask and headdress of Tut-ankh-Amun a linen headwrap was found, embroidered in a serpent design of pearls, gold and semi-precious stones, confirming this interpretation of the symbolic nature of the crown. The familiar Egyptian design of the double uraeus accurately locates the fissure between the two hemispheres of the brain, as well as indicating the ventricles. The bulged areas on the snake's body, where it touches the forehead and bends back into the brain, may indicate the interconnectivity of the orbs of the eyes with the brain. The crossing of the optic nerves is also indicated, and the uraeus is raised up on the sides of the head so as to cover the areas of the parietal lobes—those controlling verbal, analytic activity in the left lobe and geometric, temporal and spatial pattern-recognition in the right.

All of this means that the King represents a prototypic transcendent human, risen above the brain activity which creates the perception of self and world as being divided, separative and personal. Therefore the King can guide his people, not out of egocentrically shaped unconscious drives and images, but instead out of communion with the inflowing celestial and geophysical rhythmic energy-patterns of earth and sky. This royal or transcendent vision of the Human Being is the heart of the anthropomorphic doctrine in which humanity is seen as the ultimate product of the earth, carrying within it all the essential measures of earth in the form of the harmonic units which situate earth and humans as a proportional part of a universal wholeness.

To the Pharaonic sage, the Human Being was the reference for all knowledge to such a degree that the earth itself was considered on the basis of the human canon. The polar half-axis, being the reference line in the sphere, was seen as the Human Being standing on the plateau of the equator. The division between the eighteenth and nineteenth units, which separates the cranial cap, corresponded proportionately to a division on the sphere of the earth between seventy-three and seventy-four degrees North latitude. This is the latitude where the fringes of the continents collapse into the abyss of the North Sea, called the Maelstrom in legends, above which the earth's polar cap begins. In addition to this proportional coincidence between the skull cap in the human canon and the ice cap of the earth, we find in Egypt a linguistic coincidence which confirms the relationship: the Egyptian word *mh* means "cubit" (which is the measure of the King's diadem), while the word *mht* means "north" and the word *mhn* refers to the diadem itself that encircles the King's head.

Using the Egyptian measures we find that for a sphere whose circumference at the equator measures 21,600,000 armspans or fathoms (a close approximation of the earth's circumference), the circumference measured at seventy-two degrees thirty-four minutes thirty seconds will be the same number of Royal Cubits, the Royal Cubit being an essential Egyptian measure, as we shall see. Thus, in an exact, proportional symbol we have the multiple psychological and physical relationships between the icy, white, polar incrustation of the globe and the lunar, cerebral incrustation which perceptually freezes the dynamic rhythms of light and life into the separately conceived objective world.

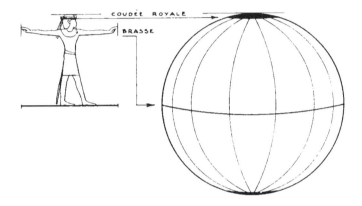

This analogy between the earth's polar cap and the cerebral mind-cap may be extended, for there are historical correspondences between the development of our brains and the greater cycles of geology and astronomy. A prime example involves the descent of the ice cap during the still unexplained cycle of the ice ages which, metaphorically, we may say performed an eclipse-like function, in that the life, growth and development created by solar energy on earth were temporarily effaced by the swelling, frozen, white mass. Whatever the cause of these ice ages, they clearly had a significant effect upon human life on earth.

H. M. Ami reports in his book *Canada and Newfoundland* that the diet of the northern races in prehistoric times did not include flesh in any form. Indeed, according to this geologist, European peoples did not become flesh eaters until they were forced to do so by the destruction of the great forests of nut and wild fruit trees by the ice cap that crept down over the northern hemisphere during the glacial period. In North America, however, there remained large pockets of wild chestnut and hazelnut trees, providing certain indigenous populations with a constant supply of protein, carbohydrate and vitamin foods without any need for hunting, agriculture or domesticated animals. European colonizers, habituated to animal protein, destroyed much of this natural food source by clearing land for grazing and crops.

Food sources and habits are, as we know, a major formative factor in cultural and behavioral patterns affecting species evolution. Ethologists and evolutionists agree that even in pre-human times the emergence of a carnivorous ape was the single most important phase in the emergence of a human-like intelligence out of primate origins. The cunning, resourcefulness and pre-calculating thought required for hunting and trapping, in addition to the necessity for the supposed pre-human primates to work together in packs with weapons and to develop a system of communication among themselves during the hunt, are considered to be the behavioral triggers which launched the processes leading to the major characteristics of human intelligence. As Konrad Lorenz points out, it was the ape-like physicality, coupled with the pack-hunting instincts of dogs, that provided the natural combination leading to the behavioral success of our ancestors as hunters. The dog, we may note, was also the first domesticated animal enlisted for the purposes of the hunt.

In Egypt, we find these details interpreted symbolically. Thoth, the Ibis-headed *Neter* who represents the principle of intelligence in both its evolving and transcendent forms, is sometimes represented as a baboon with a dog's head and is often pictured in the company of dog-faced baboons.

This power of food in shaping evolution is precisely stated in the *Taittriya Upanishad*:

> For from food alone it appears are these creatures born, and being born, they live by food, and into food they depart and enter again.

Among populations, such as certain tribes of American Indians, who were unaffected by the ice-age destruction of their food sources, and were therefore freed from the necessity of hunting, agriculture and the domestication of animals, we find linguistic concepts developed in ways quite different from our own. Benjamin Whorf has pointed out, for instance, that in Hopi and other Indian Languages there are no adjectives denoting the possession of space. Space for these non-agrarian, food-gathering peoples remained an abstraction that was approached linguistically through locational terms of a relational and orientational character. There was no concept at all for land or space divided into proprietary or objectified blocks. Even the interior spaces of the architecture had no terms for possession. In these ancient tongues both time and space, as we have said, were dealt with in purely relational terms, or with special sets of terms having to do with tendencies or intensities of movement.

It appears, then, that not only is civilized, agricultural humanity linguistically and culturally separated from those phases of human evolution which followed the cyclic patterns of natural food sources, but it has also activated, and since become dependent upon, a brain function quite other than the hormonally communicated, innate mind, rhythmically tuned to the celestial cycles of fertility. But more important to note, perhaps, is that the origin of these radical shifts in the concepts concerning time and space—which affect all the details of daily life—has been traced to the passage of the sun through the alternating dark and light spiral arms of the galaxy. According to this view, the ice-age cycle, like the sunspot cycle, is related to the sun's interaction with the dense material, compressed by the collision of gas clouds moving between galactic stars, which characteristically marks the dark edges of the spiral arms. A star passing through these gathers and draws into itself vast quantities of this compressed cosmic dust, causing an alteration in its outer layer and a subsequent decrease in nuclear burning within. But when it moves out of the dark lane, heat convection suddenly increases and heat production due to activity in the solar interior suddenly drops by ten percent.

(Our own sun, incidentally, has just—less than twenty thousand years ago—passed through the lane associated with the constellation of Orion. Twenty thousand years is not much in the solar life span and our sun is still adjusting to this instability in its convective heat balance. Many possible effects may have been triggered by this, one of which is that the sun is now, after twenty thousand years, again beginning to sprinkle, but not yet shower, neutrinos, considered by occultists most to resemble the type of energies involved in supra-rational and telepathic phenomena, onto the earth.)

Thus all is held in the spiralling arms of meta-galactic Time, recalling the vast system of *Yugas* maintained by the Hindus, those cycles within cycles shaping the outpouring of universal energy into varied patterns of rhythmic alternation and influencing the continual manifestation of life and form.

In the light of such considerations it is not surprising to find our number nineteen playing an interesting role in astronomical harmonies. Nineteen squared, for instance, is 361, a number implying the function of the division of a circle or cycle into 360 degrees, with an extra digit to complete the figure as the center point. (In Hindu thought the circumference and its center describe the relationship between *Sat*, or Existence, figured by the circumference, and *Asat*, or Non-Existence, figured by the center point.)

An example of this is the cycle of nineteen years which archeological records show was definitely observed by the Chaldeans, who called it the *Saros* cycle. This cycle involves the fact that about every nineteen years a sun-moon eclipse occurs at the same point in the sky. That is, an eclipse on the day of the winter solstice, increasing the effect of the darkening of the light, occurs again after a period of nineteen years. The Chaldeans attributed magical powers to this dark point, believing that it was an astronomical moment containing the power to end the world.

Actually, however, there are two cycles involved, both of which are indicated in the Temple of Luxor. One is of nineteen years and the other is of 18.61 years, the former canonically giving us the full height of man and the latter the exact height of man with the skull cap removed. Remembering, then, what we have already uncovered of the metaphysical principle of the eclipse, let us investigate the three elements in this synchronicity: the sun, the moon and the moon's nodes.

The paths of the sun and moon against the sky lie in planes which intersect at an angle of five degrees nine minutes, the points of intersection being called the nodes of the moon's orbit. The sun's path in the sky may be taken as being the same year after year, but the moon's orbit varies, slowing its orbital progress and hence shifting its nodal points along the sun's orbit. These nodes complete a circuit of the sun's path every 18. 61 years.

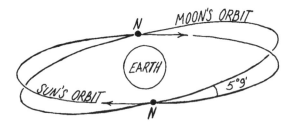

Given this situation, a lunar eclipse occurs at the full moon if the sun and the moon are within ten degrees of the same nodal point. Thus there are always three factors involved in an eclipse: the sun's position, the moon's position and the nodal alignment. In the succession of eclipses, then, we may see a pattern of solar and lunar dominance, each alternatively and "gnomonically" eclipsing the other.

Without going into the several variants in this interaction of sun and moon through the nodes, it may be said that a definite cycle is set up so that every 6585.3 days the relative relationships of sun, moon and the two nodes repeat themselves: the sun, moon and nodes have swung around bodily through an angle of ten and eleven degrees counter-clockwise from their starting points as measured against the backdrop of the stars. It follows that 6585.3 days after an eclipse there will be another eclipse at exactly the same orbital position, and it is this 6585.3 day recurrence of the solar eclipse on the winter solstice that constitutes the *Saros* cycle.

The ecliptical alignment of the earth, sun and nodal points occurs every 346.62 days, a period known as the "ecliptic year." Nineteen of these make 6585.8 days, while the sun, moon, nodal alignment of 18.029 times 365.25 days makes the 6585.3 days of the *Saros* cycle. In order to relate these two cycles, the Ancients maintained a calendar system with two successive festivals: that of the 346 day ecliptic year and, nineteen days later, that of the 365 day seasonal year. These two cycles of nineteen and 18.029 also relate to the moon's orbital cycle of 27.3 days, for there are exactly 223 lunations in the 6585.3 day cycle, so that the solar ecliptic cycle may be measured by the moon.

As Fred Hoyle points out, there have only been about 200 generations within recorded history, while more than 10,000 generations lived during prehistoric times. During this period and for much of recorded history, the sun and moon were for humankind the predominant embodied symbols of celestial influences upon earth. All religious and mytho-scientific cosmological teachings therefore gave considerable attention to the life- and form-giving forces which emanated from these two near-by and interacting heavenly bodies. Indeed, modern research into bio-clocks only confirms the almost god-like power of the solar-lunar cyclic influence in regulating life processes. Bearing this in mind, it is little wonder that eclipses held such inestimable importance to the ancient astronomer and sage.

Centuries of observation would have revealed to ancient humans that an eclipse never occurs without the factor of the nodes (which are, for instance, clearly marked opposite each other on the Aubrey circle at Stonehenge). Nodes represented a third and hidden power whose force could extinguish the dualized energies of visible light. In other words, within a symbolic envisioning of the eclipse, we may find the origins of the trinity constituted by an invisible, all-powerful, ever-present deity who proportionately polarized himself into two life-giving lights.

This is exactly the mythological doctrine of the Temple of Luxor. Amon, the Supreme Deity, whose name means the "Hidden One," or "he whose name is hidden," manifested himself in both a lunar and a solar aspect, or rather in a combination or conjunction of both. Completing this trinity are Mut, whose name means "Mother," representing the maternal, creative energy, and Khonsu, their child, the archetypal dauphin, a moon deity. Each of these three is represented in the Temple by a separate axis, and each has a slightly different geometric and astronomical orientation and value.

Resuming the numerological study of the number nineteen, let us look at an example in which this trinity is brought into contact with the gnomon and the celestial cycles, remembering that in Pythagorean thought numbers are not simply quantities but evocations of hidden energies which act formatively on matter.

From this point of view, the numbers seven and nineteen are both related to the number six in a particular way. Namely, both seven and nineteen are considered to be "hexagonal" numbers because, as may be seen from the figure, six points plus the central seventh mark six hexagons around a seventh, just as eighteen points plus a nineteenth as the central unity mark out twelve closely packed hexagons around a central hexagon. All such hexagons are cubic gnomons. The gnomon between the cube of one and the cube of two is seven, while the gnomon between the cube of two and the cube of three is nineteen, and that between the cube of three and the cube of four is thirty-seven, etc. . . , the entire series being hexagonal.

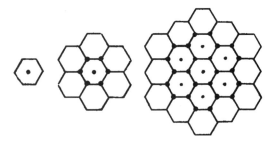

In Egyptian symbolism, again linking the number nineteen to the measure of cyclic time, the twelve outer hexagons represent the twelve locations of the sky, better known as the twelve zodiacal divisions. However, before we can discuss the Egyptian system of measuring the heavens, we must first discuss briefly the essential measure in Egyptian cosmology and architecture, the Royal Cubit.

The Royal Cubit is a geo-temporal measure; that is to say, it is precisely the distance travelled by a point on the equator in 1/1000 of a second of time due to the earth's rotational spin. The Royal Cubit measures 20.612 inches (1.71 feet) or 0.5236 meters, which is exactly the sextant arc in a circle having a diameter of one meter. Thus the Royal Cubit establishes a chord-arc relationship and the half-cubit can then be applied to the twelve divisions of the celestial vault or circle. The relationship of arc to chord in a circle is essential to all space-time calculations. But, as we have observed, in ancient thought the structural, proportional laws sprang from human physiology which was seen as a cosmic essence summarizing all the universal principles.

The Egyptian myth therefore describes the system of measuring the heavens as follows: The King or Royal Principle measures the heavens. The King is given the numerical value of half a cubit. The texts then say, for instance, that twelve Royal men measure the heavens, meaning that the circumference of a circle is given the value of 120, or ten times twelve Royal men. The radius specified by a circle of this size is 19.0983, which is also the size of the hexagon inscribed in this circle.

Let us now extend the research concerning the number nineteen into the realm of geometric volumes. The volume of a sphere inscribed in a cube will be equal to 0.5236 of the total volume of the cube. If we give the value of one to the cube, the relationship of the inscribed sphere will be 1/0. 5236, which equals 1.90983. If we inverse this order and also calculate to obtain all positive values, we can say that a sphere with a volume of ten will be circumscribed by a cube whose volume is 19.0983. That is, it is the number nineteen, the number of the cosmic human in the Temple of Luxor, which binds the relationship between the archetypal oppositional forms of the square and the circle, the cube and the sphere.

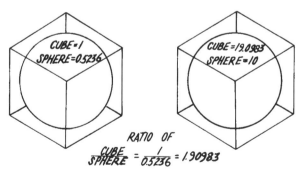

It has been demonstrated in numerous biometric measurements of the human body that the height of the upper body is in the same relationship to the total height, as the volume of the sphere is to the volume of the circumscribing cube. That is, it is in the relationship of 1:1.90983. Thus the human form embodies this universal invariant and it is the number nineteen which evokes it. Particularly interesting in this instance also is the fact that these mathematical relationships refer to the upper and lower parts of the body, which traditionally symbolize the respective locations of one's spiritual and material energies.

The pubic arch, furthermore, divides the body exactly in half, a division consistent in all known human canons. This relationship (of one to two, that is, 0.5), in relation to the relationship between the upper body and the whole body (that is, 0.5236), is the same as the relationship of a chord of sixty degrees to an arc of sixty degrees.

Consider next the full human armspan, the fathom, a measure employed in many ancient systems and still used as a nautical measure. The fathom is slightly larger than human height, the relationship most often cited being 1.047, namely that between the armspan and the total height. This relationship is equal to Pi/3, which allows us to establish four identical relationships: fathom/cubit = armspan/height of human = height of upper body/height of pubic arch = Pi/3 = 1.047.

To summarize: the height of the upper body corresponds to half the armspan and also the height of the lower limbs; the width of the shoulders correspond to a quarter of the armspan; total human height is equal to a chord of an arc of sixty degrees measured by the armspan. Thus the Human Being may be considered as the radius of the Universal Circle of invariant cosmic relationships.

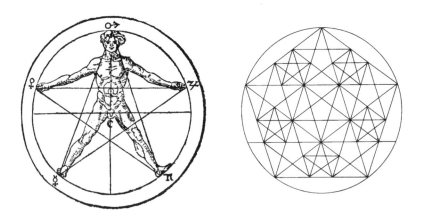

The number nineteen, finally, also plays a unique role in the measure of the pentagon. In many esoteric cosmologies the Cosmic Human is inscribed within this figure, which is the symbol of universalized humanity.

The transitory or physical human is ruled by the five external senses, and is thus figured by the exterior form of the pentagon, while the internal structure, the familiar stellated pentagram, yields the key proportions of the Golden Section, and is therefore related to the perfectibility of humankind. This proportion, as we have implied, symbolizes the "drawing near" or the "near approach" to the Original Unity.

In Egypt the evolution of the Human Being, from a creature dominated by the senses to one expressing a universal consciousness, was symbolized by the Pharaoh. The Texts say, "The King is he who becomes a star."

Now, the diagonal of the pentagon has the remarkable property of being the geometric mean between the diameters of the circumscribing circle and the height of the pentagon. These numerical relationships, which approach those of the Pharaonic canon of eighteen and nineteen, are as follows: diameter/diagonal = 20/19.021 = diagonal/height = 19.021/18.092 = 1.051.

I have mentioned in this talk only a few of the correspondences between the Human Being and the spatio-temporal geometry of earth and sky which are evoked by the division of the ground plan of the Temple of Luxor into nineteen units as the height of Cosmic Mind. This has been an exercise in the ancient, analogical mind-discipline called "stereometry" by Plato, who described it as the "likening of unlike things." To elaborate upon John Michell's *City of Revelation*: just as there were canons of architecture and physiology, so there were also canons—that is, systems of interrelated proportion—governing the formation of language, music, science and social order. All of these were based upon the same cosmic Truths, expressed in number, ratio and proportion, and were revealed in universal world order.

Celestial influences may manifest fully on earth only through the medium of the human mind and body, and it is through these instruments that these influences may be controlled, balanced, harmonized and directed towards attaining their ultimate universal goal. But in order for this instrument to be effective, an awareness is required of how these influences enter into the body-mind and activate the field of human experience and behavior. It could be said that the Human Being has the potential to structure the Universe through a conscious structuring of its own mind and body. If we consider, as does the Hindu tradition, that earthly humanity is only a momentary emanation of the possibilities contained within the Cosmic Mind or *Manas*—that is, that humanity is simply the furthest thrust of embodied self-aware perceptiveness at any one stage in evolution—then it may be said that in whatever way Humanity structures itself, so likewise it structures the manifestation of the Universe. This then is the bond between physiology and cosmology.

To quote John Michell:

> The canon was devised to promote the intense metaphoric identity of the initiate with the dynamics of geometrical and numerical relationships, wherein the world of phenomena is revealed as the product of archetypal forces.

I might add that within this consciousness the initiate may, within himself or herself, participate in the creation of the universal product for which these forces were originally intended, that is, the birth of a divine-embodied human race. With such thoughts as these emerging from the philosophic architecture of the Temple, we approach the re-centering of Humanity within the awesome expanses of galactic space.

### III. The Mythic Vision of a Sacred Science

Throughout these pages we have presumed as part of the anthropomorphic vision of the Universe that much of Egyptian symbolism, whether geometric or mythological, possesses one level of interpretation that is strictly anatomical or physiological. According to ancient logic, all of what we perceive of the evolving universe surrounding and within ourselves can only be encountered through the sensory, interfacial instrument that we inhabit. Therefore our brains and bodies necessarily shape all our perceptions and have themselves come into existence and been shaped by the interaction of the same seen and unseen energies that have shaped every perceivable thing on earth. Our bodies and minds, their architecture, processes and energies, could not be other than those of the universe that we observe, image and experience. Body, Mind and Universe must be in a parallel, formative identity. From this point of view, "Man know thyself" was the principle of ancient science, as it is also coming to be in ultra-modern science. To quote the physicist, Robert Dicke:

> The right order of ideas may not be "Here is the universe, so what must man be?" but instead, "Here is Man so what must the universe be?"

To know and achieve on every possible level this identity of self with cosmos was the prevailing dynamic of Temple education. For this reason, techniques of introspection known as yoga provided a remarkable instrument for examining not only the individual's psychology and physiology but also the characteristics of the natural and cosmic world.

Yet did ancient science, we might ask, dependent as it was upon the human body for its principle metaphor, also have a precise, empirical system of research concerning actual physiology, in addition to these more intuitive and analogical concepts? The *Edwin Smith Surgical Papyrus*, a document copied by a scribe around 1700 B. C., but attributed by tradition to the great vizier, sage, physician and architect Imhotep, whom the Greeks called Asklepios and who lived around 2800 B. C., suggests it did.

This papyrus indicates that much earlier than the magical medical texts there existed a clear, objective, scientific medicine, devoid of ritual magic, and based upon attentive, trained and repeated observation of patients. The papyrus further gives evidence of a detailed knowledge of physical and cerebral anatomy, and shows that the ancient Egyptians had an awareness and accurate measure of the pulse, and an understanding of the arterial and venous system of blood circulation. It contains in addition accurate descriptions of depressed skull fractures and compressed fractures of the vertebral column, and refers to the brain meninges and cerebro-spinal fluid by specific names.

According to the papyrus, the Pharaonic physician seems to have recognized the two forms of deafness, aphasia and hyperacusia, which accompany temporary bone fractures, and to have been aware that an injury to one side of the head causes paralysis on the opposite side of the body. It also appears that he was so familiar with this crossing of brain function with body performance that he understood that in some cases a blow on one side of the skull could cause a counter-blow or reciprocal concussion on the opposite side, thereby causing a paralysis to occur on the same side of the body as the original blow.

Experts who have studied this remarkable papyrus have concluded not only that great anatomical knowledge must have existed from the very earliest Epochs of Egyptian history, and that autopsies and dissections must have been performed under very scientific conditions, but also that the author clearly realized the relationship existing between the brain, the nervous system, the voluntary body movement and the involuntary secretions originating in the brain, as well as the fact that the location of paralysis in the body is dependent on the location of the brain or nerve lesion.

If we place this kind of evidence beside the exquisite techniques of mummification which reveal practices, such as how organs were removed from the body without disturbing other areas of the body, which still confound modern surgeons, and even beside the art of the Egyptian embalmer, who could flawlessly remove the entire brain through the nostril of the deceased, we may be well assured, despite the distortion of conventional history, that the Egyptians possessed a rich and accurate knowledge of cerebral and nervous anatomy. Indeed, it was this knowledge, acting as a guiding support for their far-reaching, holistic, analogical, geometric and mythic vision, that led them to a theory of cosmic evolution symbolically based on the forms, functions and relations of the various components of our brains and bodies.

My object for the remainder of this chapter is to attempt to show how the skeleton of this ancient science provides the symbolic motif for the architecture of the Temple of Luxor.

True symbols are not meant to change with time, except perhaps in their most external expression. They are, in effect, humanity's link with the eternal, mediating between deep nonverbal knowledge embedded from the beginning in the order of creation and the explicit reasoning of the external, sense-based, organizational faculties. Externally perceivable properties are always dependent, as we have said, upon the varied qualities of internal structure—the physical world, like the inner world of mind, being a complex system of interpenetrating sequences of hierarchical, structural levels—yet amidst this diversity of overlaid patterns all structures, as well as all dynamic processes, are characterized by order and symmetrical relationships. Science, then, can only proceed by matching a reasoned, structural model containing these aspects of order and symmetry with the physical, observable or supposed structure of matter. Art and philosophy likewise involve the matching of physical structure with sensual and intuitional patterns of perception. In both cases, all is matching and mediating. Thought is the creator and testing ground for mediating patterns, allowing a selective interaction between the whole body and the outer world of the senses, as well as between supra- and sub-sensual levels of experience.

It is reasonable to conclude from this that only models which accurately interconnect many levels of internal and external structure and experience could act as effective guides to the development of physical and spiritual knowledge. Modern physics, for instance, in its attempt to deal with the untold multiplicities and variations of particle states, is developing models which contain three major types of symmetry, all of which are based upon conserved or constant qualities in particle interaction. The first of these is of the bi-polar, oppositional symmetry type, demonstrated by positive and negative charges, matter and anti-matter, spin and iso-spin, left- and right-handed structures, etc. The second type is called "symmetrical" symmetry. This is a mathematical means of expressing all interactional particle behavior in terms of the rotation of an underlying spherical surface. The third symmetrical system, finally, is related to "co-modulation," as it was named by the Greeks. Here a web of harmoniously interrelated proportional expressions is used for describing states or locations.

This reference to the Greeks is not out of place, for the ancient Pythagorean musical metaphor or symbol is a model which contains all three of these symmetries. It is a co-modulation insofar as the notes of the scale are all internal subdivisions of one basic tone. It is a circular or spherical symmetry, due to the tonal equivalence or return as expressed in the law of the octave. And finally it contains a bi-polar or oppositional symmetry, in that the basic consonant musical ratios are derived from two numerical progressions, each of which is the inverse of the other.

This last form of symmetry leads us directly to the architecture of the Temple of Luxor.

The natural series of numbers (that is 1,2,3,4,5,6. . .) is part of a family of numerical progressions called "Arithmetic." Such progressions are generated by the continual addition of the same number-unit, which is determined by the difference between the first and second terms. Arithmetic proportion, which is established on any three terms taken from an arithmetic progression, thus has a mean term which is always halfway between the two extremes. That is, it corresponds to what we call an average.

In the arithmetic progression, then, addition is the means of growth, whereas in the progression called "Geometric" (an example of which is (2,4,8,16. . .) each successive term unfolds by being multiplied by the first term. Thus addition and multiplication remain our two most effective mathematical metaphors for describing organic growth on the one hand and physical or gnomonic accumulation on the other.

A third, closely related family of progressions is formed by establishing a mean term that results from the multiplication of any two extremes, followed by the division of this product by their average or arithmetic mean. For example: 2 multiplied by 6 = 12 divided by 4 = 3, which gives us the progression 2,3,6. This type of progression, which combines both the additive and multiplicative growth procedures of the other two progressions, is called "Harmonic," and its proportion has the characteristic that the mean term always exceeds the smaller extreme, and is less than the larger extreme, by the same fractional proportion. For example, in our series 2,3,6. . . three exceeds two by one half of two (i.e., one), and is less than six by one half of six (i.e., three).

The most important and mysterious characteristic of this form of harmonic, proportional progression is the fact that the inverse of any harmonic progression is an arithmetic progression. Thus 2,3,4,5. . . is an ascending arithmetic progression, while the inverse series (1/2, 1/3, 1/4, 1/5. . .) is a descending harmonic progression.

In music it is the insertion of the harmonic and arithmetic means between the two extremes in double ratios—such as six and twelve—representing the octave double, which gives us the progression known as the "musical" proportion: that is, 6, 8, 9, 12. In other words, the arithmetic and harmonic means between the double geometric ratios are the numerical ratios which correspond to the tonal intervals of the major fourth and the major fifth, the basic consonances in nearly all musical scales.

These two parallel yet inversing progressions not only provide the foundations of music, but more generally provide a mathematical model with which to investigate the complementary or opposed symmetries of a dualized, yet harmonically integrated, whole. For this reason the musical metaphor was the cornerstone of ancient philosophy, applicable to both physical and metaphysical domains.

There is a simple geometric method for generating a series of harmonic progressions which, as we shall see, corresponds to the ground plan of the Temple of Luxor.

Construct a line, OX, and raise a perpendicular, ZY. (In the diagram, OX is to XZ and XY in the relationship of two to one, but these lines could be in any ratio for the diagram to be effective.) Beginning, then, from the midpoint between O and X, which is designated A, raise a perpendicular to A', and from A' draw a line crossing OX to Y. This line A'Y will cut OX at B, which is exactly two-thirds of OX, and is therefore the harmonic mean between A and X. Continuing in this way, each successive proportion will be the harmonic mean between the previous proportion and the total length, and all these proportions will be musically significant: 1/2 being the octave, 2/3 being the fifth, 4/5 being the major third, 8/9 being the major tone, 16/17 being the half-tone.

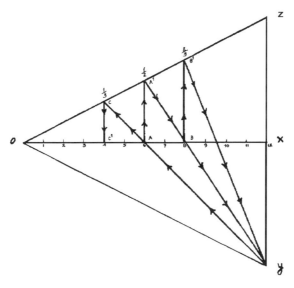

Another example is shown below. This figure is constructed in the same way as the first, but in this case we begin with A as one-quarter of OX, proceeding then with the geometric crossing as before to derive the following ratios: 1/4, 2/5, 4/7, 8/11, 16/19. These numerators are formed according to the geometric rate of two, the denominators being formed by adding the numerator and denominator of the preceding ratio. Thus, although a different series of proportions is generated by the initial division, in this case 1/4, all the ratios are still harmonic relationships.

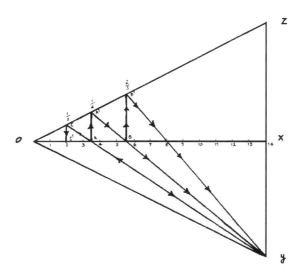

From this purely geometric gesture of a repetitive diagonal crossing within a triangular frame we can see that all the musically significant harmonic ratios may be generated without recourse to mathematics or algebra.

Continuing with this model, we may imagine our harmonically segmented triangle as a volume, i.e., as the cross-section of a spiral or cone.

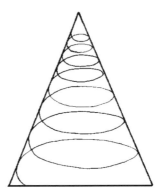

A similar cone-shaped image may come to mind in this context, namely the basic space-time diagram of relativity physics, in which the speed of light becomes the diagonal limit on a Cartesian space-time graph—a diagram also referred to as the "Cone of Light. "

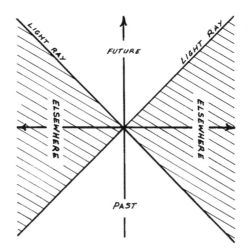

In the same vein we might also note that the angular divisions of the volume of the cone give the four most important curvatures which appear to be followed by the celestial bodies in their orbital paths.

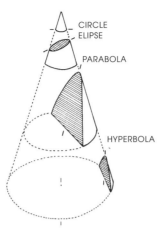

CIRCLE
ELIPSE
PARABOLA
HYPERBOLA

And if we continue to move with this image of a spiraling cone of light, constructed as ours is from the geometric principle of the harmonic crossing, we may be reminded also of the earth's gyrating spin upon its axis. This forms a double vortex, whose nodal point is the center of the earth's body and which sucks in and draws towards itself the plasmic dust radiation and the electromagnetic field of the solar system.

This gyrating movement also traces a slow-moving circle around the earth's north and south poles, causing both the shift in the pole star and the cycle of time traditionally known as the precession of the equinoxes through the twelve signs of the zodiac.

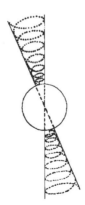

With such ideas and images of the geometry of celestial law in mind, I am reminded of an enigmatic passage from the Apocryphal *Acts of John*, in which Jesus speaks to his disciples as they circle around him. Jesus is in the center, the twelve disciples around him, as in the Sufi dances that imitate the cycle of the zodiac. Jesus says:

I have no temples, I have temples. I am a lamp to thee who sees me, I am nearer to thee who understands me, I am a door to he who knockest at me, I am a Way to thee, a Wayfarer. As for me, if thou wouldst know what I was, in a word, I am the Verb who did dance all things; 'twas I who leapt and danced. . . .

Then, later as the Crucifixion proceeds, John tells how he could not bear the sight of the event and fled to the Mount of Olives, weeping, where, at the very moment itself of the Crucifixion, as John tells it:

My Lord stood in the midst of the cave [cone] and filled it with light and said to me, "John, to the multitude below in Jerusalem, it appears that I am being crucified, pierced with spears. To thee now I speak, and give ear to what I say: 'twas I who put it into thy heart to ascend to this Mount, that thou might hear what the disciples should learn from a Master and Man from God." And having thus spoken, he showed me a Crossing of Light set up, and around the Cross a vast multitude, not having one form; and in the Cross another multitude, wherein was one form and one likeness. And I beheld the Lord Himself above this Crossing, and He had however no shape, but only as it were a voice. Not, however, this voice to which we were accustomed, but one of its own kind and beneficent and truly of God, saying unto me, "John, one there needs must be to hear these things from me; for I long for one who will hear. This Cross of Light is called by me for your sake sometimes Mind, sometimes Jesus, sometimes Christ, sometimes Door, sometimes Way, sometimes Bread, sometimes Seed, sometimes Resurrection, sometimes Son, sometimes Father, sometimes Spirit, sometimes Life, sometimes Truth, sometimes Faith, sometimes Grace. Now, these things it is called as towards men; but as to what it is in truth itself, in its own meaning to itself and declared unto us, it is the defining [patterning] and limitation of all things, both the firm necessity of things fixed from things unstable and the harmony which is of wisdom. And as it is wisdom in harmony, there are those on the right and those on the left—powers, authorities, principalities, demons, energies and threats, powers of wrath, slandering—and the lower root from which have come forth the things in Genesis [the square root of two]. This then is the Cross by which the Word has been made the way of 'cross-beaming' all things, and at the same time of separating off the things that proceed from Genesis and those below it from those above, and also of compacting them all into one. . . . Understand then in me the slaying of a Verb, the piercing of a Verb, the blood of a Verb, the hanging of a Verb, the passion of a Verb, the death of a Verb. And thus I speak, separating off the man. First, the understanding of the Verb, then the understanding of the Lord and, in the third place only, the man and what he suffered. . . ."

And when I descended I laughed at them all when they told me what they did concerning Him, firmly possessed in myself of this only, that the Lord contrived all things symbolically and according to dispensation for the conversion and salvation of man.

This quotation may give one a glimpse of how these harmonic subdivisions within a triangular or cone-shaped frame may become a matrix image for both scientific and philosophical concepts. From this point of view, which is that of Egyptian geometry, it is evident that the harmonic cone is a spiral unfolding of a sequential, musical proportion which determines what we might call the vibrational levels of being as they emerge from an apex.

In the case of the skeleton (physical human) these are shown in a descending expansion, while in the case of the Pharaoh (spiritual human) they are shown in an ascending one. This geometric arrangement implies a cosmological assumption: that of an involution, evolution or descent of energy into matter and a consequent ascent or return of the energy to its source.

In order to understand the precise application of these harmonic intervals to the human body, let us examine a bas-relief from the Temple of Luxor, as this has been analyzed by R. A. Schwaller de Lubicz (see figure on following page).

The first stage divides the height PA into 1/3 and 3/4, which defines the musical fourth on the vibrating string PA. The point is marked on the royal figure by the base of his necklace. On the skeleton it corresponds to the level of the seventh dorsal vertebra; its relations with the seventh rib—the last one directly attached to the sternum—is evident. Functionally, the dorsal sympathetic ganglions seven, eight and nine start from the three roots of the large splanchnic, the upper one being the most voluminous. This very important nerve goes towards the semi-lunar ganglions of the solar plexus which directs the entire abdominal autonomic system. It is also at the level of the seventh dorsal that a crossroad of veins is found that is remarkable in that it receives all the parietal and visceral veins.

The division of the total height by four implies also the division by two, which defines the level of the pubic symphysis. The harmonic division, having 1:1 as its point of departure, in its turn divides the height PA into 2/3 and 1/3 [c on the diagram], which is the ratio of the musical fifth on the vibrating string. This point corresponds to the base of the posterior part of the thorax, at the junction of the twelfth dorsal vertebra with the first lumbar. It is at this level that the solar plexus is situated with its semi-lunar ganglions receiving the large splanchnic. Thus the two harmonic divisions complete one another, as do the musical relationships which, on the human body, are identified both on the skeleton and by the vital centers.

The harmonic division having 1/4 for its ratio, generates the ratio of 1 to 7 [at a].

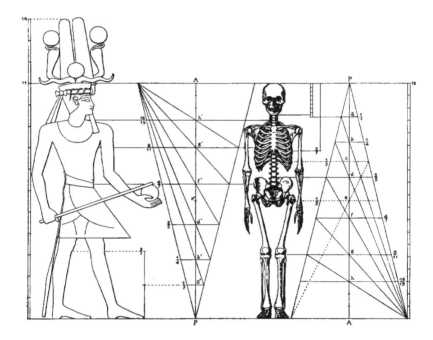

In connection with this fact, namely, that in the harmonic generation of proportion 1/4 generates 1/7, it is important to note that at birth the head to body size ratio is 1 to 4 and that, as the individual approaches adulthood, the ratio changes so as to become 1 to 7 or 1 to 7.5. De Lubicz continues:

The stage following this harmonic division divides PA into 2/5 and 3/5 [at d], the first ratios approaching the function of the 1/Phi in the Fibonacci Series. On the royal figure this level actually determines the upper level of the navel. On the skeleton it corresponds to the upper level of the iliac bone and to the disk separating the third lumbar from the fourth. It is actually there that the navel of man is placed, oscillating slightly around this line of reference. It is curious to note that the total height of man is here divided into two segments which are in the ratio of one to three to one another, while the five lumbar vertebrae are in the ratio of three to two, that is, in the same relationship only reversed.

Recall again that the co-efficient for the definition of the navel corresponds, according to anthropometric averages, to: Total height/Height of navel = 5/3 = Phi x 1.03. . . .

The stages that follow divide the total height of PA successively into 3/7 and 4/7, then 3/11 and 8/11. The femur-tibial line corresponds to this level, that is, the articulation of the knee.

The last division leading to the canonical numbers is 3/19 and 16/19. Here the Pharaonic canon imposes a reversal of the harmonic division: A corresponds to the top of the head and P to the soles of the feet. This reversal corresponds to an essential and vital function: are not the motor centers of the entire body reversed along the Roland Fissure in such a way that the motor center of the feet is to be found precisely at the vertex? The Babinski reflex reveals a rupture in the motor circuit, also confirming the relation between the head and the feet. The divisions are then read from bottom to top. . . .

The doubling of 1/4, in other words 1/2, is designated by the crossing of the sword and the triangular loincloth.

2/5 coincides with the base of the shendit loincloth overlapping the previous one.

4/7 defines the lower line of the back of the belt, and corresponds on the skeleton to the last lumbar vertebra at its point of junction with the sacrum, attached to the wings of the iliac—a very important vital zone.

8/11 passes through the level of the royal figure's breasts, which on the skeleton corresponds to the level of the fifth rib. . . .

Finally, the line 16/19, one of the most important in the Pharaonic canon corresponds to the seventh cervical, the vital point to which the ancients attached such importance that it is at this point that the Neter "gives life" to an individual when he offers the ankh to him from behind. Indeed, it is from the lower cervical ganglion and the first dorsal, the stellar ganglion, that the two roots of the lower cardiac nerve arise which innervate the heart and establish a relation with the eyes: the sympathetic nerve has a contracting action on the heart and causes a dilation of the iris [its action is thus inversed for the heart and the eye]. The whole area contained between the seventh cervical and the sternal fork is an essential arterial and venous cross-roads, accented on the figure by the level of his necklace up to the nape of the neck. This necklace, composed of many rows of pearls, often terminates at the back of the neck with two falcon heads which carry a crescent surmounted by a pearl, which strangely recalls the symbol of the reversed crescent above an oval, engraved on the hieroglyph of the heart. . . .

The King wears a high crown composed of two plumes set above two serpents which rise above the solar disk. The height of the royal crown corresponds to a co-efficient revealed by measurements to be a constant. The harmonic breakdown justifies the use of the number employed: the height of the crown is obtained by placing the 3/11 contained between the line 8/11 and the line 11/11 above the top of the head. The total height of the Crowned King is thus equal to 14/11. This co-efficient is extremely curious because it is enclosed by two functions derived from Pi and Phi. This we may demonstrate in the decimal form by the following: the square root of Phi = 1.272. . . , 14/11 = 1.2727. . . , and 4/Pi = 1.2732.

The canon of the skeleton is divided, as we know, into nineteen units, while the canon of the King is eleven units. The ratio 19/11, which is equal to 1.727272, is the relationship between the two principle Egyptian cubits, namely, the Royal Cubit (used to measure the King) and the blessed or human cubit of nineteen units used to measure the ordinary human.

8/11, which is equal to 0.727272, is the ratio which determines the pentagon and the angle of thirty-six degrees—the pentagon being, as we have noted, the traditional figure for the human being in the physical sense; the pentagram-star, contained within it, being the figure of divine or perfected humanity.

Following this analogical train of thought we may note next that in the skeleton 8/11 determines the knee, the joint which allows for individually willed movement and force. When a human being surrenders this force by collapsing the knee-joint, he or she kneels to pray. In the diagram of the King, however, 8/11 significantly determines the heart *Chakra*. The ratio 3/11, which equals 0. 272727, then becomes the ratio unifying the head *Chakra* (the cerebral mind) with the heart *Chakra* (the innate solar mind), and this unified state of consciousness then becomes the King's Crown, raised above the head by the same 3/11 ratio. Thus the Crown represents, as we have said humanity's supra-rational potential, the next phase in the evolution of consciousness.

This same ratio of 3/11, interestingly, is found in an icon of Christ in which Christ is shown with a compass, held at the heart *Chakra* with its points extending to the pelvic region, which is opened up to reveal the primordial chaos. Through the compass pour the energies of universal mind and celestial law, visualizable to the intuitive heart-mind as geometric symbols. It is as though by holding the compass, the cone of intellectual light, from the heart *Chakra* and projecting it upon the lower regions, Christ applies the knowledge-force of universal harmonic order to transform lower nature.

What we see diagrammed in the floor plan of the Temple, interwoven with musical, geometric and astronomical symbolism, is a physiological map, depicting not only the canon of the external body, but also the now familiar esoteric physiology of the ancient world which divides the body into the areas of energetic transduction called *Chakras* by the Hindus. Ancient Temple Architecture, in other words, seems to envision a harmonic unfolding of the principle of Universal Order, in parallel with the unfolding or evolution of the potentialities of Humanity—a vision able to be contemplated through symbols, proportions, symmetries and music.

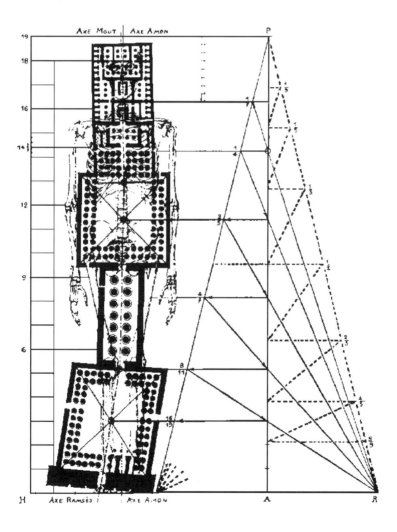

Let us now move closer to the physiological vision of ancient Egypt. From the point of view of Western anatomy, the neural circuitry serving the internal organs and glands is linked to the higher brain centers of conscious awareness and control through a chain of nerve bundles called plexuses and likened by modern research to a series of little brains.

This autonomic nervous system has been somewhat arbitrarily divided into two parts: firstly, the sympathetic system, composed of a chain of ganglia and nerves extending, just to do the subtle energy channels of *Ida* and *Pingala* referred to in Hindu physiology, down either side of the spinal column, from the cervical regions through the thoracic and lumbar regions, each ganglion being connected to a spinal nerve by a communicating branch; and secondly, the parasympathetic system, associated only with some cranial nerve on top, and some sacral nerves at the bottom, of the spine.

These two divisions act antagonistically to one another, stimulation in one set of fibers causing inhibition in the other. For example, a sympathetic nerve dilates the pupil of the eye and accelerates and strengthens the heart while, on the other hand, the parasympathetic fibers contract the pupil and weaken the heart action. In other words, we find in the autonomic system a representation of the universal Law of Inversion, that same "inverse" which, in mathematics, allows us to calculate the laws governing the intensity of sound, gravity and light radiation—that is, the fundamental forces which order celestial systems and allow for the appearance of living systems on earth.

The autonomic system controls and regulates the internal environment of the body, making the necessary autonomic adjustments to any changes occurring in the outer physical environment (such as heat, cold, air pressure and food-intake), as well as in the internal, psychological environments set up by emotions such as fear, anger, desire, joy, concentration, sexual arousal, sleepiness, etc. The autonomic system is therefore the means by which we maintain what is called homeostatic equilibrium, homeostasis being a feedback network of thermo, photo, chemical and electromagnetic receptors which work to maintain a steady-state internal body climate, with heartbeat, oxygen-intake, temperature, blood pressure and electromagnetic balance remaining fairly constant. The autonomic system, finally, is also the body's method of adjusting to extreme emergency—preparing and strengthening muscular capacity, accelerating and strengthening heartbeat, raising blood pressure, releasing glucose from the liver and epinephrine and adrenaline from the adrenal cortex. In this way breathing is made easier, digestive activity is reduced, mental activity is stimulated and kidney activity is suspended, to mention only a few of the more important, almost supra-physical aspects of our emergency control system.

It is a difficult question to assess anatomically whether the unthinking autonomic or visceral mind belongs to a more primitive stage in evolutionary organization—a bit of the "Old Adam," so to speak, somehow retaining its autonomy even after the higher brain centers were super-imposed in human evolution—or whether it is in fact a latent and yet only partially developed natural organization which may bring into existence in humanity a radically new nervous system—an addition to the cerebro-spinal system whose sensory-motor activities are more or less consciously controlled by thought, will and conscious desire.

It is possible to suggest that both these possibilities are the case: that the autonomic system is at once ancient, and yet still holds potential for a new neural organization. In either event, two factors appear to be certain. One is that as soon as humanity enveloped itself in the artificial environment and behavior afforded by agriculture, civilization and technology, the utilization of the autonomic system of responses and regulation was greatly reduced and with this naturally also the selective pressures for the system to develop further. The second certainty, which is based on ancient literature as well as on modern brain research, is that one aspect of yogic physical discipline was aimed at consciously gaining control over, and developing, the psychological and physical potentials related to the autonomic organization. From this point of view, many of the so-called miracles of yogic development (at least the ones that can be clinically investigated, such as the reduction of metabolic oxidation through respiratory control, the cessation of heartbeat, complete control over the deep and peripheral body pulses, both the willed cessation and the hyper-stimulation of mental activity, not to mention mastery over pain reactions and circulatory functions such as bleeding, etc.) can be explained by a conscious control over the autonomic mind, and a conscious coordination between it and the cerebro-spinal system. The simple fact that urination and defecation, two autonomic functions, are routinely brought under voluntary control in children as well as in pets through social and educational reinforcement gives evidence of the possibility that there may be many autonomic functions which may yield to voluntary mastery.

It has however been argued that these self-corrective controls and reflexes represent the "wisdom of the body," so that the less interference from the so-called higher voluntary mental processes the better. but research now indicates that learning and willed control need not, if approached correctly, inhibit autonomic reflex behavior, but may instead build, refine, intensify and harmonize it. These innate systems of response may then really be only the broad, partially formed limits of bodily maintenance which can be, so to speak, fine-tuned through instrumental learning, self-knowledge and deep physical as well as psychological self-awareness.

This train of thought suggests that the autonomic system might play a role in evolution. This is indeed the case. Let me try therefore for a moment to describe the important new role given the autonomic system in the presently accepted theory of evolution—an apparent digression which will prepare us for a remarkable and significant aspect of Egyptian wisdom and teaching.

The merger of genetic theory and the behavioral sciences with the dogmatic core of Darwinism has given rise to an expanded theory of evolution called neo-Darwinism. Briefly stated, the genetic view maintains that the characteristics and behavior of organisms depend ultimately on the sequences of amino acids in their proteins—from which point of view, evolution consists largely in the progressive substitution of one amino acid for another and changes in evolution occur as a result of the gradual accumulation of minor genetic mutations (i. e., structural protein alterations) accompanied by slow transitions in the physical characteristics of individuals in populations—while the Behaviorist wing argues that the appearance of any characteristic caused by shifts in genetic composition must ultimately express itself in the dynamics of behavior in order to meet the tests and pressures of selection, adaptation and survival. This Behaviorist wing believes further that patterns of innate behavior are genetically transmitted and therefore must evolve; and that the patterns that do so are the most important contingency for survival. It is at this point that we again encounter the autonomic nervous system which controls, as we have said, the homeostasis of the body-mind.

For evolutionary theorists now contend that not only innate reflex behavior, which is so important to animal survival, but also learned behavior, are both reinforced in an organism through homeostatic responses. The theory is that an organism favors behavior patterns which tend to move its internal state closer to homeostasis and refrains from those patterns which would tend to move it away from homeostasis. To quote Dr. Ralph Berger:

> Any event can be said to be reinforcing if it directly or indirectly affects bodily homeostasis. If the provoked change is toward homeostasis then it is positively reinforcing.

In this way the entire organism participates in the development of both learned and innate behavior patterns, and the brain really derives its adaptive capacities in evolution from coordinating external conditions and movements of the body with internal states of being, thereby sustaining homeostasis.

From the point of view of spiritual disciplines this theory has many implications, particularly concerning the autonomic factor in evolution. One obvious idea is that, even in nature, it is not ultimately progress in the pursuit of appetites, but rather the internal equanimity or homeostasis that results from their fulfillment that is the real controlling lever of evolutionary learning. But we need not interpret homeostasis as simply a regulator of physical drives alone; remember that all emotional elements, as well as dream and subconscious levels, are wired into this system. Of all animals, humans particularly have this capacity to build and perform complex behavior patterns in response to simple stimuli. It appears, therefore, that mastery of the autonomic controls, in other words a conscious, flowing homeostasis on many levels of life and mind, can free one to some extent from domination by the syndrome of appetite and satiation. To gain consciousness in this area, as is possible through spiritual discipline, would then give one a working insight into the major mechanics of evolutionary change for all of animal nature; and conversely the destruction, interruption or decline of such innate awareness, due for example to chemical imbalance due to dietary or emotional disturbance, or circulatory and respiratory imbalance due to poor posture or general deficiency in physical culture, is a serious threat to the possibility of future evolution in the individual or race.

This new theory of homeostasis as a key to the reinforcement of evolutionarily significant behavior returns us to the view of philosophy and physiology maintained by ancient Egyptian culture: namely, to the Egyptian physio-philosophical notion of the "heart-mind." This coincision of old and new concepts results from acknowledging that it must be through the blood, and hence by means of the heart, that information is brought to the brain and nervous system concerning chemical and other factors leading to homeostatic decline or maintenance. The heart from this point of view may be considered as the major source of reinforcement and therefore fundamental to all learning.

Since the time of Descartes, the brain has been considered the source of thought and feeling, but always some people have refused to accept this view. D. H. Lawrence expressed this reluctance as follows:

Man is a creature that thinks with his blood: the heart dwelling in a sea of blood that flows through the body always in two inverse tides is where chiefly lies what men call thought.

And to quote Norbert Wiener, one of the originators of cybernetics:

Messages which cause conditional or associative learning are carried by the slow but pervasive influence of the blood stream. The blood carries in it substances which alter nervous action directly or indirectly.

Compare now these ultramodern theories with the view expressed by a Memphite physician over 4,500 years ago.

The seeing of the eyes and the breathing of the nose bring messages to the heart. The seeing of the eyes and the hearing of the ears and the breathing of the nose bring messages to the heart. It is the heart which causes all decisions to be made, but it is the tongue which reports what the heart has thought. Thus is all action, whether simple or complex, carried out. The manipulation of the hands, the movement of the legs and the functioning of every limb. All is in accord with the command which the heart has devised and which has appeared on the tongue. Thus is determined the specific nature of everything.

These few ancient phrases summarize extraordinarily accurately the concept of mind-body relationship and its role in evolution which our contemporary Behaviorist biologists are now struggling to formulate.

There is another aspect of the function of the autonomic nervous system in evolutionary selection which also recalls ancient wisdom. The parameters of homeostasis flowing in the bloodstream—such as concentrations of glucose inciting or satiating hunger, osmotic pressure signaling thirst reflexes, carbon dioxide levels controlling respiratory rhythms and other factors, androgen concentrations controlling sexual appetites, hormones controlling sleep and wakefulness, etc.—all such parameters and others are by necessity set up in a symphony of syncopated rhythmic periodicities, each being typically out of phase with the others, but all being embedded in the circadian cycle of approximately twenty-four hours, or extensions of it, such as the twenty-eight-day menstrual cycle. In other words, since it would be selectively unbeneficial for an organism to experience its peaks of hunger, thirst, sexual arousal, etc., at the same moment of the day, we find that each homeostatic parameter, such as glucose concentration for instance, has a high and low curvature which peaks and declines out of synchronization with the other drive motivators. All these bodily rhythms then have their own phasing to the specific light, heat, humidity and other factors which unfold out of the twelve and twenty-four hour daily solar cycle. These cyclic patterns furthermore, it has been discovered, play a decisive role in our friendships, love affairs, marriages and family relationships. For example, when a man enters into an intimate relationship with a woman his bio-rhythmic pattern begins to phase with hers, so that married couples usually have coinciding peaks and lows in their metabolic rhythms within a short time. The same is true of friends or of those who work closely with each other. Thus it seems that the very mechanics of interpersonal and collective harmonies are dependent to some degree on these rhythmic life patterns which themselves are tuned to the periodicities of the sky.

Egypt symbolized this vision of life energies driven by a symphonic celestial tuning in its well-known texts concerning the twelve divisions or hours of the day and night and of the *Dwat*, commonly called the Netherworld or the world of transformations, in which transformations are depicted occurring everywhere—in food, flesh, energy, mind and spirit. The *Dwat* is the inner region of transformation beneath or within appearances, under the skin or membrane, so to speak, be it the crust of the earth or the membrane of a living cell, the skull or the face which covers the great transformer of the brain.

The introductory text of the *Book of What is in the Dwat*, which is divided into twelve chapters, corresponding to the twelve hours of the night, reads:

This is the knowledge of the powers of the Netherworld. This is the knowledge of their effects, knowledge of their sacred rhythms [or ritual]. To Re [the Solar Deity], carrier of the knowledge of the mysterious power [or unconscious drive], knowledge of what is contained in the hours as well as in their Gods. . . [Concluding]. . . O Flesh, who belongest to the Sky, but who liveth on earth, O Flesh, Glory to thee. Come Re in the form of the Living One, breathe through me here in the Netherworld of the Hours. . . . Transverse the field [or region], O Protector of the body. He shines, the great Light-giver Re drives away darkness.

Here we encounter a blending of physiology with cosmology, the transformative living field of the body expanded into a vision of cosmic transformation. Rhythms set forth in galactical space, passing through hereditary levels, are transmuted into the rhythms of incarnate life and mind. The little world of embodied life and the vast worlds of universal light are transparent metaphors, each revealing the nature of the other. To the ancient physiologist, at the core of life as at the core of the universe is an indestructible seat of homeostatic equilibrium. Through this central throne of calm flow the oscillating harmonic rhythms, rising and falling around the eternal balance point, driving this pure spirit to take on and maintain the forms and the energies of incarnation.

In Egypt this Principle of eternal balance and equilibrium at the heart of creation is symbolized by the great feminine winged *Neter*, Maat, whose representations and symbols are to be found both in the secret sanctuary of the Temple and on the musical harp and as the characteristic emblem of the judge. Maat is associated with the word *tkh*, signifying everything that oscillates or vacillates. *Tkh* is written with the sign of the plumb-bob, which is in turn often fashioned in the form of a little jug which signifies the heart and is hung from a feather, the symbol of Maat. The plumb-bob determines the vertical and symbolizes the principle of equilibrium that makes possible the mechanism of the scales, which are in turn the symbols of discretion, selection, judgment, just as in the balance of the body homeostasis is the innate selector of all behavior. (Here we may again recall that it is the oscillating neural activity, in the form of bioclocks tuned to celestial rhythms, which is the fundamental organizational factor in all life processes.)

When used as a key to the vision of universal homeostasis, the symbol of the winged Goddess Maat becomes an ever-richer source of analogical insight. Consider, for example the feather, Maat's chief symbolic attribute.

It has long been recognized that bird navigation is accomplished both by the bird's photo-sensitivity and its sensitivity to magnetic fields, but only recently have the mechanics of this magnetic sensitivity been revealed. It appears to lie in the most characteristic attribute of the bird, its feathers. Bird feathers seem to function as electromagnetic transducers, changing the dielectric pulsation received from the atmosphere into piezoelectric signals, which can be carried by the bird's nervous system. Thus bird feathers appear to be not only selective receptors and filters of the electromagnetic information contained in the surrounding environment, but also energy transducers and lines of transmission. In other words, birds use the underside of their wings for magnetic sensing: which may remind us of Maat or other winged deities, holding their feathered arms around the body of the initiate King, or protecting the four corners of the coffin or canopic chest, or, as Nut, the sky, standing with extended wings, welcoming the deceased to heaven. From this we may speculate that the King or deceased is believed to receive from the deity the initiatic technique which heightens sensitivity to magnetic fields and so leads towards a centering of the energetic body in universal rhythms.

The feather symbol of Maat supports the oscillating plumb-bob and, because vibration is nothing more than rapid oscillation, this ideogram reminds us that every living body vibrates physically and that all elemental or inanimate matter vibrates molecularly or anatomically and that, since every vibrating body emits a sound, all such vibrating bodies are thus musical in the widest sense of the word.

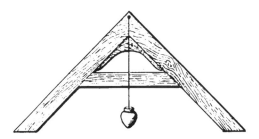

The weight at the plumb-line's end, Egyptologist Lucy Lamy points out, is often shaped like a heart, and is given the name *ib*, meaning dancer. Now, the plumb-line which oscillates in the rhythm of the human heart has a length of 0. 69 meters, while the human heartbeat itself, which is normally seventy-two beats per minute, is in effect the plumb-bob of the vibratory universe—for as the physicist Lewis Balamuth has pointed out the rate of seventy-two oscillations per minute falls exactly on the midpoint of a chart which scales all observed vibrational periodicities, from ultrasonic, subatomic vibrations up through the vast, galactical, rhythmic frequencies. The human heartbeat, in other words, is literally the center of a vibrating cosmos. The rate of seventy-two oscillations per minute of the heartbeat is, further, in a six-to-five ratio with the sixty subdivisions-per-minute rate of the earth's rotation, which is the cause of the plumb-bob's movement; and 6/5ths or 1. 2 is the ratio which connects the square of the Golden Number (Phi squared, which is equal to 2.618) to Pi, the function of all circles, spheres and rotational movements: Phi squared x 6/5 = Pi.

This same relationship of the Golden Proportion to the cyclic function of Pi may be seen again in a living sense when we contemplate the spiralling growth of plants as they reach toward the light on this day-night rotating spherical planet. The average angle separating the spiralling branch of a plant, so as to allow for maximum leaf exposure to solar radiation, is 137 degrees 30 minutes 28 seconds, which is exactly the golden division of 360 degrees (into 222 degrees 29 minutes 32 seconds and 137 degrees 30 minutes 28 seconds), or 360 degrees times 1/Phi.

The rotation of the planet, the earth's heartbeat, so to speak, is a consequence of the laws of gravity. The pendulum—a simple time-space mechanism used extensively by the Egyptians—thus teaches an important cosmic law, for the rapidity of the pendulum's movement is in inverse ratio with the square of its length. This is the same mathematical formula which allowed Newton to discover the universal law of gravity, and it also relates to the formula governing vibratory sound frequencies through the square to square root ratio: that is, the pitch or frequency of a vibrating string is inversely proportional to the square root of its weight per unit length.

This oscillatory phenomenon taking place around an eternally still central core on all levels of existence, this self-provoked, self-creative orgiastic shiver within the immutable soul of the Divine Creative Being, to put it in the metaphoric terms of ancient esoteric science, was the basis for all ancient mathematical thought, both applied and abstract or metaphysical. This system, which historians have named "Diaphantine" and attributed to the Greek mathematician Diaphantin, is found everywhere to be the thematic substructure of Egyptian architecture and of the Egyptian philosophy of nature and spirit. Undoubtedly it was selected as this governing *thema* so as to maintain the activity of mind within a parallel structure with the essential pattern of oscillation underlying all material becoming. Thus all is related in the heart of a symbol when one learns to read it. The symbol is simply the empty core, like the lacuna or blind spot in the center of the optic tract of our eyes, around which vibrate all the images and movements of vision.

In the light of all this, and to conclude these talks, I would like to discuss briefly the physiology of the Secret Sanctuary, the Holy of Holies, of the Temple of Man at Luxor. This area of the Temple corresponds, as Schwaller de Lubicz has shown, to the third ventricle of the brain, and this, in turn, is the location of the central coordinator for the autonomic, bio-rhythmic, sky-tuned chain of visceral minds called plexuses by modern research. The division of the body through harmonic proportion, as we have seen, similarly locates those centers of energetic transduction called *Chakras* by the Hindus. Indeed, ancient physiology seems to have concentrated its attention on this chain of nerve bundles that appear at harmonic intervals from the base of the skull to the pelvis. In what follows, we shall assume that there is a correspondence between these *Chakras* of ancient thought and the plexuses of modern research and that a cross-reference of some kind between the two systems is possible.

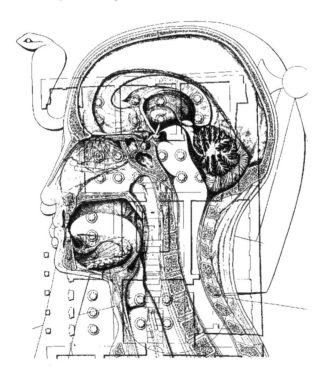

The walls of the third ventricle are formed by the optic thalamus. This is the frontal area of the cerebrum, which surfaces with the eyes and the optic thalamus and extends towards the back of the brain in two lobes whose surfaces form the walls of the third ventricle, containing the pineal and pituitary bodies. *Thalamus* is the Greek word for chamber, room or sanctuary so that, in other words, the walls of our secret sanctuary are the lobes of the optic thalamus, whose posterior portion has direct connections with the pineal body, while the floor of this ventricle is the hypothalamus, which gives the nerve signals and secretions to activate the pituitary gland. In this region of the brain, then, one finds an intense intersection of two types of life-enabling neural signal systems: namely, the system based on neuro-chemical signals which characterize all plant life intersecting with the neuro-electrical nerve reactions, which are an additional system found only in animal life and responsible for increased mobility and, in humans, for the expression of individual will and action. Since the neuro-chemical system is exclusive to plants and its signals are carried by organic chemical compounds, we may associate it with the geometry of life dominated by the pentagon. On the other hand, the electrical nervous system, made up of signals carried by ionized inorganic minerals such as sodium and potassium, we may associate with the hexagon. In fact, the doorway of Room Twelve in the Temple, leading to the secret sanctuaries, is based on the fusion of pentagonal and hexagonal geometries, the two geometries characteristic of organic and inorganic domains.

In the thalamic region, then, which is the center of the limbic or midbrain area (the ancient brain in terms of evolution), we find a connection between the eye and the glands which allows for photosensitive periodicities in the body and is also the main filter and place of mediation between the instinctual, automatic, autonomic, emotional responses carried from all over the body and the higher brain centers of the cerebrum and its cortex. The thalamic region thus monitors all powerful and instinctual reactions and retransmits them to the cerebral cortex, but in a stepped-down or diluted form, thereby preventing any over-exaggerated motor responses from the conscious cortex. This is to say that great neural self-controlling and discriminatory activity occurs here. Indeed, this region is so dominant in managing the emotional content of the mind and body that the motor controls for changes in facial expression—those which result directly from conscious or unconscious emotional states such as anger, tears, fear, joy—are all contained in the cortex in which most of the other motor terminals are situated. It is this instinctual and emotional content which, when retained unconsciously in the thalamus, sets up the tensions and lines which shape or warp the face and personality, and only when these deep, instinctual and emotional patterns are utterly removed from the thalamic system does the face reach full relaxation and become a pure, empty, timeless mask.

The optic thalamus, further, whose lobes form the walls of the sanctuary, reverses the striation of grey and white matter which makes up the brain and spinal cord—indicating an inversing of their functions. In the cerebrum, the grey matter is on the outside, while in the thalamus the grey is inside and there is a layer of pure white cellular tissue on the outside, the thalamus walls of our sanctuary. This is in contact with the cerebro-spinal fluid which floods the third ventricle and bathes the pituitary and pineal bodies. I should mention here the work of the endocrinologist Axerod, who has delineated one function of the pineal gland as being a bioelectric, neuro-chemical transducer.

It is this thalamic region with its light-sensitive, rhythmicity-forming glands that is referred to in esoteric texts as the "inner" or "single" eye, and an extraordinary development or intensification of the white cellular lining of the thalamus was supposed to have been possible through the return to it of the vital substances contained in the sexual fluids—which of course originated from the hypothalamic secretions occurring in this ventricle of the brain.

So much of esoteric writing, including even the story of the descent and resurrection of Christ, is on one level of interpretation a metaphoric reference to this supposed physiological process that could be induced by refined yogic discipline.

Greek physicians claimed that the interface of the thalamus with the cerebro-spinal fluids surrounding the pineal and pituitary bodies was the seat of the psychic being, and that all intellectual awareness was embodied in these fluid-filled ventricles. Very recently brain research has confirmed that this region of the brain is indeed where the human being lives. To quote the neurologist Nautas:

If the limbic cortex, especially the basal part of the frontal lobe, is destroyed, this causes a complete loss of the sense of self. Any other part of the brain or body can be removed or substituted for with but little effect on one's sense of self.

With this in mind, we may understand the enigmatic Egyptian phrase which states: "From the tears of Re, Humanity was born." For the cerebro-spinal fluid drips like tears into the secret third ventricle from blood vessels in the "inner eye" of the optic thalamus.

This cerebro-spinal fluid, Hippocrates, like the ancient Hindus, claimed was the carrier of the "spark of life" or *pranic* energy, which was transmitted to the mind and body by its means. Even now, scientifically, it is clear that this fluid, chemically and mechanically, protects and nourishes the entire nervous system. Remember that the cerebro-spinal fluid has exactly the same constituency as the individual's blood, relating it again to Re as the Solar principle, except that the white cells, the red corpuscles, the platelets and the proteins are removed, leaving only the ionized mineral base of the blood to come into contact with the cerebral glands. These bio-mineral substances are the conductors of the electromagnetic energy in and around the body, and therefore this crystalline fluid of purified blood, which floods the inner eye like a lens, is the ultimately refined residue of the entire mind-body-spirit condition of the organism at any moment in time.

Finally, we may note that situated just above the third ventricle, the house of the god-like glands, is the corpus callosum, the vast bundles of hundreds of nerve endings which connect the divided hemispheres of the brain—a place, in other words, where a union of the left and right divisions of perceptual modes might be achieved.

The floor of the sanctuary is the hypothalamus (*hypo* meaning beneath in Greek). This region controls the animal appetites (associated with food and sex), the pleasure and pain sensations, as well as the heat levels of the body (Sanskrit *asura*). The hypothalamus is thus the body's furnace, controlling the fires of our life and, through heat, all the metabolic rates of the organism. The thermostatic cells in the hypothalamus are sensitive to the temperature of the bloodstream, the slightest variation bringing quick responses in the form of a constant gentle vibration pervading all the muscles of the body at a rate that ranges between seven and thirteen shivers per second. This constant rhythmic vibration generates heat and replaces body warmth lost to the colder environment. The hypothalamus also controls perspiration. The lowering of the body temperature through these two mechanisms in the hypothalamus— muscular vibration and perspiration—decreases the rate at which all chemical reactions take place in the body, controlling as well the slowing of the heartbeat and breathing rate, and thereby the consumption of oxygen in both brain and body.

It is important to emphasize here the psychological importance of body heat in determining the character of both individuals and races. In the colder climates the body's blood must be retained in the organs and deeper regions of the body in order to hold its temperature at the necessary homeostatic balance. The blood is warmed by the inner fires of individual metabolism, the individual generating his own warmth by his own activity and by partaking of heat-producing nutrients such as foods rich in fats, etc.—factors which obviously lend themselves to the support of a psychology of self-containment, individualization, self-motivation and the separateness of the ego-sense such as predominates in the colder climates of European and Western culture. On the other hand, in the warmer climates of India, Egypt, South America and Africa, the blood flows in the cooler periphery of the body, near the surface of the skin. Remembering that the iron molecules in the blood are sensitive resonators of electromagnetic vibration, we may see how, among the peoples of hotter climates, there is a psychology of individual diffusion and at the same time a higher sensitivity to collective and interpersonal exchanges and flows of energy, as well as to the magnetic flux of subtle and natural energies.

The Tibetan tantric system had at its foundation the mastery of this metabolic heat, called *dumo*, and laid claim to numerous psycho-spiritual wonders resulting from it. This fire of life, this transformation of solar radiance—the mystic flame of the Vedic Hymns—is the burning altar in the heart of the Temple in the Human Being:

O Fire, mayst thou rejoice in the fuel I bring thee, rejoice in my session of sacrifice, deeply lend ear to my chant.
O Fire, who are brought to perfect birth, Child of Celestial energy, impeller of the vital force, we worship thee with this oblation, we worship thee with the chant well spoken.

It is through the reduction of body heat that catatonic states may be obtained such as are demonstrated by hibernating animals in nature and by yogis who have trained themselves to enter into similarly prolonged states of severe metabolic reduction. Again, it is a conscious mastery of the hypothalamic heat controls that allows the yogis to live high up in cold altitudes in the Himalayas with only a thin linen cloth for protection. More importantly, these states of metabolic reduction actually return the yogi to the regenerative sleep of Shiva, a living body condition parallel to the primordial state of non-polarized, non-oscillating equilibrium which preceded the inversing, alternating pulsations and rhythms of creation. This experience, it is said, is absorbed by the brain, giving the mind a depth of knowledge concerning the origin of creation and enabling a preparation for a conscious transition between life and death.

Let me note here the ancient division of consciousness into three distinct states: Deep Sleep, Dream Sleep (the equivalent, in the ancient view, to our normal consciousness) and Awakefulness (which is the growth into spiritual consciousness). Deep Sleep is the original state of the Sleep of Shiva, which we have already shown to be related to hypothalamic control. But the hypothalamus is also the seat of dreams and, as such, is extremely active during dreaming, many disturbances in the hypothalamic region causing hallucinations, visions and mental illness. This dream center of our night-time existence is also the area in humans that contains the bio-clock of twenty-four hours, which regulates all our metabolism through its sensitivity to the rising and setting of the sun. Finally, the hypothalamus also controls brain oxidation, which in turn controls certain aspects of cerebral activity and so is related to the goals of many systems of meditation.

It is not surprising in this light to find that the hypothalamus is also the pleasure center, ramifications from it spreading throughout the brain. It has been verified, further, that pleasure responses are not just connected to the satiation of physical drives, but rather that the same pleasure compensations underlie all intellectual processes, such as thinking, learning, memory and so forth, as well, which lends scientific support to the ancient concept that it is *ananda*, or bliss, that moves and sustains universal conscious evolution.

Thus the ancients saw the mastery of the autonomic brain and body functions as the means by which humankind might voyage to an entirely different manifestation of itself on earth and perhaps in the Universe, to a Supra-Humanity, conscious of and responsive to the subtle celestial messages that carry the vibratory code governing the unfolding of the universal harmonies pressing upon this Microcosm from the Cosmic Man of the Sky, the Anthropocosm, the *Purusha*.

During the Temple Epoch, as I have tried to show, there had been a collective vision of a manifestation of Humanity freed from the environmental pressures of grinding natural law. It was conceived that through a progressive inner mastery Humanity could raise itself above the contingencies of cold, famine, breeding, deterioration and death. The Supra-Human is the central collective dream that launched the dynamics of civilization with its constant impulse toward change, perfection and mastery. But the great, inner, collective image of the Supra-Human was lost. The transitory ego captured the dynamics of self-enlargement, perverting it into self-aggrandizement. The powers of self-perfection were perverted into those of self-embellishment. Humanity's internal potentials were externalized in the form of machines which tear at the earth to make it feed and comfort our unregenerated animal fears and desires. In our time, the Supra-Human, the Pharaoh, is no longer in the Temple guiding the course and development of society. He is relegated to comic books and films in a confused image, rather like a Christ in blue leotards and muscle. Nevertheless, this modern superhuman is a residue of the only dream that can make this earthly life tolerable for the Consciousness in Humanity, the golden spark that binds it to its Divine origin.

## Bibliography

Ami, H. M., *Canada and Newfoundland*. London, E. Stanford Ltd., 1915.

Aurobindo, Sri, *The Life Divine*. Pondicherry, Sri Aurobindo Ashram Press, 1965.

—— *Hymns to the Mystic Fire*. Pondicherry, Sri Aurobindo Ashram Press, 1971.

Axerod, in *Science Magazine*. May 1974.

Bateson, G., *Mind and Nature*. New York, Dutton, 1979.

Berger, R., *Cyclosis, The Circularity of Experience*. San Francisco, Freeman and Co., 1977.

Boulding, K., *The Image*. Ann Arbor, The University of Michigan Press, 1956.

Bullock, T.H., *Introduction to Nervous Systems*. San Francisco, Freeman and Co., 1977.

Chaliongui, P., *Magic and Medical Science in Ancient Egypt*. London, Hodder and Staughton, 1963.

Champdor, A., *The Book of the Dead*. New York, Garrett Publications, 1966.

Dicke, R., quoted in Misner, C.W., Throne, K.S., Wheeler, J.A., *Gravitation*. San Francisco, Freeman and Co., 1973.

Gauquelin, M., *The Cosmic Clocks*. London, Peter Owen, 1969.

Holton, G., *Thematic Origins of Scientific Thought from Kepler to Einstein*. Cambridge, Mass., Harvard University Press, 1975.

Hoyle, F., *On Stonehenge*. San Francisco, Freeman and Co., 1977.

James, M.R. (tr.)., *The Acts of John* (adapted), in *The Apocryphal New Testament*. Oxford, Clarendon Press, 1924.

Jonas, G., *Visceral Learning*. New York, Viking Press, 1973.

Kramrisch, S., *The Hindu Temple*. Delhi, Motilal Banarsidass, 1976.

McClain, E.G., *The Pythagorean Plato*. Stony Brook, New York, Nicholas Hays, Ltd., 1978.

Michell, J., *City of Revelation*. London, Garnstone Press, 1972.

Neisser, U., *Cognition and Reality*. San Francisco, Freeman and Co., 1976.

Norman, D. A. and Bobrow, D.G., *On the Role of Active Memory Processes in Perception and Cognition,* in *The Structure of Human Memory*. San Francisco, Freeman and Co., 1975.

Park, D., *The Myth of the Passage of Time*, in *The Study of Time*. Berlin, Springer, 1972.

Piankoff, A.(tr), *The Book of What is in the Netherworld,* in *The Tomb of Ramses VI*. New York, Bollingen Series, Pantheon Books, 1954.

Playfair, G.L. and Hill, S., *The Cycles of Heaven*. New York, St. Martin's Press, 1978.

Rucker, R. B., *Geometry, Relativity and the Fourth Dimension*. New York, Dover, 1973.

Rundle Clark, R. T., *Myth and Symbol in Ancient Egypt*. London, Thames and Hudson, 1978.

Sagan, C., *The Dragons of Eden.* New York, Random House, 1977.

Schwaller de Lubicz, R.A., *Le Temple de l'Homme.* Paris, Caracteres, 1957. (tr. by R. and D. Lawlor); *The Temple in Man.* Brookline, Mass, Autumn Press, 1977.

Smith, J. M., *The Evolution of Behavior,* in *Scientific American.* New York, September 1978.

Theon of Smyrna (tr. by R. and D. Lawlor), *The Mathematics Useful for Understanding Plato.* San Diego, Wizard's Bookshelf, 1979.

Thompson, D'Arcy, *On Growth and Form,* abridged edition by J. T. Bonner. Cambridge, Cambridge University Press,1961.

Ward, R. R., *Living Clocks.* New York, Mentor, 1971.

West, J. A., *Serpent in the Sky.* New York, Harper and Row, 1979.

Whorf, B., *Language, Thought and Reality.* Cambridge, M.I.T. Press, 1974.

Yadkin, J., *Sweet and Dangerous.* New York, Bantam Books, 1977.

# 3 | The Platonic Tradition on the Nature of Proportion

...................................................*Keith Critchlow*

ROPORTION IS BOTH AN IDEA AND A REALITY. It is the significant relationship between things, and therefore it is inherent in natural law, as we live in a cosmos—a cosmos being a profound unity of balance between various forces, events and elements. Proportion in the broadest sense is concerned with this balance, harmony and relatedness between things: between body and mind, nature and humanity, illusion and reality.

It is not surprising then that all ancient civilizations were concerned with proportion—by whatever name they may have called it—for the mark of a civilization is its concern for universal principles of order and the relationship of people to their universe.

The balance between parts making up the whole and the whole being made up of parts is as ancient a world view as any recorded. It has been expressed predominantly in mythological terms, whether ancient as cosmogonies and creation myths, or modern as models or likely hypotheses. What is the whole but parts? What are parts parts of? How do we come to recognize the paradox of two mutually exclusive aspects of a given set of events? One answer must lie in the nature of our cognitive faculty itself, in the construction of our instrument of knowledge currently called a brain. Yet who or what are we that are using this instrument of knowledge? What is mind that is flowing through the brain, sifting patterns, drawing conclusions of significance, recognizing? It must be our wholeness that is being aware of the parts of our experience—and possibly the most simple definition of sanity is wholeness of mind.

Thus the central theme is sense-making. This means finding the pattern or meaning in the confusion of sense data that comes avalanching in through all our sense organs. Not sense experience in itself, but finding the significance, order, repetition, pattern, rhythm—in other words, the desirable rather than the accidental. Sense-making, in fact, gives a basis of pattern by which to recognize accident, an accord by which to know discord, a life-enhancing situation by which we may judge a life-threatening one, a direction that invites rather than a direction which repulses.

But sense-making may vary on a sliding scale between the local, unique, subjective and individual (and in this sense sectionalist and partial) and the general, universal, collective and consensus. Here we have a recurrence of the paradox of part and whole, that apparent polarity or complementarity fundamental to the systole and diastole of life itself.

The human cognitive power is most easily directed to the unique, individual and subjective, because each person is at the center of his or her own experience, being the one who is central to that experience. Therefore, it is the parts of experience that are most readily appreciated, whereas it takes practice before wholes may be seen or known— although, paradoxically, they are ever-present. However, we must beware of setting up a fixed polarity in our present discussion: between the parts and the whole are parts of parts and "wholes" within the whole. This brings us to proportion.

It is not by accident that we use the common phrase "keeping a sense of proportion," for it is the very essence of "common sense" in the original meaning of the term: too much concentration on the whole can make us insensitive to the unique qualities of the immediate present, while too much concentration on the parts can lead us into a fractured state of mind in which the simplicity of the whole gets lost.

These two positions have been represented in the philosophical domain by Plato, with his insistence on the pre-eminence of the One, while yet acknowledging differentiation, and Aristotle who, while acknowledging the One, spent his life logically separating and categorizing the world into increasingly diverse species and subspecies. To treat these two approaches as mutually exclusive is fallacious, since Aristotle more significantly represents the principle of the individual reshaping philosophy for oneself, while Plato is the spokesman for a tradition—the oral, unwritten doctrines or *dogmata agrapha*— as his *Dialogues* witness.

Aristotle withdrew from Plato's Academy, and thereby the inherited tradition, to set up and pit his individual mind against the vast and differentiated parts of the universe which surrounded him. He did this so brilliantly that a contemporary Muslim dictionary of philosophy describes him as "the philosopher who most nearly imprisoned the human mind into his system of thinking." It is nevertheless the case that to use one's mind with its incomparable analytic abilities is one sure way of realizing one's gift as a human being. Yet this is only half the truth. An appreciation or experiencing of the whole is the only way to give such analytic activities meaning, significance and ultimate usefulness to the person concerned. Parts lead to complexity; wholes to simplicity and unity.

Proportion is the ratio between these two poles, these two cerebral functions. It is the key to arriving at a transcendental unity from the polarity of existence. Thus proportion as it has been consciously employed in an architectural or structural sense is traditionally symbolic of the gnostic function. Indeed, ultimately, the transcendental, proportional ratios—notably, one to the square root of two; one to the square root of three; and one to the square root of five plus one over two (Phi or the Golden Section)—are metaphysical principles which may be embodied in matter to give it significance and to enable the part to contribute to and relate to the whole.

It is important to be specific about the use of the word proportion. It may be analyzed into two simple words, "pro" meaning "in front of" or "on account of" or in some way "initial," in the sense that the second word "portion" is the dimension or aliquot part. "Pro," then, in some sense means that there is another relationship, hidden or apparent, between the portions of the whole in question; or between that whole and certain others. That is to say, it is in proportion, which implies not only with itself but also with its environmental surroundings and our appreciation of it—which is an interesting threesome.

Proportion, further, has a series of more or less specific meanings according to the dictionary (which is one guide to modern usage): comparative part, comparative relation, due relation, correlation, ratio, inherent symmetry, and a method by which through the relationships between three given quantities a fourth may be found, which is in the same ratio to the third as the second is to the first. In other words, there is one quality which pervades the different meanings of the word, which I think may be characterized by the word "subtlety." Subtlety is a quality, an essential, whole-giving quality that may under certain circumstances be qualified or described or, in Socratic terms, "circumscribed" by discussion. The curious fact is that as we get further into the mathematical aspect of proportion we begin to find those exceptionally subtle ratios known as the transcendentals, which have the rare quality of being indescribable in whole numbers, while remaining precise relationships geometrically. Such, for example, is the diagonal of the square, which is the subject of Plato's *Meno* dialogue, both exoterically and esoterically.

Since I have evoked Plato and the spirit of Socrates, it would seem consistent if not proportional to return to this Greek genesis where so much interest was taken in proportion as ratio. The common Greek word for proportion is *logos*, but a study of the use of this word in Greek philosophy shows that "proportion" had for the Greeks a far wider range of meaning than it has for us. Heraclitus, for instance, used the word *logos* to refer to the underlying organizational principle of the universe—the ultimate whole experience—through which "all things are one" and according to which "all things come to pass" (Frags. 30 and 1).

Thus the harmony or tension of opposites, so frequently associated with Heraclitus' doctrine of change, is ordered through proportion or *logos* into a stable state, "kindling itself by regular measures and going out by regular measures" (Frag. 30).

Heraclitus conceives his *logos* principle as hidden, "apart from all else," and perceptible only to the intelligence:

> Wisdom is one and unique—to know the intelligence by which all things are steered through all things. (Frag. 32)

And yet it is in some sense identical with the process of thinking for, as he says, "Thinking is common to all" (Frag. 113). Nevertheless this *logos* principle still partakes of materiality, for he also identifies it with the life-giving cosmic fire (*pyr*) which, as "the thunderbolt," "pilots all things" (Frag. 64).

Plato expanded the specific use of *logos* and used the term in relation to the mark of true knowledge (*episteme*), which is the ability to give a true account (*logos*) of what we know. (See Phaedo 76.) In the *Republic*, Plato moves the use of *logos* up the scale of significance to

> the summit of the intelligible world, reached in philosophic discussion by one who aspires, through the discourse of reason unaided by the senses, to make his way in every case to the essential reality.
>
> (*Republic* 534)

This journey Plato calls *dialectic* and he describes the "master of *dialectic*" as one who can give a true account (*logos*) of the true being or essence of something.

From the Aristotelian point of view, on the other hand, the term *logos* was used as a synonym of *horos*, that is, the division of things into definitions of genera and species. This is quite a significant contrast to the essence of a thing! And although not contrary to the essence, it gave rise to the superficiality of merely naming something in contradistinction to understanding it—particularly in relation to the whole. Yet Aristotle was also a product of the philosophical line of Plato and, by inheritance, of the Pythagoreans, for he uses the word *logos* as specifically mathematical proportion or ratio. (See *Meta.* 991.)

The Stoics, who held another view to both Plato and Aristotle, used the Heraclitean concept of an all-pervasive universal principle, which they considered to be divine. Since it was a unity, this divine presence, which they identified with fire, *pyr,* was the ground of their theory of cosmic sympathy and natural law and, by logical progression, of the ethical imperative "to live according to nature." The Stoics, further, extending the use of logos, brought the inner *logos*—intelligibility and thought— into an interesting relation with the outer *logos* as speech. Later still, Philo, sometimes called the Pythagorean Kabbalist or the Judaic philosopher, gave *logos* the definition of an archetypal light and thereby gave it a unique role in creation as the instrumental cause.

Heraclitus had implied that the universe itself was eternal, and that it was the changes which took place in it that gave rise to the experience of time, beginnings and endings. From this point of view, the concept of association (*synkrisis*) and dissociation (*diakrisis*) was considered to be the nature of genesis in the universe.

This consideration of the co-functioning of duality, of association and dissociation, accumulation and dispersion, breathing in and breathing out, gave rise to the question of ultimate wholeness, and so to the inescapable conclusion that there was a transcendental whole, within which this pulsation was a recurrent pattern. This was the notion of Unity and the Parmenidean insistence on an ultimate, partless One, a one that must be distinct from parts as this immediately implies duality—that paradoxical duality we started with. Thus the One was given distinction above or beyond "Wholeness" in the sense of wholeness of parts:

> Only one way is left to be spoken of, that it is; and on this way are full many signs that what is is uncreated and imperishable, for it is entire, immovable and without end. It was not in the past, nor shall it be, since it is now, all at once, one, continuous. . . . Nor is it divisible more here and less there . . . but it is full of what is. (Frag. 8)

Empedocles, while keeping to the Parmenidean Unity, replaced the idea of a cosmic unity with a cyclic process of transformation of four eternal "roots." The overall sphere of unity, "a rounded sphere rejoicing in his circular solitude," "stays fast in the close covering of Harmony" or *harmonia*—*harmonia* being a proportional blending of opposites.

For the ancient Greeks, harmony was as much a medical and health theory as it was a mathematical or musical one. Empedocles himself argued from a characteristically Pythagorean basis that flesh, blood, bones, as all things, are formed in fixed numerical proportions of the basic elements (earth, water, air, fire) and that, therefore, all are linked by the divine bonds of harmony or love (here *philia*, often translated as "amity").

In the Platonic and, by inference, in the Pythagorean tradition, the same principles govern our perception of, and our experience in, the universe. Humanity's relation to things is the key; and the motivation towards both *logos* and proportion arises from the need to be in the right relationship with the inner and the apparent outer essence of the cosmos.

From these basic principles Plato unfolds, most particularly in the *Timaeus*, his cosmology, in which *harmonia* is not only a soul, but geometric shape as well. Bodies thus become matters of proportional association of "solid" relationships, which relationships can be appreciated (by *analogia*) in the proportional relations between the regular (equitable) solid figures—the Tetrahedron (fire), the Octahedron (air), the Icosahedron (water) and the Cube (earth).

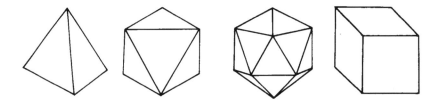

From such constituents, four in number, the body of the universe was brought into being, coming into concord by means of proportion.

(Timaeus 32c)

Plato argues for polarity as the nature of our experience and our universe, and symbolizes this polarity by fire, which makes the world body visible, and by earth, which makes it resistant to touch. Proportion is the bond that holds these two and their complementary elements, water and air, both together and apart—a proportion best understood as a geometric proportion between the above regular solids. This Plato calls *analogia*.

Geometric proportion or *analogia* is essentially demonstrated in number by a three-term set, in which the middle term is greater than the first by the same ratio or proportion as it is smaller that the third—as in 2, 4, 8.

Plato was at pains to make clear that a whole is more than a sum of its parts, as is obvious when considering the crucial issue of the positioning (*thesis*) of the parts—a true holon has parts which have a fixed spatial relationship to each other and to the whole. (See *Laws* X, 903ff.) This becomes clear when one envisages a collection of, say, flat squares jumbled in random positions to each other in space, and the same collection arranged in sixes as cubes. Even when ranged together there is a difference between jumbled and neatly packed cubes. Taking this Platonic *analogia* a little further, the cubes could pack into a large cube making a proportional increment, or set of proportional increments, according to how many cubes were in the larger cube. Proportion here must be taken in its broadest sense, because from the point of view of modern mathematical usage objections could be made on the grounds that the cubic volumes increase in additive, not proportional, increments. But this is a problem of modern mental conventions and not a matter of the truth or falsity of the example given.

Reasoning by *analogia* was then the Greek way of reasoning by wholes rather than by parts, the fruits of which method are embodied in the monuments of intelligent activity we call the classics of ancient Greece. Underlying it is the doctrine of the fundamental unknowability of matter, and the consequent necessity of understanding it by analogy. As Aristotle said:

> The underlying nature is an object of scientific knowledge by an analogy. For as bronze is to the statue, the wood to the bed...so is the underlying nature to substance, i.e., the "this" or existent.
>
> (*Physics* 191a)

A significant summary of the roots of this conclusion may be found in Heraclitus' insistence that "nature loves to hide," and that this hidden reality is clearly beyond the reach of men who trust implicitly in their sense perception—an apt comment on modern so-called empiricism. Diogenes of Appolonia came to the same conclusion from another perspective when he argued that the intelligent and divine *arche* (the maintenance principle) is continuously present in all things that are, but in varying degrees:

And there is no single thing that does not have a share of this; but nothing has an equal share of it. (Frag. 5)

Reasoning by analogy is primary also, and for these reasons, to Plato's doctrine of the sensible and intelligible routes to knowledge. The Soul (*Psyche*) for Plato—the pure unitary Soul—is the means by which we have access to true knowledge (*episteme*) and is thus the correlative of the *eide*, or the realm of the archetypal ideas (*eidos*). The Soul, then, is the *arche* or principle of all knowing or cognitive activity, and different in kind to the body which it informs as well as en-forms. Yet the principle of proportional ratio is that which relates sense (*aesthesis*) and opinion (*doxa*) to true knowledge (*episteme*). The proportional mean between *doxa* and *episteme* is *dianoia* (thinking or understanding). *Dianoia* has as its object the mathematicals (*mathema*) while the activity of *noesis*, the eternal aspect of the *psyche*, has the *eide*, the archetypal ideas, as its object. *Noesis*, then, has some equivalence to what we might call today "intellectual intuition"; while *dianoia* is discursive reasoning subject to the laws of logic and the "objectivity" exemplified by the information brought into the *psyche* from the sensations—that is to say, true empiricism. *Doxa*, accordingly, is plausibility based on outer experience, and *dianoia* is the bridge through discursive reasoning to *noesis*, the direct contact with, or cognition of, the Truth.

| THE GOOD or THE ONE | | | | | |
|---|---|---|---|---|---|
| Intelligible World or World of *Nous* | Indivisible or Partless Realities: World of Ideas, Numbers, Forms | D | *Noesis*/ Intelligence or Intuition *Episteme*/ Knowledge | Gods | Fire |
| | Mathematicals (Geometry) | C | *Dianoia*/ Thinking or Understanding | Winged Things | Air |
| World of Appearances or Sensation or Opinion or Becoming | Visible and Divisible Things | B | *Pistis*/ Belief *Doxa*/ Opinion | All that dwells in water | Water |
| | Images | A | *Aesthesis*/Sensation *Eikasia*/Imaging | All that goes on foot | Earth |

In the *Timaeus*, Plato puts into Timaeus' explanation the cosmological description of how the principles of the World Soul operate, both macrocosmically in the cosmos and microcosmically in humankind.

The Cosmic *Nous* or World Soul is called by Plato the "maker" or *demiourgos* to distinguish the made world from the ungenerated or self-sufficient archetypal world of pure *eidos*. The known world is thus the work of *nous*. *Nous* is the law (see *Laws* 875d); it governs all circulations, cycles, transformations; and it is the moral paradigm for humankind (see *Laws* 897ff)). As Timaeus states (*Tim*. 30a–b), our cosmos is the work of an intelligent cause, arranged to be "as good as possible" an image (*eikon*) of the intelligible realm of which it is a reflection.

The Platonic cosmos, then, in the words of Timaeus, was created by a "maker" who,

> wishing to make this world most nearly like that intelligent thing which is best and in every way complete, fashioned it as a single visible creature, containing within itself all living things whose nature is of the same order. (*Timaeus* 30d)

And his reasoning goes on to assert that the cosmos is one, unique, and could not be otherwise, as it reflects the Oneness of its Cause.

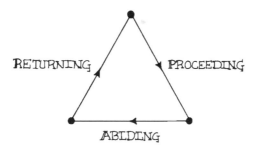

Timaeus next introduces the procedure of unfoldment into being, initiating the principle of manifestation, or the outward projection of intangible principles into our world, through polarity:

> Now that which comes to be must be bodily, and so visible and tangible; and nothing can be visible without fire, or tangible without something solid, and nothing is solid without earth. Hence the god, when he began to put together the body of the universe, set about making it of fire and earth. (*Timaeus* 31b)

This polarity of radiance (fire) and solidity (earth), however, as we have seen,

> cannot be satisfactorily united without a third; for there must be some bond between them drawing them together. [Why else would Eros be the first of the Greek gods?] And of all the bonds the best is that which makes itself and the terms it connects a unity in the fullest sense; and it is of the nature of a continued geometric proportion [*analogia*] to effect this most perfectly. (*Timaeus* 31c)

Accordingly, the "maker"

> set water and air between fire and earth, and made them so far as was possible, proportional to one another, so that as fire is to air, so is air to water, and as air is to water, so is water to earth, and thus he bound together the frame of a world visible and tangible. (*Timaeus* 32b)

In this way the "fourness," a natural bifurcation principle in the proportionals 2,4,8, comes into being in the Platonic cosmology, for Timaeus goes on to say, as quoted above:

> For these reasons, and from such constituents, four in number, the body of the universe was brought into being, coming into concord by means of proportion, and from this it acquired Love. (*Timaeus* 32c)

This Love is *Philia*, another *analogia* like *Eros*, alluding to the affection of love or amity, not only as the universal bond, but also as the only proportional means of differences living or subsisting together.

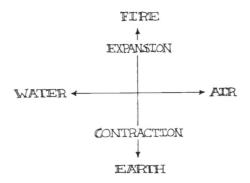

The world, then, is "a living being, whole and complete of complete parts. "(*Timaeus* 32b)

And as to the form appropriate to this living being, the "maker," Timaeus explains,

> turned its shape round and spherical, equidistant every way from center to extremity—a figure the most perfect and uniform of all; for he judged uniformity to be immeasurably better than its opposite. (*Timaeus* 33b)

This precise definition of the boundaries of the created cosmos—a finite creation—is followed by an equally precise definition of what we call today the balance of nature or ecology:

> And all around on the outside he made it perfectly smooth for several reasons [all of which result from there being no need of anything "outside"].... For nothing came out or went into it from anywhere, since there was nothing: it was designed to feed upon its own waste and to act and be acted upon entirely by itself and within itself; because its framer thought that it would be better self-sufficient, rather than dependent upon anything else. (*Timaeus* 33d)

The role of *psyche* or soul and that of proportion are unfolded next, in order to explain the relationship of the complete completeness-yet-partness of parts within the whole:

> And in the center he set a soul and caused it to extend throughout the whole. (*Timaeus* 34b)

This extension is a permeation similar to that of light as it permeates a translucent sphere. Light makes the body evident and the body gives light resistance so that it may be known. *Perichoresis,* implying a total permeation, is the analogical term used for this qualitative relation between soul and body, Creator and creatures.

> On all these accounts the world he brought into being was a blessed God. (*Timaeus* 34b)

Timaeus then explains that the "maker" made the soul

> prior to the body and more venerable in birth and excellence, to be the body's mistress and governor. (*Timaeus* 34c)

Because until two things are in proportion, that is related through a third, they cannot be known, the composition of the soul is also primarily a threeness, as it is the motivator or "governor" of the body. Plato describes this threeness to the origin of things in deliberately obscure terms, since it is the most essential and primary subject we can engage our minds upon, one not conducive to everyday language and usage and yet not outside it either. Here, indeed, is the essence of the paradoxical mystery of whole and part:

> The things of which he composed soul and the manner of its composition were as follows: Between indivisible Existence that is ever in the same state, and divisible Existence that becomes in bodies, he compounded a third form of Existence composed of both. Again, in the case of Sameness and in that of Difference, he also on the same principle made a compound intermediate between that kind of them which is indivisible and the kind which is divisible in bodies. (*Timaeus* 35a)

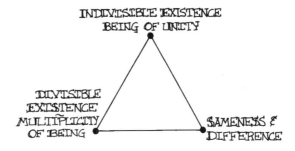

The whole is the "indivisible Existence," which is ever in the same state. "Divisible Existence" is that which becomes in bodies or parts. These two are necessarily compounded by a third beloved of Plato: "Sameness" and "Difference." And he makes these necessary relations an intermediate, that is a proportion, between the extremes.

> Then, taking the three, he blended them all into a unity, forcing the nature of Difference, hard as it was to mingle, into union with sameness, and mixing them together with Existence. (*Timaeus* 35a)

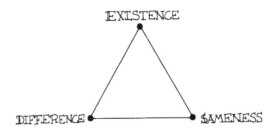

There is a simple, direct, or what one might call intuitive, way of comprehending the profundity of Plato's primary triad of Sameness, Difference and Existence, as well as an analytical, discursive way. A study of Plato's *Sophist* provides the directive for the second approach, as does also the *Commentary* of Proclus, to whom we will turn for a reminder of the reflective and reciprocal nature of our appreciation of the principles put forward in the Platonic tradition, and those principles themselves. Proclus writes:

> The Soul, having an intermediate existence also fills the [proportional] gap between reason and irrationality. With the highest part of herself she consorts with Reason [*Nous*]; with the lowest, she declines towards Sensation [*Aesthesis*]. (*Commentary* 1. 251)

And again:

> Since the soul consists of three parts, Existence, Sameness and Difference, in a form intermediate between the indivisible things and the divisible, by means of these she knows both orders of things.... For all knowing is accomplished between the knower and the known.
>
> (*Commentary* II.298)

This last is a reminder to the reader that consciousness itself, and even the meaning of these words, is dependent upon the triad of consciousness without which knowledge cannot take place: that is, the triad of the knower, the known and the act of knowing; in other words, the necessity of a knower (reader), a known (a text) and the act of knowing (reading) as proportional relations.

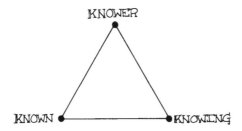

Aristotle clarifies this point of view when, referring to one of the many lectures by Plato that he attended, he writes:

> Again he puts his view in yet other terms: Mind [*Nous*] is the Monad, Science or Knowledge [*Episteme*] the Dyad (because it goes

undeviatingly from one point to another), Opinion [*Doxa*] is the number of the plane, Sensation [*Aesthesis*] the number of the solid; the numbers by him are expressly identified with the forms themselves or principles, and are formed out of the elements; now things are apprehended either by Mind, or Science, or Opinion, or Sensation and these same Numbers are the Forms of things. (*De Anima* 404b)

However we approach the soul's triadic structure, the procedure, according to Plato, continues to unfold in proportional divisions:

Having made a unity of the three, again he divided this whole into as many parts as was fitting, each part being a blend of Sameness, Difference and Existence. (*Timaeus* 35b)

Next, Plato describes the famous Lambda, although this is a later name, based on the Greek letter (Lambda), for the portioning system employed by Timaeus:

And he began the division in this way. First he took one portion [one] from the whole, and next a portion double of this [two]; the third half as much again as the second and three times the first [three]; the fourth double of the second [four]; the fifth three times the third [nine]; the sixth eight times the first [eight]; and the seventh twenty-seven times the first [twenty-seven]. (*Timaeus* 35b,c)

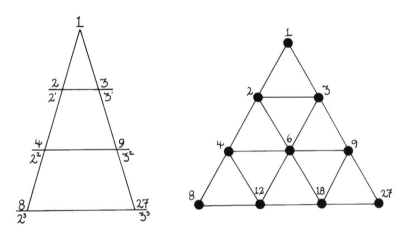

These two progressions of "even" (two) and "odd" (three), through "square" and "cube," he proceeds to "fill up" with both double and triple intervals, cutting off yet more parts from the original mixture and placing them between the terms, so that within each interval there were two means, the one [harmonic] exceeding the one extreme and being exceeded by the other by the same fraction of the extremes, the other [arithmetic] exceeding the one extreme by the same number whereby it was exceeded by the other. (*Timaeus* 36a)

In other words, he inserted a harmonic mean where the proportion was fractional, and the arithmetic mean where the proportion was numerical. For example, if we take the extremes six and twelve, the first or harmonic mean will be eight, as eight exceeds six by one third of six (that is, two) and is exceeded by twelve by the same fraction, that is one third of twelve, which is four. In the second instance, the arithmetic mean between six and twelve is nine, which exceeds six by three, and is exceeded by twelve by the same number. Timaeus continues:

These links give rise to the intervals of $3/2$ and $4/3$ and $9/8$ within the original intervals. (*Timaeus* 36a)

At this point the musical analogy comes in, without, as Cornford judiciously points out, pretending or claiming the phenomenon to be a music theory in the sense some critics have assumed:

And he went on to fill up all the intervals of $4/3$ [i.e., fourths] with the interval $9/8$ [the tone], leaving over in each a fraction. This remaining interval of the fraction had its terms in the numerical proportion of 256 to 243 [the semitone]. By which time the mixture from which he was cutting off these portions was all used up. (*Timaeus* 36b)

This simple language about subtle matters evidently alludes to research and methods of reference which remain the mysteries of the tradition from which they arose.

The point central both to Timaeus' doctrine of creation and to the subject of our study is the cardinal position of proportion: proportion both in the unfolding of the cosmos and in the unfolding of our awareness of it. This is evident as Plato continues in the *Timaeus* to relate the seven major intervals to the rotations of the heavens in a manner requiring intelligent and concentrated interpretation.

Having thus completed the proportional divisions of the World Soul, Timaeus proceeds to explain the relation of the Soul's proportions to the World's Body or "all that is bodily."

When the whole fabric of the Soul had been finished to its maker's mind, he next began to fashion within the Soul all that is bodily, and brought the two together, fitting them center to center.

(*Timaeus*. 36d,e)

The important thing that Plato is at pains to establish through Timaeus is that the invisible motions of the Soul's circulations are imparted to the bodily circulations of the cosmos:

The Soul, being everywhere inwoven from the center to the outermost heaven and enveloping the heaven all around on the outside, revolving within its own limit, made a divine beginning of ceaseless and intelligent life for all time. (*Timaeus* 36e)

At this point we may note that Proclus in his *Commentary* states his belief that the phrase "for all time" here means the Great Year as the "single period of the whole":

This period has as its measure the entire extent and evolution of time, than which there can be no greater extent, save by its recurring again and again, for it is in that way that time is unlimited.

(*Commentary* II.289)

Since for things to sustain in space they need time, time as much as space is a vehicle for proportion. Plato therefore goes on to assure us that time, as the moving image of eternity, was co-extensive with the coming into being of the Heavens:

At the same time he ordered the Heaven, he made, of eternity that abides in unity, an everlasting likeness moving according to number—that to which we have given the name Time. For there were no days and nights, months and years, before Heaven came into being.... These have come into being as forms of time, which images eternity and revolves according to number.... Time came into being with the Heaven, in order that, as they were brought into being together, so they may be dissolved together, if ever their dissolution should come to pass; and it is made after the pattern of the ever-enduring nature, in order that it may be as like that pattern as possible; for the pattern is a thing that has being for all eternity, whereas Heaven has been and is and shall be perpetually throughout all time.

(*Timaeus* 37d-38c)

The Heaven, in other words, is co-extensive with time—all time, past, present and future. If time should cease as the moving expression of eternity, then so would the Heavens or the created order itself.

When the "father," as "generator," had brought this self-moved creature, the world, thus into being, he rejoiced in that it was

> a shrine brought into being for the everlasting gods. (*Timaeus* 37c)

Here Cornford has embodied the true spirit of the word *agalma* by translating it as "shrine." The shrine is the cosmic prototype of the Temple, and this aspect of the created cosmos is again clarified by Proclus:

> Plato speaks of the cosmos as an *agalma* of the everlasting gods because it is filled with the divinity of the intelligible gods, although it does not receive those gods into itself any more than cult images receive the transcendental essences of the gods. The gods in the cosmos are, as it were, channels conveying a radiance emanating from the intelligible gods. (*Commentary* III.4)

Indeed, in his succinct formulation,

> The cosmos is the holiest of shrines. (*Commentary* I.124)

Next, Timaeus defines the Sun, Moon and the five "wanderers," or planets, as being brought into being to "preserve the numbers of time."

> Having made a body for each of them, the god set them in the circuits in which the revolution of the Different was moving—in seven circuits seven bodies. (*Timaeus* 38c)

And having thus accounted both for the macrocosm and for the preservers of the numbers of time—the planets, and the Sun and the Moon—Timaeus goes on to explain the categories of the microcosm.

This he does by unfolding the four forms of intelligence proportionally contained in the "living creature." These forms of intelligence, corresponding to *Episteme, Dianoia, Doxa* and *Aesthesis,* he symbolically represents as: firstly, "the heavenly race of gods"; secondly, "winged things whose path is in the air"; thirdly, "all that dwells in the water"; and fourthly, "all that goes on foot on the dry land." (See figure on page 138.) Stones are body, space is soul. These beings of air, water and earth are therefore of the realm of generation: that is, birth, growth, change, maturity and death.

Then, moving on to a description of the human soul, Timaeus says:

> Having received the immortal principle of a mortal creature, they [the gods], imitating their own maker, borrowed from the world portions of fire and earth, water and air, on condition that these loans should be repaid. (*Timaeus* 44d)

Repaid, that is, on the physical level as ecological awareness, on the level of belief or opinion as the submission of emotion to pure intellect, and on the intellectual level as the submission of human consciousness to divine consciousness.

The resultant bodies were then joined by a multitude of valencies ("rivets" in Cornford, which I find too mechanistic) too small to be seen, but making of each body a unity of all the portions.

> And they confined the circuits of the soul within the flowing and ebbing tide of the body. These circuits, being thus confined in a strong river, neither controlled it nor were controlled, but caused and suffered violent motions. (*Timaeus* 43a)

Plato goes on to state clearly that this disproportion is effected by the onrush of sensations, that "perpetually streaming current . . . stirring and violently shaking the circuits of the soul."

> It is, indeed, because of those affections that today, as in the beginning, a soul comes to be without intelligence at first, when it is bound in a mortal body. (*Timaeus* 44d)

The remedy for these disruptive and shaking movements is to be found in harmony, which in this context we may take to be the expression of proportion.

> Harmony, whose motions are akin to the revolutions of the soul within us, has been given by the Muses to him whose commerce with them is guided by intelligence, not for the sake of irrational pleasure, but as an ally against the inward discord that has come into the soul, to bring it into order and consonance with itself. (*Timaeus* 47d)

At this point in his monologue, Timaeus returns to the "probable account"—"no less probable than another, but more so"—of the generation of the four elements.

As our world is a copy of the intelligible, eternal pattern, and a copy is not self-subsistent by definition but needs a support, a medium in the same way that a reflection needs a mirror, Plato proceeds at length to invite the reader to join with him in accepting a stable ground of being for all the four elements which are themselves of course constantly changing. Whatever the material nature of the ground of being is,

> for the present we must conceive three things: that which becomes; that in which it becomes; and the model in whose likeness that which becomes is born. (*Timaeus* 50d)

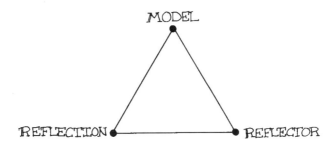

The "Recipient" he then compares with a mother, the "Model" with a father, and the "nature that arises between them"—"that which becomes"—with an offspring.

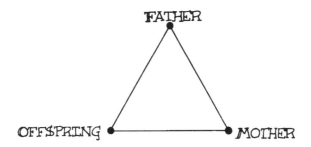

The Recipient or the Receptacle, as he comes to call it, must not in itself be called air, earth, fire or water. It is rather the *materia prima* or ground of substance, that is virgin matter before the differentiation into earth, air, fire or water:

> So far as its nature can be arrived at...the most correct account of it would be this: that part of it which has been made fiery appears at any time as fire; the part that is liquefied as water; and as earth or air such parts as receive likenesses of these. (*Timaeus* 51b)

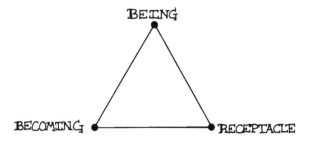

This "mother" aspect to virgin matter survives in the interesting etymology Mary, Mare, Mater, Mother, Matter.

After describing Form, here the unchanging, ungenerated, indestructible, invisible thing "which thinking has for its object," Timaeus goes on to juxtapose that which also bears the name form but is its "Different" aspect. This is the world of change, of sensible existents perpetually in motion, "coming to be in a certain place and again vanishing out of it," that aspect of things which is to be apprehended by belief and sense perception.

The third member of this particular triad, with Form and Copy (form), is Space itself which, like Time, is an everlasting quality, "not admitting destruction," and providing a situation for all things that come into being. It is indeed proper that all things should come into being "in" something else—"clinging in some sort to existence on pain of being nothing at all"—so that Space for Plato's *Timaeus* occupies a curious intermediate realm, which is best understood as being the ground of being to the geometrical forms of atoms, for in this way its bridging nature between sensible and intelligible can be appreciated.

In this connection we may note also that Space as the Receptacle (Mother) of the proportionals is a proportional herself, that is between the realms known by intelligible gnosis (*Noesis*) and sense experience (*aesthesis*) and opinion (*doxa*).

The triad that Timaeus finally outlines is Being, Space and Becoming, "three distinct things—even before Heaven came into being."

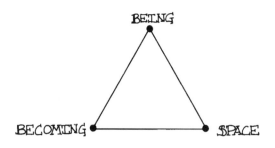

A state is then described in which all the four kinds or elements were without proportion or measure (space and time), motion acting like a winnowing-sieve causing like to aggregate (*synkrisis*) towards like, the lighter to ascend and the heavier to descend. At this point the "maker" began to give them distinct configurations, both by means of shape (space) and number (*arithmos*, time) with the "greatest possible perfection." Plato warns us that the account will be "unfamiliar." Yet for a modern it is curiously familiar since we have become used to atomism and the geometrical account in space and number of the elements of our physical world as expressed in the periodic table.

It is at this point that Plato, through Timaeus, asks us to enter into the *analogia* of space and the orders of space as regular and expressed as geometricals. This account of the permeation (*perichoresis*) of the sensorial turbulence of fire, air, water and earth by reason (*Nous*) is to be understood in the atomistic sense as being microscopically at the root of each element, thus recalling Heraclitus' principle that "Nature loves to hide."

Fire, water, earth and air possessed indeed some vestiges of their own nature, but were altogether in such a condition as we should expect for anything when deity is absent from it. Such being their nature at the time when the ordering of the universe was taken in hand, the god then began by giving them a distinct configuration by means of shapes and numbers. That the god framed them with the greatest possible perfection, which they had not before, must be taken, above all, as a principle we constantly assert. (*Timaeus* 53b)

Plato consistently proceeds in triads, having demonstrated the necessity of doing so as an essential property of Mind (*Nous*), Cosmic Intelligence and the minimal conditions of human consciousness. Now, having evoked order in space, he proceeds to demonstrate triads as triangles to be the minimal expression of perceptibility in shape. Surface, or the second dimension, is the minimal condition of visibility (aesthetic, sensorial) and the triangle is the minimal expression of the plane expressed geometrically:

Fire, earth, water, and air are bodies; and all body has depth. Depth, moreover, must be bounded by surface; and every surface that is rectilinear is composed of triangles. (*Timaeus* 53d)

For this purpose the equal-sided triangle is "best," as it is the most regular, and so as to demonstrate the ultimate symmetrical expression of this "perfect" triangle, Plato draws attention to its half-division as the ultimate triad. In doing so, he implicitly introduces the proportional relationship between one, as the base side, two, as the length of the hypotenuse or sloping side, and the transcendental proportion, the square root of three, as the length of the upright.

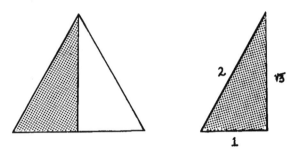

This upright proportional side unites the left-handed and right-handed triangles, which have the remarkable property of being able to create further triangles by addition. Six of them, for instance, create an equal-sided triangle that is proportionally bigger by the ratio of one to the square root of three in a square root of three progression: that is, by proportional increments in terms of scale.

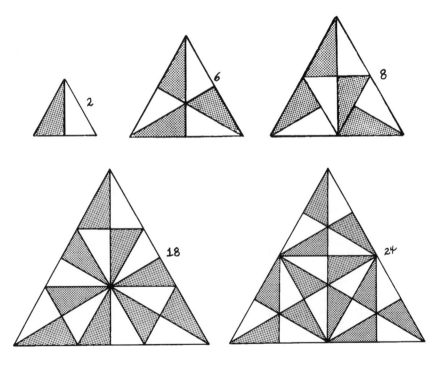

Timaeus continues:

> Now all the triangles are derived from two, each having one right angle and the other angles acute. Of these triangles, one has on either side the half of a right angle, the division of which is determined by equal sides [the right-angled isosceles]; the other has unequal parts of a right angle allotted to unequal sides [the right-angled scalene].
>
> (*Timaeus* 53d)

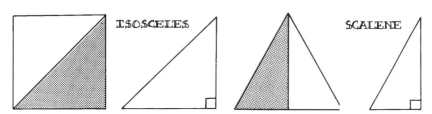

During this exposition Plato does a curious thing—a necessity forced upon him by his intention to conform to the procedure of unfolding creation in terms of triads which in turn make up the four elements. He clearly says that every surface that is rectilinear is composed of triangles. But then he correctly chooses to say that all plane triangles are derived from two kinds, the right-angled isosceles and the right-angled scalene. (It would be necessary to bifurcate irregular triangles to demonstrate the consistency of this fact.) As we shall see, however, these two kinds of triangles in fact embrace a triad of triangles. Having thus stated the triadic genesis of order in plane space, Timaeus says:

> This we assume as the first beginning of fire and the other bodies, following the account which combines likelihood with necessity.
>
> (*Timaeus* 53d)

Timaeus then goes on to add a particularly significant passage:

> The principles yet more remote than these are known to Heaven and such men as Heaven favors. (*Timaeus* 53d)

This is almost a definition of grace in modern theological terms. It certainly cannot be taken in the merely specialist mathematical sense, because who is to say that Heaven necessarily favors such a specialist? There is good reason, for the present writer at least, for the introduction here of such a statement that seems to bear directly on the question of the relation of written and unwritten doctrine *(Dogmata*

*Agrapha*) and to support the hotly contested thesis that Plato did not commit all his knowledge to writing. To the present writer this is an obvious fact on many grounds, yet we may confine ourselves to one example, namely that which is the subject of the construction of the basic elements of our experience: fire, air, water and earth. This geometrical doctrine is currently held by moderns in the theory of atoms, molecules, elementary particles and so on—even if with a naive silence on intelligible causes.

Plato gives Timaeus a question to proceed with:

> What are the most perfect bodies that can be constructed, four in number, unlike one another, but such that some can be generated out of one another by resolution? (*Timaeus* 53e)

Adding,

> If we can hit upon the answer to this, we have the truth concerning the generation of earth and fire and of the bodies that stand as proportionals between them. (*Timaeus* 53e)

This demonstration of the continuing pre-eminence of proportion is followed by a curious "evasion," which we can only assume is a covering up of the fifth body:

> For we shall concede to no one [does this mean "divulge" to no one?] that there are visible bodies more perfect than these, each corresponding to a single type. (*Timaeus* 53e)

For, having constructed the Tetrahedron (the four-face pyramid) of four equal-sided triangles, the Octahedron (eight-face) out of eight equal-sided triangles, the Icosahedron (twenty-face) out of twenty such equal-sided triangles, and the Cube out of six squares (twelve isosceles right-angled triangles, although Plato chooses twenty-four), Plato admits of a fifth construction which

> the god used for the whole, making a pattern of animal figures thereon [the Zodiac]. (*Timaeus* 55c)

Now, is it really consistent to allocate to the Heavens a solid figure (there are only five such regular solid figures as is common mathematical knowledge today) which is less perfect than those allocated to the four elements and which is not the Heavens of Light? And if the Pyramid

(Tetrahedron) is fire, then of what nature is this other light? This is not a matter to gloss over lightly (forgive the pun), as we have here a contradiction in Plato's own principle of triads.

In order to construct the pentagonal Dodecahedron (twelve-face), the fifth solid, a third type of triangle is needed.

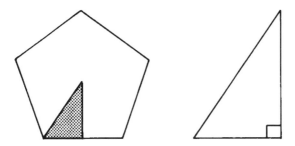

This would make up the triadic principle so fundamental to the tradition expounded by Plato until now. And yet Plato has said that we will need only two kinds of triangles. To solve this quandary we must refer back to the original passage quoted earlier where Plato introduced the idea of the two triangles with the preliminary remark concerning "principles more remote than these" which "are known to Heaven and such men as heaven favors." Later, he asked us to join him in judging which right-angled scalene triangle was the "best," and as part of this procedure he stated:

> Now of the two triangles, the isosceles is of one type only; the scalene of an endless number. Of this unlimited multitude we must choose the best, if we are to make a beginning on our own principles. Accordingly, if anyone can tell us of a better kind that he has chosen for the construction of these bodies, his will be the victory, not of an enemy, but of a friend. (*Timaeus* 54a)

This qualification is his logical let-out, since he does not specifically say in this instance "four bodies," but only "these bodies." Certainly, given the whole context, those "favored by Heaven" and "a friend" can hardly be antagonists in the search for geometrical and cosmological truths. The fact is that the triangle which is one tenth of a regular pentagon, and which is the basic constituent of the pentagonal Dodecahedron, has been quite deliberately obscured by avoidance, and that when the fifth solid which makes up "the whole" is mentioned, the mention is significantly brief, occupying only one sentence. And yet this figure, the pentagonal Dodecahedron, the fifth solid, is immeasurably more important than the others, because it is not only "the whole" but also the Heavens of the animal belt or the zodiacal constellations, and so constitutes the limits of our sense-perception *(aesthesis).*

So much ink and paper and unnecessary *(doxic)* energy has been expended attempting to prove an esoteric doctrine in relation to Plato and Pythagoras, that to add to it seems futile. Yet the indications seem clear enough from the above that there was a great deal "unsaid" in the *Timaeus* "myth"—which echoes Aristotle's allusion to Plato's *Agrapha Dogmata* in his *Physics* (V, 209b) where he says that Plato's account of the Receptacle in the *Timaeus* differs "from what he says in his so-called 'unwritten teaching'." There is no way that one may know much more about this. Plato's contemporaries seem to have observed the injunction that these teachings remain unwritten. With the exception of a public lecture "On the Good," that Plato gave and which was attended by, amongst others Aristotle and Simplicius (who both later published their notes—see Simplicius, *Physics*, 151, 453), little reference remains. And this anyway says little, since it was a public lecture and so contained material of and for "publication."

Most conclusively, unless one chooses to reject the authenticity of *Epistle VII*, there is the passage in which Plato explicitly states that he would never publish anything on ultimate principles. Consideration of this statement must take into account the positive reason for the oral tradition—that only in direct one-to-one dialectic can a transmitter be as certain as is possible that the truth has been received and thereby take the fullest responsibility for the transmission—and also, as we shall see, the "unspeakable" nature of proportional knowledge itself. Before making his statement, Plato gives a description of the true student of philosophy:

> This is the state of mind in which such a man lives; whatever his occupation may be, above everything and always he holds fast to philosophy [the love of wisdom] and to the daily discipline that best makes him apt at learning and remembering, and capable of reasoning soberly with himself; while for the opposite way of living he has a persistent hatred.
>
> (*Epistle VII*, 340d)

Plato then goes on to state:

> So much at least I can affirm with confidence about any who have written or propose to write on these questions, pretending to a knowledge of the problems with which I am concerned, whether they claim to have learned from me or to have made their discoveries for themselves: it is

impossible in my opinion that they can have learned anything at all about the subject. There is no writing of mine about these matters, nor will there ever be one. For this knowledge is not something that can be put into words like other sciences; but after long continued intercourse between teacher and pupil, in joint pursuit of the subject, suddenly, like a light flashing forth when a fire is kindled, it is born in the soul and straightway nourishes itself.... What I have said, in short, comes to this: whenever we see a book, whether the laws of a legislator or a composition on any other subject, we can be sure that if the author is really serious, this book does not contain his best thoughts; they are stored away with the fairest of his possessions. And if he has committed these serious thoughts to writing, it is because men, not the gods, "have taken his wits away." (*Epistle VII*, 342c, 344d)

As further evidence of the partial nature of Plato's disclosures of the tradition he is describing (due to factors related to the esoteric and to the indescribable transcendental nature of proportion), consider Numbers emanating from the One in the order of the Quadrivium—that is, Number or Arithmetic, Geometry, Harmony or Music, Astronomy—as the means by which the "maker" arranged our world, and through the correct study of which we are able to liberate our souls from the ensnaring illusions of the sensory world of shadows.

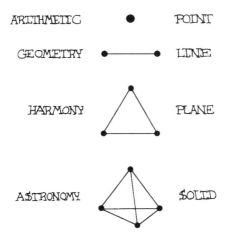

Thus when we get down to the subtle world of the atomic and molecular arrangement of the four elemental states, which becomes solidity when sensed as earth, liquidity when sensed as water, gaseousness when sensed as air, radiant light when sensed as fire, we find Plato moving to the second language of creation, namely geometry.

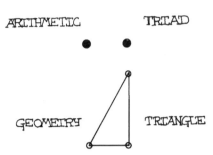

ARITHMETIC      TRIAD

GEOMETRY      TRIANGLE

We are given elementary particles, or particles with a triangular (geometric) nature and a triadic (arithmetic) valence, but without reference to number relations of side length. Only the numbers of such triadic particles per specific atom are given, so that when Plato "suggests" this "likely explanation," he is adhering strictly to a language that is beyond sense testing (*aesthesis*) or empiricism, for the atoms are microscopic and indivisible individually. In other words, it is the "subtle" world as we have just observed.

Here proportion of quite a different nature comes about. The triangular relationship of the prime elementary particle has side lengths of one, one, and the square root of two, which is a transcendental proportional number that is not expressible in whole integers.

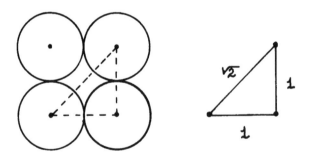

This was obviously too complex a subject to be exoteric since the "vulgar" would use (and have used) this transcendental property against the wholeness of number itself, by arguing from sensory data (*aesthesis*) and opinion (*doxa*), whereas Plato himself was well aware that the subject was not fully appreciable until the student was working at an awareness of the *dianetic* or *noetic* levels and so was appreciative of the metaphysical levels through which all being and becoming emanate. In this case the student would not fall into the simple, or vulgar, error of "judging the foot by the shoe," as Michelangelo was fond of putting it.

To judge the hidden intelligible source, or the principles of our world (whether we choose to call these the laws of nature or the intelligible principles of being), by sense experience is as intelligent as attempting to deny that there was such a phenomenon as electricity in times before it was studied and quantified and harnessed as energy.

Let us return to that "subtle" world we know sensorially as solid, liquid, gaseous and radiant. As we have seen, in Timaeus' description of the "logic" of the allocation of the most regular and beautiful forms to the four elements, he reasons that two primary ingredients are required: solidity (revealing that "earth" or solidity is at a symbolical level the physical plane itself) and light, simultaneously to "see" and to see by (again revealing the dual symbolic nature of light or "fire" as the source of creation on the one hand and as the spirit of cosmic and human intellect on the other).

For the solidity of earth, Plato "suggests" the isosceles arrangement of the one, one, square root of two, triangular elementary particles, arranged in a set of twenty-four so as to make up a regular cube—that is, an atom of earth as a solid figure, made up of six squares, whose "fourness" reflects the fourness of the elements on a physical plane, and whose "sixness" reflects the six days of creation. (See Philo, as a source for this interpretation.)

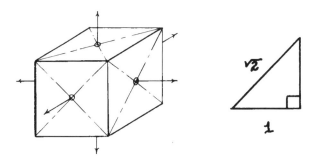

Thus Plato uses a transcendental proportion, the square root of two, to demonstrate the inherent square-root-of-two proportionality of the Cube, as expressed in the length of an edge of the Cube in relation to the diagonal of its face. Yet he only discusses the more easily appreciable numerical aspect of there being twenty-four such elementary particles in the make-up of this cubic atom of earth. It is quite significant that though the Cube can be made up of twelve such particles, Plato chooses twenty-four, which gives the symmetry lines of the figure.

Next, the Tetrahedron, with three sloping faces on a triangular base, is allocated fire or light. This figure is the minimal expression of the third dimension, which is the dimension necessary for something to be in our world, according to Plato, and therefore "first," in the same sense that light is "first" in the emergence of "our" world. This radiant or light source for our world is, in fact, as orthodox today in so-called astrophysics as it is in Biblical exegesis.

The Tetrahedron is made up of four equal-sided triangles, yet Plato has asked us to accept the half equal-sided triangle as the most beautiful and significant triad in the make-up of elementary particles. The reason can only be that this triangle gives us another fundamental geometric transcendental proportion, and in so doing draws attention to the inherent square-root-of-three construction of both the equilateral triangle and the Tetrahedron itself.

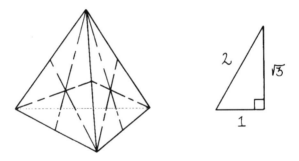

This reinforces the hidden or inexpressible nature of Platonic proportioning—which is nevertheless transmissible to the knowledgeable or work-willing student, as stated in the *Seventh Epistle*. A system of transcendentals is hidden both in the simplest of polygons (the square and the equal-sided triangle) and in Timaeus' explanation. Again, it is the numerical aspect by which Plato draws the reader up, constituting the Tetrahedron from twenty-four such particles. Of course, the Tetrahedron at its most essential can be made up of eight such particles, but this would not give the full lines of symmetry marked out on each surface (just as in the case of the Cube twenty-four were chosen when minimally twelve would have sufficed).

Plato then proceeds to place water, the twenty-faced Icosahedron, and air, the eight-faced Octahedron, between earth (solidity) and fire (light), since it is necessary that there be a proportional relationship between opposites to enable them to relate to each other. In this instance again, curiously, it is possible to assemble Plato's geometric cosmology in two ways, which we may perhaps call esoteric and exoteric, from the same text.

The proportional and concentric model of what Plato suggests, which we might call the macrocosmic model, is based on the idea of the whole of an element compressing down into its own sphere, until the whole is completely filled—the whole representing the cosmos. This gives us the Cube in the middle, as earth, surrounded by the light (space) of the Tetrahedron in such a way that the centers of the faces of the Tetrahedron are the contact-points of four of the nodes or corners of the Cube.

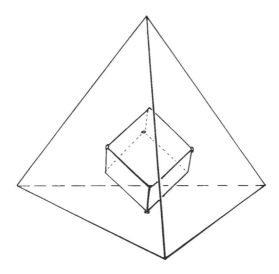

This placement enables a proportional and logical superimposition of the remaining geometrical figures so that they sit in correct concentricity between the Cube of earth and the Tetrahedron of fire or light.

Next to the Cube comes the Icosahedron, as the surrounding waters, in such a way that the centers of eight of the twenty faces hold the nodes of the Cube exactly in position.

Around the Icosahedron (water), and related by the Golden Mean proportion, is the envelope of air, the Octahedron, made up of eight equal-sided triangles which, like those of the Tetrahedron of fire and the Icosahedron of water, are made up of the half triangles or the one, two, square-root-of-three triadic particles, but this time in a set of forty-eight, whereas the Icosahedron uses one hundred and twenty. Needless to say, the Icosahedron could have been made up of forty such particles and the Octahedron of sixteen. The reason for the choice in both cases, however, is consistent: to give the full rotational lines of symmetry on each figure's triangular faces.

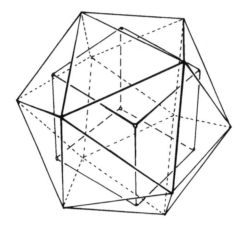

A significant proportional relationship emerges once again in the relationship between the Cube and the Icosahedron, through the transcendental square root of three, which was the significant dimension in the elementary particle or triad of fire. In this instance, the edge of the contained Cube is the square root of three long in proportion to the vertical height of the face of the containing Icosahedron, thus demonstrating in another way the part-whole nature of these proportionals.

Finally, the Octahedron of air, which surrounds the Icosahedron of water, is in turn contained by the all-enveloping Tetrahedron of fire or light, and therefore needs to relate geometrically to both.

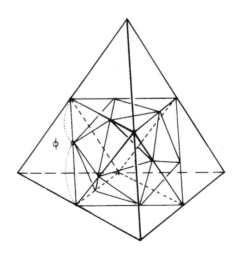

Now, if the Octahedron of air is related to the contained Icosahedron of water in such a way that its edges are divided in the Golden Mean proportion (Phi or the square root of five plus one over two) by the nodes or points of the Icosahedron, it can also precisely relate to the containing Tetrahedron of fire or light by touching exactly halfway along the edges of the Tetrahedron.

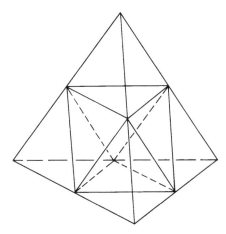

That is, the nodes or points of the Octahedron of air lie exactly in the centers of the edges of the Tetrahedron of fire or light, setting up a square-root-of-two proportion between the edge of the Octahedron and half the edge of the Tetrahedron—thereby relating all the four elemental geometrical proportionals from Cube to Tetrahedron.

Water (Icosahedron) relates to earth (Cube) by the transcendental square root of three. Air (Octahedron) relates to water (Icosahedron) by the Golden Mean proportion, the transcendental Phi or the square root of five plus one over two. Above this, fire (Tetrahedron) relates to air (Octahedron) by the transcendental square root of two.

Here we have demonstrated at the most essential and equivocal level the fundamental proportionals (the square root of two, the square root of three, and Phi or the square root of five plus one over two) which Plato shows hold together and differentiate the basis of our experience of the world, the cosmic structure, this holy shrine we inhabit. Thus it should come as no surprise to find just these exact proportionals present in the sacred and traditional Temple, Mosque and Cathedral structures throughout human history, for it is precisely through these proportionals that the Sacred Buildings, as the cosmos, could become shrines, the same proportionals maintaining the greater cosmos as maintain the microcosmoses of our bodies.

There is one more relationship to establish in the Platonic tradition: namely, "that certain fifth figure" which took up the whole, the Dodecahedron of the Heavens with its twelve five-sided faces. There are five ways in which the Tetrahedron of fire, with all the other elemental figures within, may fit regularly inside the Dodecahedron. All of these are symmetrical and all entail relating the Tetrahedron edge as a Golden Mean proportion to the edge of the enclosing Dodecahedron. If all five Tetrahedra were inside at the same time, the effect would be to have a five-pointed star or Pentagram on or "in" each pentagonal face of the Dodecahedron, thus giving rise to the Golden Mean spiral path to each face.

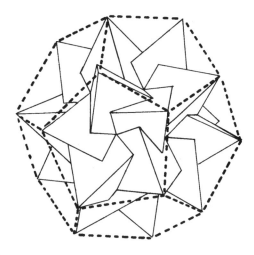

So we can see that Plato "hid" in the *Timaeus* with careful deliberation, because of the inherent, hidden and transcendent nature, the transcendental proportionals of the square root of two, the square root of three and the square root of five plus one over two. Further evidence of Plato's "esoteric" use of these transcendentals may be found in the *Meno* dialogue. This dialogue is central to the Platonic doctrine of *anamnesis* or recollection, which maintains the inherent ability of the soul to recollect or remember the archetypal *eidos* or ideas, as knowledge intrinsic to one's eternal human nature. The diagrams that Socrates uses in the *Meno* to elicit important mathematical concepts from the unschooled slave Meno are squares and their diagonals, which as we have just seen are proportional to each other as one is to the square root of two, thus giving rise to the primary triangular relationship of the elementary particles which make up the atom of earth (the Cube). (See *Meno* 20c-86c.) These diagrams occur again in the *Republic*.

These instances also demonstrate that Plato was not ignorant of the fact that a transcendental number is not expressible in whole numbers.

More than a few commentators, finally, have drawn attention to the recurrence of Pythagorean and Platonic ideas in modern physics and its approach to ultimate particles or those microscopic, uncuttable "building blocks" of our world. The periodic table of the elements, for instance, is an arrangement according to the geometry of space, and it is remarkable that the ultimate particles currently under discussion (1980) are triadic in spin, so that the smallest quarks are triadic in ultimate nature. Yet whether these entities are "physical" or "metaphysical," or whether we should take it that "uncuttable" means "not to be cut," as in the ancient wisdom, is another matter.

What is evident, however, is that the figures used by Plato in the *Timaeus* are the same as those used to "model" the atomic patterns in modern physics, whether in spherical, partially spherical, or planar linear form. Hence, the transcendentals recur as the determining relationships: the square root of three in the Tetrahedron, the square root of two in the Octahedron and the Cube, and the square root of five plus one over two in the Icosahedron and the Dodecahedron.

In microbiology, the smallest and most elemental entity that can behave as if living, the virus, is commonly found in Icosahedral form; but perhaps the coincidence here of life or living matter with the vehicle of water is too broad an analogy for the modern mind. There is no doubt, that the Cubic form is recurrent in the solid state, and so too is the Tetrahedron and the Octahedron, yet the interdependency of light-energy and mass have been shown to be fundamental to the modern view of physics.

Space and time and the laws of number are certainties for us. How the transient forms of manifestation reflect these is a matter of approximation and hence uncertainty. Thus a view that believes it is directed outward to empirical reality will be less by far than one that takes in the viewer as the recipient of the facts of experience, and so attempts to integrate the inner and the outer into a whole. Certainty must precede for there to be a lack of it in uncertainty. And so we can understand the value of the Platonic creation myth in the *Timaeus* when we appreciate the fact that Plato was indicating "intelligible" certainties, yet "sensible" likelihoods.

In our experience few things are more invisibly tangible than our relationships with our fellow beings, yet these are above all nonmaterial. These bonds of affection, love, loyalty and so on are as much the cohesive forces of our social sphere as the proportionals are the cohesive forces in the cosmic drama as Timaeus unfolds it in the Platonic dialogue. This is the most important aspect of the whole doctrine. That which is most important is least tangible. It is ultimate matter and ultimately inexplicable. The role of proportion is to aid us in understanding the mysterious way in which Unity unfolds into multiplicity so that we can use this knowledge to reintegrate ourselves by the same mystery.

# 4 | What is Sacred in Architecture?

................................................*Keith Critchlow*

To RAISE THE ISSUE OF THE SACRED immediately causes a response in the modern mind which conjures up its opposite—the profane. The traditional unitive view on this, however, can be summed up by the response of the ancient Chinese Sage who, when asked, "Where is the Tao?" replied, "Where isn't it?" The reason we find the concept of totality difficult is that the whole of our education is based upon contention, polarities, and the nature of categorization; naturally integral, unified thinking and experience are difficult for us. Yet they are both our birthright and intimately related to our sanity.

We are told an undivided mind is a good thing but never how to achieve it. This indeed is where the Sacred becomes relevant. Sacred and sacrifice are closely connected here, the sacrifice being directly related to the giving up of our patterns of thinking that cause us to approach totality either with the energy of the separate ego or with the categorical preconceptions that always get between us and experience. The part cannot experience the whole until it dissolves its separateness in that whole.

To societies rooted in the Sacred, that is, in the ideals by which the greatest majority of humankind live and have lived over the greatest majority of the life of the human family, the created order is sacred. Therefore all in this order is sacred. The relative is recognized, however, since once one observes the coming into being of something, its maintenance and its inevitable dissolving again, then one is said to be observing the relativity of things within an eternal flux. Both the *prima materia* (energy/matter) and the cyclic recurrence of the form are permanent; it is only the sensible form that is relative and subject at all times to change.

No better example of this understanding can be found than the Shinto shrine of Ise in Japan, where two sites stand side by side. Every twenty years the same form is rebuilt on the adjacent site, and the decayed temple is taken apart to await its turn, in twenty years time, to hold the form again. The form is eternal; the temples rise and fall.

The relative only has meaning and becomes measurable against an absolute background. Therefore, it is always a measure of change. That which does not change is not of the sensible order and is called a principle. Principles and the domain of natural law Plato called the intelligibles. In the present context then, we must say that the profane is concerned only with appearances and not essence, and at worst sets out, as profanation, to obscure the hidden essence of things. The Sacred, on the other hand, as complementary to the profane, embraces both relative (as expression) and absolute (as pure principle), and sets out to reveal the absolute within the relative and transitory.

The profane is provisional in time and exhaustible. The Sacred is providential, inexhaustible and eternal. Therefore, the profane mentality is bound to be outside the sanctuary, outside the temple, outside *temenos*, for it is by definition concerned only with passing time, not with the essence of time. What this means in terms of individual responsibility was put most directly by Lao Tsu:

> Embrace the Way [Tao] and the Way
> will welcome you,
> Embrace abandonment of the Way
> and abandonment will welcome you.

Happily or sadly, one has only oneself to answer to or blame when it comes to the choice.

Each essential human need has its sacred origin and is sacred for all tradition-based societies, whatever part of the world they may reside in. Architecture, agriculture, mid-wifery, healing and the rest of the essential living crafts are skills transmitted throughout all cultures and times in their various ways.

The Sacred in Architecture has common ground with health and cosmology, since the inner essence of correct and appropriate form in Architecture is based on a resonance of harmony and health. Total healthiness comes from wholeness, which is holiness. This resonance enables a consonance to sound from microcosm through mesocosm to macrocosm, and is the root and secret to finding unity and the unified experience.

The material world is subject most dramatically and universally to the laws of gravity—in human experience that which "pulls down" to earth. The realm of life, however, is dominated by *levity*, a word meaning "uplift" that has significantly fallen out of use in the English language since the Industrial Revolution. If the material world is essentially about "pulling down" (entropy?), then the human world, particularly as understood in the inspiring philosophy and ideals of a sacrad tradition, is essentially about "lifting up." As all life draws up to the light, so is the human psyche attracted to the elevating principles which act as constant regenerators to the forms and beings of our world.

Architecture, as sacred expression, is concerned with the power of levity in the physical, emotional, intellectual, inspirational and ontological realms, always dedicated to raising experience to a more inclusive and comprehensive unity and integrity. Therefore, it is not without relevance that the vertical dimension is so often the dominant one in so much of sacred architecture.

There are architectural principles that transcend different cultural expressions. These are based on elemental and primordial factors and demonstrate how structure on the physical level is integral with structure on the metaphysical level. They are analogous to the universal anatomical and physiological laws, transcending culture or race, that rule our human bodies: the blood groups, for instance, are a most insistent symbol of human unity on a physical level despite all the differences of skull shape, skin color or hair texture. We must not lose sight, however, of the fact that the Anthropos is the collective archetype for the whole human family—without which to be human has no meaning.

The metaphysical laws that are of a universal language and are the fabric of all sacred traditions in Architecture are Number, Geometry, Harmony or Music, and Astronomy/Astrology (Cosmology). This quadrivium of sacred sciences is taken as evidence of the universal intellect in and with which human intellect participates to a greater or lesser degree. These sacred sciences have been the vehicle through which the esoteric principles of each society were transmitted.

In fact, it is difficult to know how and on what basis one may call a society "civilized" in any intrinsic sense (beyond the civic agglomerations that pass as cities in contemporary industrial society) if it does not have the cohesive metaphysical and regenerative principles as an active and vital ingredient. Only from this integral viewpoint can traditional architecture be understood. By the same yardstick, we can view the malaise and poverty of our own time with its "little boxes" in the international style.

That our own times are predominantly profane or "outside" is evidenced in our current stockpiling of weapons, the destructive power of which is closely linked to the violations of the green world and the natural order, as demonstrated by the statistics on extinctions of species. All are indications of diabolic activity, increasing the entropic potential, accelerating the winding-down of form—feeding gravity and the grave. (Diabolic here means literally "to throw apart"; symbolic, "to throw together.")

Whereas, when the Sacred predominates, "The war horses are put out to grass," as Lao Tsu says. Peace and disarmament are the objectives, not "defense." The relationships between peoples are increased in harmony and understanding. This in turn raises up and gives birth to expression in the arts in the form of inspiration and beauty. Great feats of architecture rise up, symbols of edification built as much by the need of the people to express their elevated feelings as by any economic or political pressure.

The writer knows of no Scriptures that advocate war as a way to integrality—and if one wants to know of the most elevating, inspired and "energetic" revelations that have been expressed through the human vehicle, it is to the Scriptures of the world that one has to turn. They have generated the real energies, the coherent life-giving energies that have moved millions of people through thousands of years and have left legacies of elevative energy in the form of the great sages, sagas, music, paintings, objects and architecture, and not less the profoundly healthy agricultural and medical systems based on co-operation and husbandry. If we choose to abandon these eternal energies as eternal resources and to destroy life on earth in the greed for finite resources, then we have only our own ignorance to blame.

However, the evidence is sufficient that there is an irreversible movement afoot, especially among the young, who are determined that life will survive and that essentials will become more important than luxuries. Our hosts to the conference at Green Gulch demonstrated this beautifully. Anything less than one's Buddha nature is anything less. Anything less than the whole is anything less.

# 5 | Twelve Criteria for Sacred Architecture

*.............................................................................Keith Critchlow*

$T$HE FOLLOWING ARE A SELECTION OF CRITERIA which either may be presumed to have existed for the designer/builder of the sacred architectural traditions of the past or may be brought to bear on any sacred building as an aid in unraveling its mystery and design. Further, they may be taken as guidelines by which to test a projected design for a future sacred building, and therefore were the concern of the design team for the Lindisfarne Grail during the evolution of form as it developed in 1979 and 1980.

## 1.
### As a Mesocosm

*The whole world is the outward form of universal reason.* [1]

We take it as a first principle that we not only live in a cosmos but are ourselves a total reflection of this cosmos. After we acknowledge this reflective principle, the next step is to see the necessity of fabricating or expressing a means whereby we can appreciate the unity between ourselves and the whole, and thereby potentially become whole ourselves. This introduces the principle of the Mesocosm, the Temenos or sacred space into which we enter to contemplate the unity between ourselves as creatures and the One we conceive as Creator. This sacred space,

---

1. This and the following epigraphs are taken from Rumi, *The Masnavi*, in *Teachings of Rumi*, trans. E.H. Whinfield (New York: E.P. Dutton & Co., Inc., 1975).

which represents the paradigm of all time and all space, is the Temple. Naturally it is called by the name appropriate to each genuine revelation, be it Shrine, Temple, Synagogue, Cathedral, or Mosque, yet each expression is intrinsically dedicated to the act of contemplation of ultimate reality. This defining of the Temenos or sacred precinct is in itself subject to universal laws and is therefore also a reflection of the cosmos. Thus we call it a Mesocosm, the link between the macro- and microcosmos. The Mesocosm is an instrument by which the part can appreciate the whole and thus appreciate the wholeness of itself.

## 2.
## As an Anthropocosm

*In outward form thou art the microcosm,*
*But in reality the macrocosm.*
*Seemingly the bough is the cause of the fruit,*
*But really the bough exists because of the fruit.*

The Anthropocosm is one of the most helpful concepts to aid our understanding as to the disposition of parts in a sacred space which is integrated through proportion.

In brief, the head, heart, guts, and limbs division of our bodies is fundamental. The limbs are for motility, poise, and communicative work or movement in the world. The head, heart, and guts aspects are symbolic as well as physiological, the symbolism being triadic and interdependent. Thinking, feeling, and willing are one such symbolic triad, based on the body cavities. Facts, values, and execution are another level of expression, while science, art, and technology are another. All are expressions of the fundamental triad of the ideals toward which those three aspects of our being are directed and upon which their most essential appetites are based. The mind is drawn quite naturally to the ideal of Truth; the heart or our values, is quite naturally drawn to the ideal of Beauty; the guts or will is quite naturally drawn to the ideal of the Good. Each affinity in turn gives rise to one of the triads of the conscious modes of approaching reality: skeptically as in the scientific mode, mystically as in the artistic mode, and dogmatically as in the moral or active mode. These are not restricted to the empirical nor to the ideal, but relate to the scale between the two and include both. Meditation is the craft of the soul, the craft being the contemplative refinement of right action.

In the sacred space we find not only the three ideals cogoverning each part and the whole of the design of the building, but also each expressed as a spatial quality, and in certain cases becoming part of the sequential experience of consecutive spaces in the building itself. The Temple is your body as your body is the Temple.

Thus, the concept of the Anthropocosm expresses the appreciation of the essential human condition as archetype and as the expression of the principle of the Mesocosm in reverse. That the Universe is also a living being with soul and spirit is a traditional doctrine expressed more or less in all revelations, but a misunderstanding of this principle in recent centuries has led to quite unwarranted criticism of the anthropomorphizing of the Creator. Limitation to the purely literal interpretation of the traditional doctrines is virtually guaranteed to debase their meaning. William Blake stated, after Dante and Swedenborg before him, that all scriptures have at least a fourfold meaning. The literal level is not incorrect, but is inadequate and misleading if taken as the sole meaning.

## 3.
## As the Intervals between One and Two

*But within the outward sense is an inner secret one.*
*Beneath that secret meaning is a third,*
*Whereat the highest wit is dumbfounded.*
*The fourth meaning has been seen by none*
*Save God, the Incomparable and All-sufficient.*
*Thus they go on, even to seven meanings, one by one.*

Fundamentally, this is a musical analogy that expresses the idea of the relation between unity and diversity. Music teaches us that there are basic ratios or intervals defining the principle of the octave within sound. A single note and its recurrence either above or below in the sliding scale of sound subject the human ear to an inherent sense of the rightness of eight intervals—the octave.

These notes, or the intervals between the notes, represent a universal law of eightness—or the profound relation between seven and eight, From this law of the octave are developed the thirteen notes of the chromatic scale, or the relation between twelve and thirteen.

The proportional intervals of sound, which we call tuning, are analogically related to both the sevenfold and the twelvefold progressions that characterize the natural qualitative divisions between one and two. One represents a point on the scale of sound, two its octave recurrence.

These intervals are expressed not only in the acoustics of any given sacred building but also in the common ground of number as dimension, symmetry, and proportional ratios between elements of that building.

Plato gave us the finest exposition of the relation between musical intervals and the soul in his cosmological dialogue, the *Timaeus*. The analogy between the sacred space and a musical instrument is implied in the sense that wholeness and harmony can be helped by correct tuning. Health has a common root meaning with wholeness and holiness. In canonic tuning there is a consonance between the architecture and our own bodily and psychological perceptions, not least in the attuning of mind and spirit. Atonement affirms this.

4.
As Containing Its Own Soul

*Though earth and water have cast their veil upon us,*
*We retain faint reminiscences of those heavenly songs.*
*But while we are thus shrouded by gross earthly veils,*
*How can the tones of the dancing spheres reach us?*

This refers to the analogical mode of the soul as the perfect form— the sphere. Both as a principle of unity and a model of the cosmos, the sphere represents the ultimate undivided, undifferentiated whole. Each sacred building exists within its own sphere, which is its metaphysical perfection and from which it represents the physical limitation.

As space is to the soul of the sacred building, so the materials are to the body. It does not follow that sacred buildings should be spherical but that the sphere is the primary and essential form from which differentiations take place. From this point of view all solid figures are special cases of the sphere. There are only five mathematically regular solid figures; they bear the name of Plato, who first committed their facts to writing in his *Timaeus*. In this dialogue, analogy is drawn to the geometric mode of the four states of matter/energy and to the fifth as the ground of being or heavenly whole—the ether. For instance, the Cube represents the molecule of earth in the language of Plato, an analogy which contains both the language of spatial crystallization on the one hand (becoming physics on the manifest level) and the symbolic expression of material perceptibility on the other. Thus "earth" is the symbol of the physical plane. The scale of symbolic allocations of the regular solids relates both to the physical expression as elements and to perceptual psychological bases in the planes of consciousness: the Icosahedron as "water" and the emotional or rhythmic plane; the Octahedron as "air" and the intellectual or ordinative plane; the Tetrahedron as "fire" and the spiritual, inspirational, or intuitive plane; the Dodecahedron as the ether of the divine level and the ontological state that unifies, embraces, and permeates the other four planes or states. Space thus defined becomes a crystalline, harmonic symbol of the psychic modes.

Form in the sacred space is founded on principles emerging from these archetypal forms. The three fundamental proportional scales emerge from the three primary triangular solids. The Tetrahedron gives birth to the $\sqrt{3}:1$ proportional ratio; the Octahedron gives birth to the $\sqrt{2}:1$ proportional ratio; and the Icosahedron gives birth to the Golden Mean proportional ratio of $(\sqrt{5} + 1)/2:1$. Each of these three relates to bodily proportions within the sacred edifice; together they are the means whereby the principial Anthropocosm can be related to the Mesocosm.

# 5.
# As Reflecting the Steps of
# Jacob's Ladder or the Stations of Wisdom

*Acts, words, and faith are the food of the King,*
*So that in this ascent one attains to Heaven.*

In all genuine traditions there is the recognition of the stations of wisdom that express the stages of discontinuity in the scale between Heaven (Unification) and earth (differentiation and uniqueness). Jacob's Ladder is such an image or icon arising out of the Abrahamic tradition of the Old Testament. It has been specifically conventionalized into a form upon which certain aspects of the Kabbala are taught. This image is based on a series of ten stages and eleven intervals, with the ten sephiroth or spheres of light placed on a central axis on a model which is called the "extended tree." This tree of knowledge, or gnosis as it is called, is a scheme upon which the ten interpenetrating levels of subtlety of universal laws are demonstrated. These levels represent the stages, as far as they are defined or definable, of the ascent of the soul to reintegration with its Creator, which may be described as a state of complete unification.

These stages are more or less explicit in the design of a sacred edifice.

# 6.
# As Parts Relating to
# the Whole and to the Subtle Body

*Its glory is not derived from stones or mortar,*
*But from being built without lust or strife.*

The parts of any building must by necessity relate in some way to the whole of that building. The significance or profundity in this relationship is dependent upon the subtlety and state of being and knowledge of the designer or designers. However, even this is not enough, as the most profound sacred edifices are also expressions of the fulfillment and perfection of the art of building and craftsmanship. The mark of all truly sacred and profound buildings is an integral dependency and interdependency of part to whole, of design to execution, and of theory to practice.

In the Hindu tradition it is expressly stated that the souls of both the donor and architect are inseparably involved in the success of the final form. This involvement of the subtle bodies of those responsible for the Temple brings the responsibility into a life or death relationship with the Temple's form. The subtle body works on laws of its own which we can take in this instance as those principles that ensure the integration of the spiritual and physical planes. In fact the soul itself can be described as the linking factor between the timeless domain of pure principle and the bodily domain in time—hence its vital significance. The role of the subtle or psychological body is to relate the whole through a direct connection with the spiritual domain.

# 7.
# As the Heart of the Community

*When the body bows in worship, the heart is a temple.*

Although a hermit's humble cottage or cell is as profoundly a sacred space as a magnificent cathedral or temple, this in no way diminishes the fundamental symbol. The very sacredness or dedication to spiritual values of such a dwelling is as much the heart of the community in the intrinsic spiritual sense as a more obvious major edifice which is also the visual center, such as the cathedral church of a medieval Christian town.

This symbol of the heart is analogically connected to the sun in our solar system—the source of life and light. In the sense of spiritual nourishment, the divine liturgy and meditational activities which realize the divine presence within the daily life of the hermit-monk and the community are as vital as any bodily nourishment. From the spiritual perspective, such activities are fundamentally vital because they represent the link between the source of the creative order and the creative order itself—a link as vital in the subtle sense as the flow of blood to every tissue in the bodily organ. The analogy of the permeation of spirit to the permeation of blood in the body relates to the Platonic Christian term *perichoresis*, which specifically defines the total permeation of all matter by spirit as the maintaining principle. This cardinal maintaining principle is the only guarantee that all creation is not either dissipated through the action of the proceeding principle or withdrawn completely due to the returning principle—these principles together comprising the fundamental threefold aspect of the creative unity itself.

In summary, whether the heart of a community is the religious hermit or holy man of the village, or whether it is focussed in the divine liturgy of the central temple or cathedral, the important factor is the spiritual presence represented in either case. Sacred space is, so to speak, designed to be as irresistible as possible to spiritual and intelligible presence—the locational heart in the spatial sense and the central organ for the dispensation of grace in the metaphysical sense.

# 8.
## As a Grace-Receiving Space

*What is first in thought is last in act.*
*Thought is the special attribute of the Eternal.*
*That product goes forth from heaven very swiftly.*

The word most appropriate for spiritual presence is *grace*. The grace-receiving space is therefore the space that is specifically designed with the intention of being a receptacle capable of receiving the blessing of spiritual presence. Grace can be variously described as state of consciousness or a state of understanding or a state of serenity out of which specific psychological energies flow. These states have the effect of aligning one's way of life, or the communal life, which results in a more wholesome and enriched existence. Descriptions of grace in itself are not possible, since it is a cause which is effective in a multiplicity of unique ways, yet the common factor is a life-enhancing positivity and sense of rightness and affirmation.

In the Hindu tradition it is stated that if the proportions of a sacred image or building are correct then worship is not only permissible but most likely to be effective. The accent is more on proportion and less on form. Grace cannot be legislated for, yet canonic rules are a common occurrence, like prayer formulae, which the perennial philosophy and the lives of the saints affirm to be effective.

# 9.
## As the Integrality of Permanence
## and Change in the Time Dimension

*You issue from God's attributes at first;*
*Return again back to those attributes with all speed! ...*
*You begin as a part of the sun, clouds, and stars,*
*You rise to be breath, act, word, and thought!*

There is nothing more timely than the timeless, as S.H. Nasr has said. An understanding of time as the flowing image of eternity is fundamental to understanding the way in which the outer form of a sacred building relates to its inner essence. Traditionally there have always been inner, intrinsic, and hidden rules which govern consciously or transcendentally the layout of outer forms of sacred spaces. These rules are expressed through number, geometry, harmony, and the laws of cosmology.

Architecture has been called frozen music, an analogy bringing out the static mode of the principles of harmony in built form, in contradistinction to the necessity of the time dimension for the expression of music. As music is to moving time, architecture is to eternity; through this analogy the principles of harmony common to both can be appreciated as symbolizing the archetypes outside time and reflected in time.

In a similar way the center of sacred space is without dimension, as the central moment of time is without duration. The architecture of the sacred frames the paradigms of both space and time *in potential*. The unfolding from the center of space sequentially reveals the three dimensions, and the periodic repetition of the moment unfolds the dimensions of duration. By analogy, the inner harmonic laws of architecture in time unfold from the architectonic principles outside duration. Thus style and cultural expression are the outer manifestation of principles, laws, and proportionals that are timeless and styleless. Nevertheless, principles cannot exist without manifestation and manifestation cannot be formed without principle, so the two are inseparable in reality. Therefore, we cannot posit a syncretic archetype outside or separate from the precise emergence of the specific sacred edifice in its time. The hidden cannot be the revealed, as the revealed cannot by definition be the hidden; therein lies the mystery of unity in diversity and the paradoxical nature of unity, as well as the unquestionable rightness of each unique sacred edifice of each unique revelation.

# 10.
## As Placing

*Distance and nearness affect only the body*
*What do they matter in the place where God is?*

In a similar way that time is the flowing image of eternity, place is the unique expression of all space, and the means whereby we can experience the conditions of pure space. Each place is unique yet answers as a central point to the three dimensions of all spatial differentiation. To experience the significance of space as a sacred center, each person is encouraged by the design of the sacred place to experience simultaneously the uniqueness of his or her situation and the unifying significance of this place with all places. Hence each experiencer of the sacred space becomes not only central to his or her own ground of being but potentially becomes absorbed into the totality and thus oblivion of all space—a state of nondifferentiation. In this way each place within the sacred area is a potential source of identification with the essence of the individual and with the creative principle itself. To be "placed" is to know where one is in every sense of the word. To be centrally placed gives one a balanced view of the conditions of existence—hence the value of symmetry in the sacred edifice.

# 11.
## As Canonic Proportion

*But if you want an instance of this secret knowledge,*
*Hear the story of the Greeks and the Chinese.*

The essential role of canons of proportion is to develop a state of being or a state of mind that is poised between the principles of existence and existence itself. There are a variety of ways of describing this proportional thinking and action: entunement, atonement, right action, and so on. It is also based on the perennial wisdom of the sages who set out rules for conduct that release the spirit rather than imprison, that reduce the numbers of laws of cause and effect rather than increase them. Canonic law is traditionally based on objective laws of harmony, cosmology, number, and geometry which act as a framework for the multitudinous melodies of individuality to discover the common scales on which all melodies are based. All of the senses by which we must experience the physical world have canonic prescriptions which aid the transmutation of impressions into perception, perception into knowledge, and knowledge into wisdom.

It is also an axiom of the oral tradition that each realization of the universal laws requires a unique channel, since realization is based on the co-necessity of the unique and the unified, the part and the whole. Canonic prescription links the knower to the known, the participant in knowledge to the principle of knowledge.

The ancient wisdom would posit that a knowledge of canonic laws is not necessary to an existence but that an access to the significance of existence would require an understanding of canonic law. The true meaning of tradition lies in this knowledge—tradition here meaning that core of truth that is "pulled through" the multifarious outpourings of history, that which makes the permanent knowable in the midst of the changing.

## 12.
## As that Wholeness Embodying
## the Highest Knowledge Available to be
## Carried within the Form for Future Generations

*The knowledge of men of heart bears them up,*
*The knowledge of men of body weighs them down.*

A sacred edifice in the highest or fullest sense is a crystallization of the principles of the civilization that it expresses. This means that the frozen melodies are available, so to speak, to the conscious awareness of any receptive experiencer, regardless of time. The experiencer becomes the musician who is able to release or appreciate the meaning within the sacred building. In this way it is as true to say that a magnificent cathedral is built as much for the single individual's enlightenment as it is for the experience of a collectivity. It also follows that the wholeness of the edifice or its decay, mutilation, or remodeling in time has a direct bearing on the fullness or lack thereof of the experience of the indwelling spirit. Yet it is also true that even a fractional part can release the significance of the whole to the timely meeting of a receptive soul. Essential knowledge in the sense intended here signifies an understanding of what it means to be fully human: that is, from a theological or wholeness perspective, a cosmological perspective, and an anthropological perspective. Each leads to an integral state of being as well as an outward harmonic expression. This essential knowledge simultaneously answers the three major challenges: How did things arise? What is their nature? How will they resolve? The answers lie not in particular details but in laws that govern particulars, intangible laws that become clad in more or less clarity with the particulars of the age. Such answers specifically unite the outer with the inner, which is the key to the integral state of harmony.

Finally, the definition of a profane space is one that is seen as a falling short of this ultimate knowledge of expression: either a willing or ignorant denying of the principle of wholeness and thus of the realization of the state of integrality. It is not necessarily in opposition to sacred space, but rather a partial state and "false ceiling" to the wholeness of things.

From the perspective of wholeness all space is sacred: it is up to each of us whether or not this is realized. This is the real meaning of *response*-ability.

*This adaptation therefore of souls was procured by him through music. But another purification of the dianoetic part, and at the same time of the whole soul, through all-various studies, was effected by him as follows: He conceived generally that labor should be employed about disciplines and studies, and ordained like a legislator, trials of the most various nature, punishments, and restraints by fire and sword, for innate intemperance, and an inexhaustible avidity of possessing; which he who is depraved can neither suffer nor sustain. Besides these things also, he ordered his familiars to abstain from all animals, and farther still from certain foods, which are hostile to the reasoning power, and impeded its genuine energies. He likewise enjoined them continence of speech, and perfect silence, exercising them for many years in the subjugation of the tongue, and in a strenuous and assiduous investigation of the most difficult theorems. Hence also, he ordered them to abstain from wine, to be sparing in their food, to sleep little, and to have an unstudied contempt of, and hostility to glory, wealth, and the like: to have an unfeigned reverence of those to whom reverence is due, a genuine similitude and benevolence to those of the same age with themselves, and an attention and incitation towards their juniors, free from all envy. With respect to the amity also which subsists in all things towards all, whether it be that of Gods toward men through piety and scientific theory, or of dogmas towards each other, or universally of the soul towards the body, and of the rational towards the irrational part, through philosophy, and the theory pertaining to it; or whether it be that of men to each other, of citizens indeed through sound legislation, but of strangers through a correct physiology; or of the husband to the wife, or of brothers and kindred, through unperverted communion; or, whether, in short, it be of all things towards all, and farther still, of certain irrational animals through justice, and a physical connexion and association; or whether it be the pacification and conciliation of the body which is of itself mortal, and of its latent contrary powers, through health, and a diet and temperance conformable to this, in imitation of the salubrious condition of the mundane elements—of the appellation of all these, which are summarily comprehended in one and the same name, that of friendship, Pythagoras is acknowledged to have been the inventor and legislator.*

IAMBLICHUS, *Life of Pythagoras*

*The importance of the Tetraktys (quaternary) that is obtained by addition (that is to say, 1,2,3,4) is great in music, because all the consonances are to be found there. But it is not only for this reason that the Pythagoreans gave it the greatest honor: but also because it seems to comprise the whole nature of the universe. It is for this reason that the formula of their oath was: 'I swear it by he who transmitted to us the Tetraktys, the source of eternal nature.' He who transmitted this was Pythagoras and all that has been said about the Tetraktys seems indeed to have been derived from this philosopher.*

THEON OF SMYRNA, *Exposition*

*Pythagoreans limit number to one kind, the mathematical; they do not take it to be separate, but say that sensible beings are composed of it. For they build up the whole universe out of numbers, but not out of number consisting of abstract units, for they take units as having spatial magnitude.*

ARISTOTLE, *Metaphysics*

*Now the Pythagoreans, seeing that many attributes of numbers belong also to sensible bodies, believed that things themselves are numbers, not separate numbers but composed of numbers as their elements. Why? Because the attributes of numbers belong inherently to musical scales, to the heavens, and to many other things.*

ARISTOTLE, *Metaphysics*

# 6 | Pythagorean Number as Form, Color, and Light

................................................... *Robert Lawlor*


THE PYTHAGOREAN SYMBOLISTS ASSUMED what may seem an obvious cosmological ground for their numerical procedures: that God has manifested himself in this universe as light, and that the first formation of light is color. Therefore all formation must be fundamentally of the nature of color, that is, a spectral continuum of hierarchical organization. Certainly spiritual texts from many cultures abound with the association between light and the universal creator. But Pythagoreanism, like its Egyptian sources, is an instance in which this association may be taken not only as an inspired metaphor, but also as a proto-scientific analogy. Leibnitz beautifully restated this Pythagorean theme, saying, "The exquisitely orderly behavior of light indicates the underlying radical patterned order of reality." And in recent years, Prigogine's "self-organizing biology" likewise asserts that the fundamental nature of matter is organization, and that all observable organization is hierarchical. Long before this, however, Dante said, "The elements of all things that Nature begins, whatever be their mode, observe an inner order. It is this Form that makes the Universe resemble God."

This essay intends to demonstrate how some of the curious modes of Pythagorean number symbols, transmitted by the Platonists, grew out of this cosmology of light. I will particularly examine the disconcerting proposition attributed to Pythagoras: "Color is Form, and Form is Color."

In addition to the rather subtle and esoteric concepts which may stand behind this radical identification, there are some common sense observations which may have led to its formulation: There is no form which has no color. All bodies absorb and retransmit light and in so doing define the edges of our objects of visual perception. Through colors and their shade differences, a field of vision is divided into objects in space. No one has ever seen a color by itself or a form without a color. Color and configuration arise codependently because the nature of form and color are the same.

Number, like any other language, arises as a descriptive emulation of the phenomenalization of light and sound. It follows, therefore, that the efficacy of the language of number, as with other languages, is dependent upon its ability to imitate syntactically the nature, laws and relationships observable in light and sound. In other words, the question is how well does a language map the *basic reality* it is intended to symbolize. There are reasons to believe that the Pythagorean philosophers had already intuited in a detailed way the unification of energetic forces which James Clerk Maxwell theorized in 1861 as the "rainbow of electromagnetic radiation." This may explain why Pythagorean science attempted to build an entire cosmology on observations of the laws of sound frequencies in vibrating strings and vessels, assuming a fundamental qualitative identity between light and sound.

Thus the idea that "the light shineth in the darkness" is part of the age-old philosophical tradition which we associate with Pythagoras. All visible light is light which is transiting between emission and absorption. It is light which has been warped by either collision with or entanglement in Form. Visible light is of the same nature as sound except that it has attained a critical velocity. The expression of this velocity in perception is form-color. Audible sound is then analogous to invisible light (pure light, or darkness), but at a lower octave of vibration and in a preformative or rudimentary phase of form expression. The fact that sound is a form-bearing stage of vibratory organization has been amply verified in our day by audio-holography and by the science of cymatics. Likewise in many traditional texts, sound is seed and the fruition of sound is embodied form.

As we discuss some of the elements of Pythagorean number and geometry, let us continue to bear in mind that the theoretical logic of these mathematics is based entirely on the appearance and interrelationship of Number and Form in the context of vibratory phenomena. Elements of this logic are *proportionality, reciprocity, cyclic recurrence and equivalent resonant affinity, integrality of partials with fundamentals,* and the *codependent origin of quantity/quality as is found in frequency, amplitude and phase.* Therefore the Pythagorean inquiry into the relationship between symbol and reality does not have an historic termination, but continues whenever we understand more precisely the world of light in which we live and which lives in us.

# I. Number and Counting

As a result of Pythagorean influence, Plato's writing contains many deliberations on the nature of "counting," which in Greek is *arithmos* (the numbering of assemblages). These arguments contain the foundation of Platonic philosophy and, taken in conjunction with Aristotle's criticisms, reveal how Plato was both transmitting and modifying the teaching of his enigmatic predecessor.

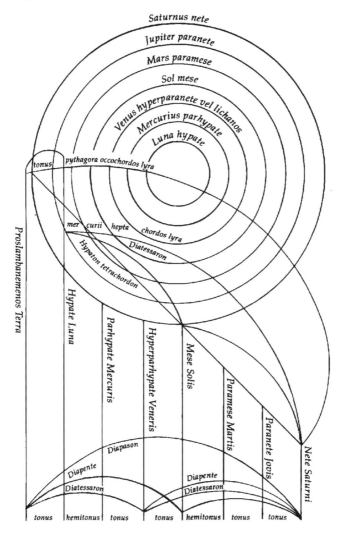

In the Renaissance the Seven Circles defined by the tones of the musical scales were placed in relation to the seven planetary orbs, demonstrating an intuitive awareness of the relatedness of time-space organization.

Why was the humble activity of counting held to be of such importance by the Greek philosophers? One answer oddly enough comes
from modern brain research. All our perceptions begin from an innate
capacity in the brain/mind to recognize (count) periodic patterns of
energy frequency which our nervous system has transformed into neural
rhythms. All distinguishments which we experience in perception begin
from this counting of pattern, recognizing one pattern-unit as distinct
from another and in relation to another, within spectrums of sensorial
sensitivity. The first act of perception is thus a *quantity* recognition of
temporal periods which are then transformed, in the case of vision, into
spatial fields and qualities set in a spatial context. Even smell, touch,
taste and hearing elicit an image-formation response, though it is subjective and often amorphous. Intelligence *counts* and then views these
tabulations of time as spatial images. If we assume then that qualities are
derived from this innate counting, then intelligence can be understood
as a process of transformations back and forth between two inseparable
ways of being, quantity and quality. This may be the conceptual intuition
which guided the Platonic emphasis on counting, for in Platonic philosophy, as in Hindu philosophy, counting and calculation are proper to
humans (the Sanskrit word *manas*, man, means "measuring") and relate
them to the intelligible world. This in turn must be connected to the
Pythagorean influence, where ontology itself was defined as that which
is countable.

The simply act of counting depends upon a faculty which continually
relates to and makes distinctions between numbered things as well as
between numbers themselves. This combination of distinguishing and
integrating defines very well the activity of mind itself. On the assumption that this level of quantification is initial and a necessary aspect of
creation, the Pythagorean philosophy begins with the examination of
the structure of number and geometric symbol, exploring their inner
relationships with the natural world and the worlds of mind, both of
which are, in the Pythagorean sense, fabrications of light.

All counting presupposes the existence of some homogeneous field
of units. In order for counting to work these units must be invariable,
unchanging, indivisible and infinite in number. Counting is matching
(or measuring with) units from this universal set with other items,
assemblages or extensions.

For Plato a number of key philosophical ideas emerge from positing
a homogeneous field of ultimate, invariable units (called *monads*). First
is the necessity for hierarchy in the symbolic practices of both language
and number. One branch of mathematics then contemplates the "Ideal"

(monadic) level, which is in no way subject to change or becoming or passing away. (This fact initiated the famous Platonic dichotomy between the "Ideal" and the "sensory.") This ideal mathematics itself falls into two areas of research. The first is that of Ideal Numbers and the natural organization of discrete positive integers. The second is Geometric Ideas, referred to as "continuous magnitudes," consisting of the simple geometric volumes and the components which delimit these volumes, such as points, lines and planes. After 2400 years we still find it necessary to rely on these same geometric components and numbers for our language of science, although radically altered by the intentionality of application. Ideal or theoretical arithmetic supposes that practical calculation and rules of reckoning arise from the *a priori* relationships and qualities of Number, and that these qualities of Number themselves arise from the relationship of Number to Form (square numbers, hexagonal numbers, etc.). Ideal mathematics studies the properties and kinds of numbers (odd, even, amicable, perfect, prime, abundant, etc.) as Form-Ideas (*eidos*), while practical mathematics applies this syntax to the material expression (*hyle*) of number. In Platonic thought, Number as proportion and principle should never be separated from the concept of geometric form. The reasons for this will be developed in the course of this essay, but for now we should understand that Plato believed that this maintained the connectivity between the changing, perishable world of particulars and the world of eternal, intelligent Being (*Eidos*). Plato intended mathematics to be a method of activating our capacities of counting, reasoning and, as well, intuition. The division between the Ideal and the sensible extended also to the studies of Harmony and Astronomy, which were considered branches of mathematical thought. (For details of theoretical arithmetic and Platonic number theory consult Thomas Taylor's *Theoretical Arithmetic of the Pythagoreans*, Theon of Smyrna's *Mathematics Necessary for Understanding Plato*—Theon is a second-century Pythagorean—and, most importantly, for the origins of Pythagorean thought in Egyptian mathematics see R.A. Schwaller de Lubicz's study of the Rhind Papyrus in *Le Temple de l'Homme*.)

The concept of an oceanic, monadic milieu upon which the procedure of counting is based recalls the undifferentiated cosmic sea in ancient mythology, and it brought mathematical thought into direct confrontation with the naked singularities of limitlessness and ultimate limit. Regarding the finite or limited, the monadic concept led to an image which has had a dominant role in Western thought. The monad, in order to be the *archai* of the unit, must be indivisible, that is, its singularity is *not* made up of any component parts. This of course in materialistic thought became the theoretical physical atom. And in this sense the ultimate unit is really an attempt to find the *limit* of material divisibility. But in the Platonic or Pythagorean mind, for which number logistics, we recall, were based on harmonic motion, the unit was first of all Ideal. Then, coming to the level of the particular, the unit finds its expression not as a particle, but rather as a wavelet. Thus limit becomes a perceptional limit of vibrational experience, not a material one, and limit is reached through consciously heightened perception rather than through the analysis of matter.

However, the atom as a discrete, ultimate unit, although surpassed by Particle Physics, has been a magnetic and enduring concept, and we find reiterations of it in many basic symbolic procedures. The idea of the atom, combined with the idea of matching or counting, is the dominant organizational principle behind the standardization of phonetic languages. By this I mean that phonetic languages take what is seen to be an inclusive set of the most rudimentary sounds (atoms), and then match these sounds with a set of equally rudimentary symbols—one particular sound matched with one particular symbol. This is basically an atomistic concept of counting where a one-to-one equational sense of relationship is the basis of organization, just as one musical tone is matched with one notational symbol, or one tick of the clock with one second of time. This form of relationship can also be extended to become "anatomical" thinking, in which any system is comprehended by the association or identification of one component, a cell or organ, for example, with one physiological process or function. In recent times the usefulness of anatomical thinking has fallen short in many instances, but particularly as a means of describing the human brain. It has been shown that higher brain functions, such as memory and other forms of intelligence, are not housed or located in any particular section or component of the brain. The failure to understand the brain as anatomy has given rise to an interesting new model for the mind/brain complex, based on holographic encoding patterns.

The purpose here is not to discredit one-to-one anatomical equationalism, for certainly our science has applied it successfully in describing many levels of organization. But the problem is that atomism and anatomical thought as the basis of our processes of symbolism have had extended implications in our science which are just recently being understood.

Atomism as it presently exists in our number system means that we obtain wholes by linearly adding together discrete units, such as $1 + 1 + 1$.

In systematizing number in this way we forget that number continuity really only progresses through a wave-like alternation (odd-even), that there are no discontinuous magnitudes nor discrete parts, that a unit can never exist outside of a contiguous form/flow. This is why the Greek word *arithmos* denotes the definite and discrete, but also means rhythm and unbroken interrelatedness. To conceive of any unit in Platonic thought is to evoke its Ideal archetype, the monad, and is never understood as a simple, empirical fact. Whenever the spell of one-to-one "anatomical" thinking is broken then wider intuitions open out, as in the case of Einstein's use of the continuous curvature from Reimann's geometry, or the flow cusp patterns of Professor Thom's catastrophe theory.

In contrast to audio-phonetic "anatomical" language organization we have hieroglyphic languages, where the meaning is associated with a visually rendered structure. In the existing modern forms of Chinese ideograms the sound aspect is relatively arbitrary. Hieroglyphic languages in general are not organized on a one-to-one equational basis to the extent that modern phonetic languages are. Each ideogram represents a clustered continuum of concepts, modulated according to the context or level of contemplation. Originally phonetic languages were more like aural hieroglyphs, and not so dependent upon a one-to-one equation between sound and symbol or word and idea. They made use instead of clusterings of acoustical analogues. But in all cases these two major language types place a distinct emphasis on either the visual or the aural perception. In ancient Egypt both a hieroglyphic (visual) and a hieratic (aural) system were co-maintained, perhaps to avoid the dichotomy of sight and hearing. This seems consistent with our contemporary awareness that sight and sound, like time and space, are only superficially separate. An organism can sense and respond to sound and light through means other than the eye and ear. These phenomena, called non-visual light perception and non-aural sound perception, indicate that the whole body may be an instrument for seeing and hearing. The recent science of ultrasonics has verified what meditating sages intuited long ago: where there is light there is at the same time sound, and reciprocally. The language of chanting, found in so many ancient cultures, integrated hearing and vision: never a sound without a visualization, never a vision without a sound vibration. In learning to listen we project what we have heard of the universal vibratory continuum and it becomes what we see of ourselves (our experience). The clarification of this process is vision and it requires a multi-sensorial language as support.

It is fashionable today to discuss the ways that language structure affects and limits our perceptions and concepts of the external world, but we are now beginning also to grasp how deeply it affects our internal instruments of consciousness, both brain and body. Recent brain research is showing that children before the age of two or three show little or no bilateralization in the brain. In other words, left-right hemisphere differences develop with subsequent symbolic education, and it may be that language and mathematical systems make it necessary for the brain to channel certain kinds of activities or information to one side of the brain or the other. Active inhibition is a proven characteristic of our nervous system, and this may be one explanation for the origin of the dual-lobe condition of our brain/mind; it may also indicate the extreme mutability of brain/mind functions in the face of the symbolic orders which are impressed upon it. Neural energy is moved and distributed throughout the brain in relation to symbolic procedures. Symbols, in this sense, use us more than we use them. Perhaps this understanding of mind-symbol relationship prompted Plato's great concern to link numerical practice not only to reason but to intuition and imagination.

## II. Being and Non-Being

Plato's monadic ontology implies that every number presupposes a definite and discrete unit taken from a limitless, homogeneous field. Contemplation of it thus provides access to the contemplation not only of a limit, but also of the limitless. These extremes are the fundamental tension in Pythagorean thought, rather than the terms "Being" and "Non-Being." In Pythagoreanism, Being is limited and countable (perceivable); Non-Being is limitless and uncountable; Being and Non-Being can only be linguistically considered in terms of the *limited* and the *limitless*, and thus take on a particular conceptual tonality. Non-Being (the limitless), is not an opposite to Being (limit), but is only other than Being. In numerical practice, the relationship between the limited and the limitless, or between Being and Non-Being, is not fixed. Religious thought, we might say, is predominantly based on a fixed Being/Non-Being relationship, while what may be called spiritual thought, like true scientific thinking, must apply a dynamic, changing relationship. In Pythagorean thought the principle which effects a change between limit and the unlimited is the imaginal power of perception. Non-Being then is only the yet unimagined, unperceived portion of Being. There is no other Non-Being except the yet-to-be.

What "has been" remains eternally resonant in form/fields of ceaseless transformation. As in monadic number theory, everything perceived is an interfusion of both the limited and the limitless. The universal movement is a diminution of Non-Being in the progress towards total Being. It is Being embodying itself.

## III. The Ideal World

Another major philosophical as well as semantic problem which Plato encountered through the contemplation of Number is that of *predication*. The results of counting rely on predication in the same way as other languages do in communication and observation. Any statement using the verb "to be" as a copula is a predicative form, whether it be "this thing is six" ($x = 6$), or "this thing is beautiful." Plato recognized a problem which has never, in over two thousand years, been explained away. The problem can be simplified as this: "This marigold is beautiful." We know that marigold signifies a particular existent yellow or orange flower. It is necessary also to ask whether the word *beautiful* signifies something. Is there an entity whose name is beautiful? The same type of question can be extended to ever more complicated modes of predication, such as: "Moonlight is similar to the whiteness of a pearl." Moon and pearl are words signifying entities, but are there entities standing behind the words "similarity" and "whiteness" to which these words are referring? As is well known, Plato answered this question affirmatively, by postulating the existence of a realm of pure Ideas, so that beauty, similarity, whiteness, and all such qualities refer to noetic objects, similar to the pure monads of number theory. These essences or form-ideas belong only to an imperishable supersensible world of thought, and a sensible object reflects this higher realm because to some degree it participates in the Idea, for example, of beauty, similarity, or whiteness.

Plato's Ideal world is no doubt a modification of the Pythagorean concept, except that Plato brings to both his mathematics and philosophy a bias towards the superiority of the purely noetic thought realm over the somatic, a predisposition which certainly did not exist with Pythagoreanism or its sources.

Let us briefly survey some of the historical modifications of predication and the concept of an Ideal world of pure essence.

In early Sanskrit and also in ancient Egyptian there is *no enforced predication*. A sentence in Sanskrit would only note a cohabitation in the field of vision of a flower and beauty, or of marigold and orangeness, each appearing with no fixed copula between them. The object and the quality and the perception of both of them are not differentiated, but all remain as pure experience, a musing, with an open possibility of relationships between them. The verb in Sanskrit denoting existence has several forms. The predicative form adopted by European languages is from the root *vrt* which means "to be" in the sense of a vibrational happening, a shimmering, unevolutive eventfulness. The Yoga Sutras of Patanjali begin with a warning of the necessity to restrain the *vrtti*. To the Hindu sages a word vibration connects its user to the archetypal field generating that root sound, which then, by affinity, influences and shapes the emitter.

In contrast, the way our language is presently employed, "to think is to predicate." This overemphasis directs our thoughts and observations away from musing and the imaginal towards description, definition, classification, explanation. Plato seems to be aware of the problem of excessive predication and the assertiveness which it gives to language and thought. This assertive disposition enhances the sense of individual separateness and habituates thinking into patterns with which we identify ourselves through a constancy of fixed associations, such as "this is that," "this will be that," "this won't be that," "this was that." Predication, when extended in time, becomes prediction, and certainly our science carries the imprint of the tendency towards definition and prediction which is concurrent with predication. Predication, with its demands of thinking ahead and thinking back, supposes that reasoning and designing are intellectual activities capable of dealing with future time and space. The older languages, which offer possibilities other than predicative reasoning, allow for the apportioning of a variety of mental processes. Perhaps one cannot predicate the future or even the present except in very limited ways, but undoubtedly predication imposes an association between the concept of orderliness and the concept of predictability; while Pythagorean thought might allow for a sense of fundamental organization which is utterly wide, simple and precise, yet less predictive than even so-called randomness. Brain research has shown that excessive stress placed on assertive, predictive and recollective thought patterns causes excessive cerebral blood flow, which we experience bodily as imbalances in blood circulation and psychologically as anxiety. Again we find that a language imbalance has a serious and complex physiological implication.

Aristotle, who is cast alternatively as the villain or the hero in the piece, refuted the independent existence of a world of Number and Idea as form-essence. He claimed that the existence of numbers and qualities are dependent upon the existence of the sensorial object which exhibits these measurements and characteristics. Symbols can thus become collections of arbitrary and standardized mental notations having no being of their own. Aristotle also claimed that quantities and qualities may be separated or lifted off (abstracted) from the whole. He replaced the Platonic Ideal reality with a theory of mental abstractions which enables scientific investigation to detach or isolate either qualities or quantities from the whole and from any or all of its content. The extended implication of Aristotle's thought technique is well-known: objects of sense wither away and become only items or carriers of useful data. They are deprived of their full sensorial as well as their Ideal being, which even in the simplest object is a simultaneous and multidimensional experience. While Platonic ideals provide for an elevated detachment from the sensorial world, Aristotle's thought opens onto a strange, possessive yet indifferent view of matter.

One obvious comparison between Aristotle's theory of abstraction and the Platonic notion of the Ideal is that with the former language becomes almost entirely word equations: the use of words to define other words without the Platonic contemplative reference to the permanent nonsensorial Form or Ideality which the words evoke in order for there to be a communion of understanding. Another comparison reveals a curious reversal in the concepts of the abstract and the concrete. Because Plato founded his Ideal or noetic reality upon the primary language of geometry and number, the closer one comes to the sensible the less exact and less concrete one's discernments become. With Aristotle concreteness and exactitude belong to the sensible, empirical world, and the movement from the concrete sensible world towards abstraction means an increase in vagueness and imprecision in some instances, or precise but reductionist schemas in others. Certainly this proves, if nothing else, that the concepts of abstraction and concreteness cannot be dealt with through a simple oppositional approach.

In modern language Plato's Ideal world could be thought of as a primary level of organizational potential whose precision and simplicity insure clear, imageable relationships between absolute universal invariables and their corresponding particular variables. Increased complexity of variables and particulars becomes a veil obscuring Ideal essence and requires the vision of transparency to again reveal it. Plato proposed that perfect instances of these universal, primary patterns were the five regular geometric volumes, the tetrahedron, octahedron, cube, dodecahedron, and icosahedron. Pure geometric Form is to symbolic, utilitarian and natural form as pure sound is to language and music.

Anders Wedberg's book *Plato's Philosophy of Mathematics* presents two diagrams which show the three hierarchical levels of Plato's concept of the Ideal as it relates to geometric and numerical order:

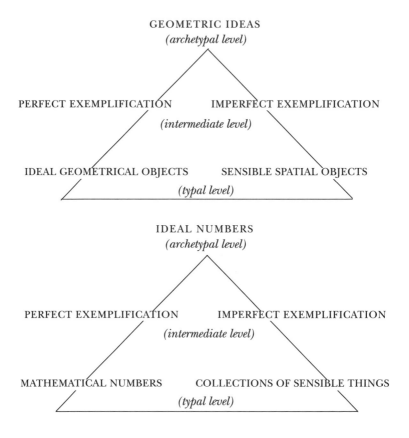

GEOMETRIC IDEAS
*(archetypal level)*

PERFECT EXEMPLIFICATION          IMPERFECT EXEMPLIFICATION
*(intermediate level)*

IDEAL GEOMETRICAL OBJECTS        SENSIBLE SPATIAL OBJECTS
*(typal level)*

IDEAL NUMBERS
*(archetypal level)*

PERFECT EXEMPLIFICATION          IMPERFECT EXEMPLIFICATION
*(intermediate level)*

MATHEMATICAL NUMBERS        COLLECTIONS OF SENSIBLE THINGS
*(typal level)*

These diagrams are reproduced here with the additional note that the three levels are designated as the archetypal, the intermediate and the typal. The first diagram demonstrates that the idea of the circle, for example, has two aspects: on one hand it is the abstract property of circularity (cyclosis) and on the other hand it is a *circle*, the ideal, perfect, standard circle. In other words, there are two assumptions at work here, that of the pure geometrical Idea and that of the Ideal geometrical Form. Plato approached these realms through contemplation, whereas Pythagoras, in a heightened form of seeing, envisaged them as attributes of the gods.

The next most important aspect of Pythagorean-Platonic metaphysics to consider is the connection between geometric form-ideas and the Ideal Numbers.

IV. The Philosophy of Form/Color

Pythagorean ontology begins with a homogeneous field of imperishable monadic units, analogous to the cosmic aether of Western science, and to the mythic image of creation arising from a vast, undifferentiated vibratory ocean. This primary beginning has also been alluded to as universal consciousness, that is, as pure Unity infinitely replicating itself as monadic units. The epistemology or knowledge of this world, however, is dependent upon form (*eidos*). This word *eidos* also translates as *idea*. Creation only becomes manifest through both *ontos* and *episteme*, being and knowledge of being, and knowledge of being arises from the contemplation of the laws of organization which we experience as form.

All form is generated from the archetypal principle of volumation, by the five greatest *génos* which are exemplified by the five unique, perfectly regular geometric polyhedra. To the Pythagoreans, the nature of the whole in-forming world was polyhedraic. "Polyhedron" means a form with many faces. The world then is not probabilistic, it is not indeterminate, it is not approximate. It is in essence many-faced. The undifferentiated monadic field must be configured as Form-Idea in order to express its being. Everything which exists has a form. Form is the antagonist of limitlessness and makes possible both quantity and quality. Form is the fixing of Number into realized relationships. Form is innate or original knowledge, and also makes possible all learnable knowledge, because it determines genus, species, subspecies, the entire hierarchy of "kinds." Form is the force of organization and organization is the very *ontos* of creation, the being of things. The cosmos is the ordering of number. Perception is the imaging of form contained in the potential of number. The homogeneous monadic aether becomes form through three original, *a priori* forces, called in Sanskrit *sattwas*, *rajas* and *tamas*, and in modern scientific language the protonic force, the electronic force and the neutronic force. In the Christian Trinity they were called the Son, the Holy Spirit and the Father; in the Hindu Vishnu, Brahma and Shiva: the movement towards centrality, the movement away from centrality and centrality.

So in ancient thought as today, all form begins with an inseparable, inexplicable triadic force, which the ancient Pythagorean geometers observed in their diagrams as $1/\phi^2$, $1/\phi$, 1. These Golden Mean proportions, along with the set of proportions related to the square root of 2, the square root of 3 and the square root of 5, are all the proportions needed to form the complete world of the geometric solids. These proportions, known as "irrational numbers," were for the Pythagoreans the only abstractions. But they had no existence apart from the forms which they generated. Form was understood as the realization of these involved principles of relationship. These primary irrational ratios embedded in the structure of the Ideal Volumes, 1: √2, 1: √3 and 1: √5, are immutable and irreducible in the hierarchy of formal proportions, and are therefore considered to have the imprint of the Divine Unity or monad. Hence they are his primary creative powers (the *Neters* or Gods). These ratios, in the continuum of proportional unfoldment, are necessary and prior to all numbered (countable) relationships, such as 1:2, 1:3, 1:5 or their permutations, beginning with 2:3, 3:4, 3:5, which in Pythagorean thought comprise the world of audible music and visible form, the secondary level of creative executors.

There is then a harmony of Sound and Form perceptible to the senses, as well as a harmony of both on the pure, noetic or hypersensorial level apprehended through ideal number and geometry. Music is the dream of a transforming body.

The form-generating relationships were considered to be active powers of creation, just as we have discovered, for example, that the square, the inverse square, and the square and cubic roots are functions in the laws of light, sound and gravity, or that the double square is the ordering principle in the periodic Table of Elements, or that the square root of 2 function is necessary in compression ratios in various mechanical methods of power generation, or that it is only necessary to multiply the speed of a spacecraft by the square root of 2 in order to lift it out of a confined orbit and free it from the pull of gravity. . . .

All of existence is a form-process: pre-forming, in-forming, per-forming, de-forming, re-forming, trans-forming, re-preforming, a seven-fold cyclic form/process which houses the entirety of being. But to understand more deeply the Pythagorean concept of form we must cultivate further their postulate of an identity between form and color. As is often the case, modern science is useful in opening up the essence of Pythagorean reasoning. To the Pythagorean the visible order of visible things is of the same organization as is found in any of the invisible realms of substance or mind. The basic quality of substance is order, and everything that participates or resonates in this quality of order is substance. Therefore to the Pythagoreans, thought and even feeling is very refined substance, that is to say, an organized and envisionable quality of vibration. For this Aristotle condemned the old teachers as being "sense-bound physiologists"! But our senses inform us only of spectrums and octaves, these scales of differences which are basic to all distinguishment. In contemporary science we find the atom is modeled as a spectrum or octave of seven shells or thresholds of energy, similar to the energy variations in the seven-fold spectrum of natural light. Light is found as geometrized electromagnetism (atomic substance: the limited) or as emissions radiating between states of substance as wave frequencies (the unlimited). Substance is the morphological possibilities of light. Physical color is the result of the interaction of electromagnetic wave frequencies (radiation) with atoms and molecules organized into hierarchical wave structures, with each level having a discrete energy quantum. Physical chemistry is thus a morphological study of electromagnetic behavior within the inner geometry of a particular molecular field. The individualities of these geometries express themselves as color. These views make up part of the quantum mechanical philosophy of matter and they help provide an explanation for the Pythagorean identification of form and color.

Light and other forms of radiation can only be absorbed if they carry precisely the right amount of energy to promote an atom from one rung to a higher rung. As the atom falls back to its fundamental state the absorbed radiation must be removed, carrying away the difference between the two levels. This released energy appears as a photon or a quantum of light having a particular wave-length determined by the energy difference in the rise and fall within the structure of the atom. This entire interaction of a substance-form with a radiating field is color, and it gives information about the relationship of a substance-geometry to a radiating field of energy. Color, then, speaks of an affinity of form and field. It should be noted that these instantaneous fluctuations in energy level are concurrent with alternating changes in the geometry of atomic structure, and that this endless color/form activity is not arbitrary but occurs according to a very precise rhythmic scale. Every atom possesses a preset harmonic energy scale, "a musical organization": an in-formed vibratory gradation, which gives birth to the thousands of color variations discernible to the human eye. (Cf. *Scientific American*, Oct. 1980.) Color is not, as Aristotle thought, a separate quality carried by or painted on an object. It is rather a message of inter-relationship/process. Color images the chemistry of this flame of universal life which we call substance. Color is substance transforming itself. We have been assured by practitioners of advanced meditation that these models (or similar ones) of submicroscopic organization—analytically revealed in our physics—are accessible in deep meditative visualization.

The end of the last century saw the Pythagorean concept of form/ color intuitively expressed in the beauty of Impressionistic painting. At the end of this century we may witness its return as the foundation of a new philosophy of science. A very similar image of the relationship of form and field is used by Rupert Sheldrake to form a powerful new model, for biological philosophy. Sheldrake is proposing an ancient model only with fresh information from modern research. His hypothesis could be interpreted as follows:

All apparent form may follow the same structural essence as the atom or molecule. The visible form is only a nucleus in a spectral nest of related morphic fields which resonate and conduct the information which controls the self-organization and development of the form. Each formation or morphic unit results from the organizational capacity of the morphic field, and each form reciprocally contributes to the continuation (nourishment) of that field. If energy is defined as a quality of being, then it is possible to image reality as a spectral sequence of internested thresholds of energy, similar to the spectrum of natural light, where a shift in frequency level generates the perception of a completely new quality of being: a new color. A form and its morphic field are different octaves in a resonant continuum. Periodic resonance is the law of life and it is this which is causative in all formal organization, regulation and development. Rhythmostasis is the sustaining power of formal organization and we may consider form of all types, including the helical DNA as wave-guide antennas, receiving and transducing information from fields having a resonant affinity. Fields never die, so no form is ever extinct. To experience one's entire field-body would be to experience the fullness of mind, because they are identical. Light and sound and all kinds of radiation may only be encodements of form/organization, just as a holographic phase plate is an encodement of an entire three-dimensional image.

Holographic concepts of mind propose that mind, nature and light all share the same ideal or abstract analogue. This common analogue consists of the characteristics of wave phenomena: frequency, amplitude and phase.

This inseparable relationship between form and color, or in more modern terms, between form and field-frequency, through the principle of resonation, is the essence of Pythagorean thought. Whenever it re-emerges in history it inseminates a new vision of natural science. Frequencies have form, and form and frequency are inexorably interrelated, as are gravity and mass. This new "field biology" and the holographic field theory of mind are marked by what is a general shift in our scientific view, a moving away from the emphasis on mass, location and motion as being the primary qualities of substance. Science is now finding that the so-called "secondary qualities" of matter—color, form and tone—are equally important. In Newtonian and Einsteinian physics these qualities had been labeled "secondary" because they were considered to be partly psychic, that is, more an aspect of the appreciation of matter rather than qualities inherent in the physical object itself. Because color, form and tone are both physical and psychological they are difficult to abstract and quantify in Aristotelian fashion. But it is now felt that this classification of primary and secondary qualities no longer holds, as *all* qualities are currently seen as effigies created by the sensorial and perceptual responses of living consciousness.

## V. Form and Image

Substance and light are of the same electromagnetic energy; they are fields of force whose movement/form is detectable as wave phenomena. Substance varies from radiated light in that it has been organized into relatively stable geometric vortices by the three primary principles of organization, the protonic, the neutronic and the electronic: the movement towards centrality, centrality and the movement away from centrality. The varying proportions of these three powers determine the geometry of the substance.

All light is invisible until it has encountered a substance. All substances to some varying degree absorb and re-emit light. This interaction is color, and it is the signature of the inner form of the substance.

Holographic brain theory proposes that the phenomenon of mind can be seen as a similar process. Mind and memory function through the absorption of light where the phase-interference patterns of light are encoded as spatial transforms stored within the living substance of the brain or other tissues of the body. All the forms of the world can be holographically projected from encoded phase-patterns of light. We can generalize this theory and say that substance itself may be a holographic memory process in which the consciousness of living substance—and perhaps of all substance—(its geometry) builds itself from the stored transforms of living experience. And experience, in view of the holographic theory, can be designated as the absorption and re-emission of light.

The unique quality of electromagnetic radiation is that within the space-frame of the earth it travels in straight lines. These straight lines make possible reflection and refraction which in turn make possible the perception of invisible light as form and color. The Pythagorean philosophy of symbols calls attention to this basic fact of reflection. Everything that exists does so by being duplicated as an image. And an image is always other than that which it represents. A mirror-image is very emphatically not the object being mirrored; it is a transform of the form, or the beginning of a succession of transforms, each indicating a shift in medium, or a shift in the basic co-ordinates which describe a medium. Self-repetition, self-imaging, self-mirroring, self-imitation are all words describing the basis of the process through which *ontos* must pass to become *episteme*. The nature of light shows that being creates by counterfeiting itself—and confronting itself—as image. Therefore imaging, which is the very basis of similarity recognition, is also inherently contradictory and oppositional.

The symbol continues this natural process of the imaging of light. Symbols become one of the namesakes of being. In the Pythagorean sense, symbols must mirror the proportional character of a phenomenon, that is to say its form-essence, rather than its perspective character, that is to say its seemingness or appearance.

Self-mirroring sets up a situation of infinite regression: an image within an image, a spectrum within a spectrum (spectrum in Latin means image), an octave within an octave. This infinite regression, translated into our mentality, becomes the notion of a quantifiable infinity of number, time and space. Paradox, self-reference and infinite regress are beyond the boundary of our Aristotelian logic. But the logic of Pythagoras is the logic of light and vibration. It is inclusive of the concept of an octave contained within an octave, but it also understands that the essential form-nature of an octave (the consonance of its proportions) is connected to all other octaves through resonance.

The symbolic science of the Pythagoreans concerns itself with understanding how it is possible that one Idea, in its unity and wholeness, is distributed over so many things which partake of it, the participation of the particular, the individual, in the Ideal, the universal. How do fields of pure being in-form themselves, and how do the forms of being enfield themselves in a contiguous process?

The Platonic approach differs from that of Pythagoras in that it sees the access to the Ideal realm as being through the purely noetic experience of thought and mind, that is to say in the transcendence of sense and perception and the aesthesis of the visible world. But for the Pythagorean, what is beyond aesthesis was attained by hyperaesthesis: in the education, extension and intensification of the sensorial capacity, of which our normal senses are a lower but integral octave. This difference means that Pythagoras belonged to the older, mystical and yogic tradition, while Plato, using the same body of knowledge, begins the path of philosophy and contemplation.


## VI. Form Perception and Death

For the Pythagorean, this universe is a universe of perception. Perception is the transformation of light into forms of itself. And light is consciousness imaging itself. So each particular is a tiny holographic image of self-perception within a larger, anthropocosmic formation of self-perception.

Perception is the unceasing activity of existence. The universe is created in perception: it evolves through the evolution of perception; and its goal lies in the perfection of self-perception.

In this philosophy, death is only a shift in the ground state of perception. In the experiments which have been done with sensory deprivation, particularly the experiments of John Lilly, it has been shown that as soon as the flow of information has been cut off completely from our five external senses, then the experimenter immediately begins perceiving and sensing other levels of experience. Our psychologists call these experiences visualizations or hallucinations or dreams, or some kind of distortion of our normal sensory activity. But it has now been proven that both psychologically and physiologically there is no difference between these inner perceptual experiences and the ways that we perceive our so-called external environment. So we are beginning to establish that inner seeing and inner observations are observations of tangible, formal worlds, which are simply out of the frequency threshold of ordinary sensing. As a matter of fact, our ordinary senses can block the processing of those other levels.

The first books on philosophy written in traditional cultures are consistently about death. Plato, in one of his dialogues, has Socrates announce that any true philosophy is a philosophy of death. Then Plato has a young man in the group laugh at old Socrates for this archaic view. The Egyptian Book of the Dead is one of these early texts. Like the Tibetan Book of the Dead it is about death but is a completely different view of death than ours today. The title of the Egyptian book is a mistranslation. It is not "the book of the dead," but literally translated means "The Book of Coming Forth by Day." We can interpret this as the entry into the visible spectrum of light.

Now a basic part of initiatic education in ancient cultures was a training of how to function consciously within the perceptual modes which are available to us during the transition we call death. So philosophy was not originally an activity of mental speculation, but rather it was actual instruction concerning procedures to follow at death. The Egyptian Coffin Texts, for example, are instructions and injunctions on how to change consciously one's perceptual ground state in order to function consciously in experiences such as sleep and death. It was understood then, by these ancient practitioners of perceptual philosophy, that a conscious life is not possible without a conscious death.

There is of course a biologically necessary relationship between fear and death. But the problem is that both as a race and individually we obstruct with fear the memory of our last death, as well as the ability to image positively the one that we must face next. This is the source of the great cosmic amnesia that we are undergoing, the forgetfulness of our identity: where is our origin, why we are here, and where we are going. The new education and the new science must try to overcome this stifling amnesia by disclosing or remembering the immortality of the vibratory worlds of form to which we are harmonically and eternally connected.

### The Circles of Form ➤

Here the regular polyhedra are determined by nine concentric circles whose pattern, like a concentric wave-front, contains all the proportions for the construction of these five principles of geometric symmetry. Each volume is holographically encoded in three circles: its inner circle (tangent to its faces, radius r), its intercircle (tangent to its edges, radius p) and its outer circle (tangent to its vertices, radius R). But in the nesting of forms one circle may serve for both the outer circle of one form and the intercircle of the next form, thereby reducing the number of circles to nine. A further reduction occurs because the inner circle and intercircle of the innermost form (the octahedron) describe a recurrence of the initial (outer) form (the icosahedron). See The Circles of Form as Nucleus. These two circles mark the end of one octave of form-genesis and the beginning of a second. These two circles being the coinciding of beginning and end become analogous to the nucleus or seed, thereby leaving us with seven circles surrounding a dualized nucleus as is imaged by the structure of the atom.

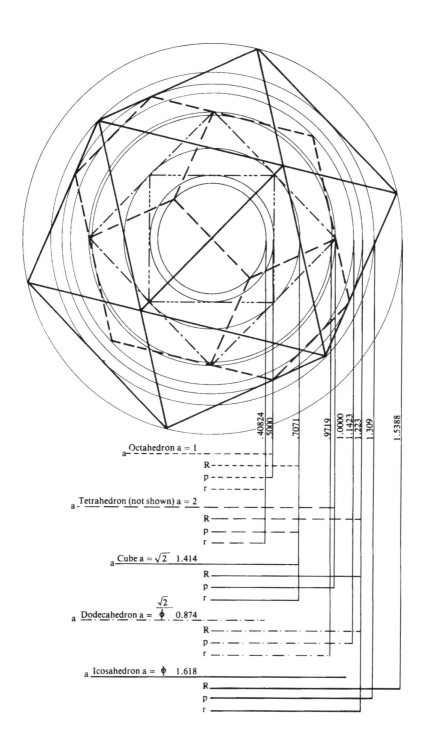

Octahedron a = 1
a
R
p
r

Tetrahedron (not shown) a = 2
a
R
p
r

Cube a = $\sqrt{2}$   1.414
a
R
p
r

Dodecahedron a = $\frac{\sqrt{2}}{\phi}$   0.874
a
R
p
r

Icosahedron a = $\phi$   1.618
a
R
p
r

.40824
.5000
.7071
.9719
1.0000
1.1423
1.223
1.309
1.5388

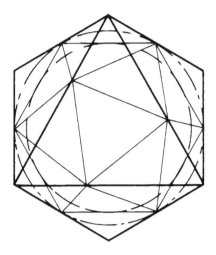

*The Circles of Form as Nucleus*

The inner circle and intercircle of the innermost form, the octahedron, represent the reappearance of the icosahedron, and thus the
overlapping of the beginning and ending of the cycle. In nature this coincidence of beginning and ending is the seed or nucleus. The nucleus
is the perfect continence of polarity: the androgyne. It is root/germ,
neutron/proton, etc. Therefore the Circles of Form are analogous to a
nucleus sustaining a seven-fold orbital field of polarized interactivity.
This is the same basic cosmological model as that of the Kabala, both
Greek and Hebrew, and it is also found in Hindu and other cultures. It
is also a central organizational pattern of light and sound differentiation: the atom and the solar system. Thus traditional cosmological
unifying models can be associated with the generation of volumes.

*The Circles of Color*  ➤

The seven circles can be metaphorically linked with the seven colors.
Just as each frequency level of light evokes a new quality (color) so each
concentric circle in turn evokes a new quality or genus of form/organi-
zation, or a new electron orb evokes a new family of substance in the
Periodic Table. All the circles are co-dependent: the loss of one dissolves the entire encodement. The inner black circle with the floating
white circle represents the continence of the nucleus, yet still having its
polarity in potential.

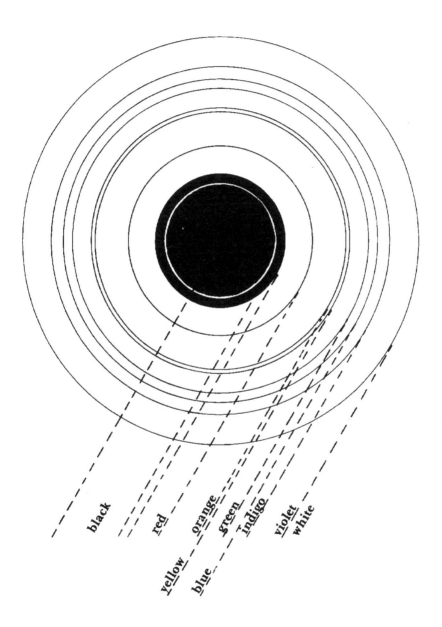

black

red

orange

green

indigo

violet

white

yellow

blue

*Wise men, Callicles, say that the heavens and the earth, gods and men, are bound together by fellowship and friendship, and order and temperance and justice, and for this reason they call the sum of things the "ordered" universe, my friend, not the world of disorder or riot. But it seems to me that you pay no attention to those things in spite of your wisdom, but you are unaware that geometric equality is of great importance among men and gods alike, and you think that we should practice over-reaching others, for you neglect geometry.*

PLATO, Gorgias

*They very much honored the memory, abundantly exercised, and paid great attention to it. In learning, too, they did not dismiss what they were taught, till they had firmly comprehended the first rudiments of it; and they recalled to their memory what they had daily heard, after the following manner: A Pythagorean never rose from his bed till he had first recollected the transactions of the former day; and he accomplished this by endeavouring to remember what he first said, or heard, or ordered his domestics to do when he was rising, or what was the second and third thing which he said, heard, or commanded to be done. And the same method was adopted with respect to the remainder of the day. For again, he endeavoured to recollect who was the first person that he met, on leaving his house, or who was the second; and with whom in the first, or second, or third place discoursed. And after the same manner he proceeded in other things. For he endeavoured to resume in his memory all the events of the whole day, and in the very same order in which each of them happened to take place. But if they had sufficient leisure after rising from sleep, they tried after the same manner to recollect the events of the third preceding day. And thus they endeavoured to exercise the memory to a great extent. For there is not any thing which is of greater importance with respect to science, experience and wisdom than the ability of remembering.*

IAMBLICHUS, Life of Pythagoras

# 7 | The Two Lights

................................................................*Arthur G. Zajonc*

I
N THE DIALOGUES OF PLATO and the lectures of Aristotle we recognize ourselves in inspired infancy. The dialogues seem warmed and illumined still by an ancient, perennial source grown feeble with time but which flourished again in Plato's hand. By contrast the learned and probing mind of Aristotle appears bent on illuminating and enumerating the entire cosmos, its contents, structure and Creator by the methodical brilliance of the human mind alone. When we place Aristotle against the background of Pythagoras, Homer, Hesiod and the Mysteries—that is, against the backdrop of myth, epic, ritual and initiation—the contrast is the greater. A profound transformation of the human psyche is foreshadowed in ancient Greece. It will take long centuries of neglect at the beginning of our era, rediscovery in Arabic Spain and Sicily in the twelfth century, and vigorous explication and elucidation at the hands of Arab and other scholastic commentators before the singular accomplishment of Greece grows and diffuses into the mode of reflection common to Western thought. Once this heritage has become a commonplace, it can be challenged, for example, in mechanics by Galileo or in methodology by Francis Bacon and René Descartes. With them and their contemporaries another cognitive stage is begun in the midst of which we ourselves stand.

The transformations have been many and profound, yet for all the monumental accomplishments in science, art and social life, many contemporaries have spoken of something precious as fallen away from our culture, especially since the rise of the scientific world view in the sixteenth century and its rapid diffusion in the eighteenth seemed to obscure and overshadow certain of humankind's noblest visions and aspirations rather than to foster the "enlightenment" which it proposed to advance. Even during the steady expansion of science in the eighteenth and nineteenth centuries, we may hear dissenting voices which speak to us of the losses incurred through the assumption of a narrow, mechanistic science. We think immediately of Blake or Keats, the romantic poets of Britain and Germany. Even in the provinces of transcendentalist New England, echoes of the same sentiments arise. Lamenting the prevailing science as myopic and impoverished, Thoreau would make the following entry for Christmas 1851 in his journal.

> I, standing twenty miles off, see a crimson cloud in the horizon. You tell me it is a mass of vapor which absorbs all other rays and reflects the red, but that is nothing to the purpose, for this red vision excites me, stirs my blood, makes my thoughts flow, and I have new and indescribable fancies, and you have not touched the secret of that influence. If there is not something mystical in your explanation, something unexplainable to the understanding, some elements of mystery, it is quite insufficient. If there is nothing in it which speaks to my imagination, what boots it? What sort of science is that which enriches the understanding, but robs the imagination?. . . If we knew all things thus mechanically merely, should we know anything really?[1]

Thoreau gives voice to one of the great tensions that not only animated the romantic poet but which also has stimulated controversy and provoked persecution in nearly each century since at least the time of Plato. We are reminded of Plato's suggested sentence for atheistic atomists, five years in solitary confinement and, if unreformed, execution. The tables have slowly turned so that now the sincerely held convictions that the cosmos is spiritually based and that our human species shares in the divine, these carry with them the sentence of intellectual isolation. Between our time and Plato's we encounter struggles similarly driven in the antagonism between the Cambridge Platonists and the rising materialism of Locke, Descartes and Hobbes, or again in the attempt to reconcile Christian or Islamic doctrine with Greek philo-sophy during the Middle Ages. Often it is the fight between the reactionary and avant-garde of society. Yet occasionally a period or individual, while fully dedicated to advancing a new world view, becomes poignantly aware of a spiritual, moral or intellectual loss. Then there arise great and noble attempts at reconciliation and synthesis rather than reformation or return to a "purer," ancient state closer to God, whether biblical or

---

1. Henry D. Thoreau, *The Journals of Henry D. Thoreau*, ed. Francis H. Allen and Bradford Torrey (Boston: Houghton Mifflin Co., 1906), Vol. III, pp. 155-56.

hermetic. It is, I think, something of this that has brought this conference together around the person of Pythagoras. We look back to his community in Croton and recognize elements which seem extremely modern: mathematics and acoustical studies for example. Yet the ritual and form of daily life appear rooted in a deep and ancient tradition. The tension between scientific investigation and a religious life which creates so much discord in our age seems to have produced harmony for the Pythagoreans.

In his opening address Christopher Bamford suggested that after Pythagoras something very precious did fall away from Western consciousness. In mythopoeic terms it might be called the loss of Orphism. By this I understand a final loss of our one-time native, unconscious participation in the phenomenal world, called by Owen Barfield "original participation." In this ancient mode of consciousness the subject/object split of Cartesian dualism is nonexistent. The soul-spiritual content of the world is experienced in unity with the phenomena it presents outwardly. It was a slow fall from grace, one which the mysteries and the community of Pythagoreans doubtless knew and attempted to forestall, yet it does seem, as Chris suggested, that with the fall of the community at Croton and the subsequent development of Western thought, we witness a profoundly symbolic change not only in world view but in the mode of knowing practiced by the intellectual West. I cannot accept that this transformation was an unnecessary aberraton or tragic deviation in human evolution. It may just as well have been the "discovery of mind" which, while promoting an individualized humankind, may lead to a genuine human freedom. Yet it does seem abundantly clear that individuation can and must lead to anarchy unless a new harmony is established between the sacred and the profane. We must not imagine the reconciliation as the triumph of a divine knowledge over a worldly one but rather as Novalis saw it, as a reciprocal raising and lowering in which the divine takes on the countenance of the mundane and the world becomes the visage of God.

The world must be romanticized. In this way one rediscovers the original meaning. Romanticizing is nothing other than a qualitative potentization. In this operation the lower self becomes identified with a better self—just as we ourselves are a series of such qualitative potentizations. This operation is still entirely unknown. By giving the common-place a high meaning, the familiar a secret aspect, the finite the appearance of the infinite; thus do I romanticize it. —The operation is just the opposite for the high, the unknown, the mystical, the infinite—it becomes "logarithmitized" through this process. —It receives a familiar countenance, romantic philosophy. *Lingua romana.* Reciprocal exaltation and descent.[2]

In one sense, we must regain what we have lost, we must descend like Orpheus in search of the shade of Eurydice and bring her to the light of a new day. Yet to merely run time backwards, to create a new Croton, to re-enact a sacred tradition, is to deny what twenty centuries of honest toil have given to humankind. That is to say, it avoids a critical responsibility, namely, to evolve a tradition in keeping with our time. Pythagoras traveled to many centers of ancient culture and sacred knowledge, yet he created a ritual and practice uniquely his own, suited for his people and age. Is it not incumbent upon us to do likewise? Certainly, we also may travel to temples and study the traditions of sacred knowledge, but must we not also likewise master the knowledge and methods of our own age? Through the confluence of these we may truly unearth, not an eclectic muddle of imported doctrines, but the sacred knowledge of our epoch. Such is possible only when all has passed through the alembic of the seeker and reappears in the dress both of our time and eternity.

In what follows I shall not guess what will become the content of a new sacred tradition. Rather I would like to address the nature and healing of the rift between the traditional sacred and profane modes of knowing. For I feel that only when these two join in a common endeavor in each individual knower, can a new tradition be founded. The world-historic struggles between sacred tradition and a rising scientism move likewise in the psyches of each of us. We each know the ebb and flow which brings us one moment to the tranquil heights of spiritual reverie or again to the brilliant clarity of well-reasoned discourse. Are these truly complementary modalities? Or is the split not rather a reflection of our present cognitive stage which by conscious effort may be changed? If there was an "original participation" in which no rift existed, is there not a "final participation" towards which we may labor? In this work we shall each find mentors who articulate our hopes and provide insights into the means and content of what I have been calling a new sacred tradition. For those who know the contributions of Rudolf Steiner to this task, my debt to him in what follows will be obvious.[3]

---

2. Friedrich Von Hardenberg, *Novalis Schriften*, ed. P. Kluckhohn and R. Samuel (Stuttgart: Kohlhammer Verlag), Vol. II, p. 545. (Translated by A. Zajonc.)
3. See especially Steiner's lecture cycle *Grenzen der Naturerkenntis*, English translation: *The Boundaries of Natural Science* (Spring Valley New York: Anthroposophic Press, 1983).

# Of Craftsmen and Priests

As a framework allow me to adopt a terminology which has arisen in this conference. In characterizing the split or epistemological gap, as Chris Bamford called it, which occurred after Pythagoras, Joscelyn Godwin introduced the terms positive and negative gnosis. I understand by these two polar relationships or attitudes which an investigator or seeker may have to the external world. Positive gnosis admonishes us to engage the world if we would find true knowledge or "gnosis." By contrast, negative gnosis considers the earth as a dark illusion, a prison from which we must seek release. In this view, gnosis is only to be found by inner illumination. To gain a clearer understanding of these terms, we could remain within the esoteric tradition and contrast the two disciplines of alchemy (as positive gnosis) and mysticism (as negative gnosis). However, I will choose another approach. In many exoteric disciplines we may see a reflection of these same attitudes. The history of medicine is a wonderful instance of the varying attitudes its practitioners have had towards the world, emphasizing in turn positive or negative gnosis.

In the writings that come down to us as the Hippocratic corpus from about the time of Pythagoras, we find descriptions of a rich and varied relationship between medical theory and medical practice. On the one hand one finds there descriptions of philosophers who propose sundry theoretical schema for the understanding of illness and disease. These may take the form of humoral pathology, the explanation of illness in terms of an imbalance of the four elements, or atomism, but in all cases the philosopher remains remarkably distant from "clinical" experience. At the opposite pole we learn of the barber-surgeon or nurse who without benefit of theoretical knowledge attempts cures by the most varied and often radical means. Between these two resides the true physician as a Hippocratic ideal. He is admonished to go to the bedside of his patients and carefully observe their surroundings, the weather, and especially to inquire after the history of the illness. Prescription of a careful regime and diet along with certain purgatives or laxatives are then given and frequent, even daily monitoring of the patient's symptoms is practiced. In addition, each physician struggles to integrate his own experience through theory. As a consequence each will usually adopt a theoretical framework according to his individual disposition so that a certain happy contention exists among practitioners. Perhaps because of this, theory rarely rises to the status of dogma. In our imagined Hippocratic physician we find the two poles of theoretical and practical knowledge seeking reconciliation.

The physician may be deeply reflective but he is also engaged with human disease and misery.

The Hippocratic corpus reflects, however, only a passing phase in medical history. With the great compilation of medical knowledge executed by Galen (circa A.D. 200) the ephemeral union of positive and negative gnosis ruptures. In place of the bedside physician acting as both nurse and philosopher, we find the physician off in his study or at the podium, with his barber-nurse following directives. Diagnoses usually were made by visual inspection of a urine sample alone which had been collected by the nurse and brought to the physician's study. All treatments, including necessary surgery, were performed by the nurse. Before the time of Vesalius, dissections, when allowed, also were performed by the barber-nurse. The attending physician would read the appropriate sections from Galen while students looked on. This is a striking image of the separation of positive and negative gnosis, of craft and theoretical knowledge, which was prevalent during the Middle Ages. The physician stood above reading from a book whose contents were dogma for centuries, while below a technician practices his craft. Through intimacy with the phenomenal world the craftsman-artisan widened and deepened his positive knowledge of the world. By contrast, the scholar turned away from the sense world, revering Galen and Aristotle with nearly as much ardor as holy scripture. It became the work of the scholar to explore and unravel the truths within these texts unfettered by challenges from natural knowledge.

Not until the time of Paracelsus do we find individuals who again struggle with both positive and negative gnosis. Paracelsus recognized two "lights," the light of revelation and the light of nature. Although clearly the lesser of the two lights, the "light of nature" seemed to him, at least at times, to be the only mode open for human inquiry. One could study the documents of revealed knowledge, indeed he studied them deeply, but the days of revelation were past. Thus we find Paracelsus in the mines studying the formation and powers of minerals, we see him seeking out the folk remedies in village and country in search of the lost craft of medicine, and we find him in the town square of Basel burning the near-sacred books of Galen. Paracelsus was a heretic in his own time, yet we may see him as someone deeply committed to the study of nature in the light of a sacred tradition, Christian and alchemical.

In the history of medicine then, one witnesses a reflection of the fragmentation of knowledge. A great schism seems to separate the scholar and the practitioner during the Middle Ages. We should remark, however, that together with this fragmentation there arises the possibility for an extraordinary cultivation of thinking on the one hand and artistry on the other. Perhaps it would have been impossible for the West to develop the formidable intellectual powers it did during the scholastic period, had the schism never occurred. We must recall that when the world view and theology of this period projects itself through the positive genius of architect and craftsman into stone and glass, the Gothic cathedrals result. As the spirit of the scholastic rises through dialectic and the seven liberal arts to embrace a divine order, so also does the craftsman master masonry and stained glass as never before—or since. Through his art an earthly edifice may embody that same spirit. The pristine unity of knowledge was broken, yet the loss can also become the means for transformation and reunion. Can we not learn something from this? Let us be wary of a premature union before we have fully experienced the joys and struggles of both pure thinking and an intimate worldliness. Then perhaps we may find the goal of a unitary knowing nearer at hand. We will learn to know fully once we have known partly.

Allow me to re-emphasize the dangers associated with the premature synthesis of theoretical and empirical knowledge by an example drawn from contemporary physics.

In his Nobel acceptance speech, the physician Edward Purcell recalls his emotions upon seeing the world in the light of his discovery of nuclear precession.

> Professor Block has told you how one can detect the precession of the magnetic nuclei in a drop of water. Commonplace as such experiments have become in our laboratories, I have not yet lost a feeling of wonder, and of delight, that this delicate motion should reside in all the ordinary things around us, revealing itself only to him who looks for it. I remember, in the winter of our first experiments, just seven years ago, looking on snow with new eyes. There the snow lay around my doorstep—great heaps of protons quietly precessing in the earth's magnetic field. To see the world for a moment as something rich and strange is the private reward of many a discovery.[4]

One must not discount the power of such a vision. It is often just this which has filled countless scientists with enthusiasm for their work. Yet we should also be fully conscious of just what such a vision, taken literally, purports.

---

4. *Nobel Lectures—Physics 1942-1962* (Amsterdam: Elsevier Publishing Co., 1964), p. 219.

Through painstaking, detailed study of experimentally produced phenomena, Purcell and his colleagues saw confirmation of a certain theoretical model of reality. A spinning top which is tilted slightly will precess around a vertical axis. We all know this motion from playing with tops. The model elaborated by Purcell and others saw the proton as executing an exactly analogous motion. In this case the magnetic moment of the proton would precess around the axis of a laboratory magnetic field, with the precessional motion inducing a small voltage in a detection coil. By measuring the detected voltage as a function of magnetic field strength, for example, one could compare measurements with predictions of the theoretical model. The work of Purcell is a classic example of the methods and explanations offered by physics. Let us focus a little more carefully on several features it possesses, as these will be important to our discussions much later.

First of all we find that laboratory phenomena, like meter positions, are interpreted through a chain of more or less conscious inferences as providing confirmation or falsification of a particular theoretical model. Of course, one never sees a precessing proton. Rather, certain meter positions are understood as indicating the motion of electrons in the detection circuit under an induced electromotive force acting in accord with the laws of electromagnetism. Any measurement, therefore, entails a complex of theories not just a single one. As Pierre Duhem pointed out at the beginning of this century, each experimental observation is "theory-laden."[5] That is, when we say, "The meter reads three volts," all of electromagnetic theory is implied. The scientist, for the most part, assumes the validity of established theories unconsciously in even the most elementary observations. We can, therefore, say that contemporary experimental science is not concerned with essentially pure phenomena, but with very elaborate theory-laden observations. In the last part of this paper I will discuss Goethe's scientific studies which, by constantly remaining with the seen phenomena, differ markedly from the above characterization of contemporary experiments.

Let us turn to the theoretical component of Purcell's discovery. Physical theories are developed, of course, at various levels of abstraction, but perhaps the most common form is exemplified by the model which Purcell discusses. With it one is to understand the dynamics of nuclear magnetism as very much like the dynamics of spinning tops. Experience

5. Pierre Duhem, *The Aim and Structure of Scientific Theory*, trans. P.P. Wiener (Princeton: Princeton University Press, 1954).

we have gained in the mechanical realm of tops is to be transferred to the atomic level. Clearly implied in this is the assumption that the world is inherently mechanical at all levels, microscopic as well as macroscopic. Very often this same assumption is extended to become the unifying element of all scientific explanation. Then biology, human behavior and much else besides are all conceived as inherently mechanical. All science is reduced to physics. Such a view is both extraordinarily arrogant and naive. Limiting ourselves to Purcell's model, however, we can say that he draws the features of his theory from the sensory realm of spinning tops. These abstracted tops are then projected back into the phenomenal world. The result is that a snowfield becomes a field of gyrating magnetic tops. Physicists insist that this is meant only as an analogy, an aid to understanding the relationships which obtain between magnetic fields and atomic moments. Yet all too frequently our models become our reality. As with all models, they are never congruent with reality but become a Procrustean bed which severs from nature those qualities and features so precious to the poet. Certainly the poet is no stranger to metaphor and simile, but the impressive applications of science and the simplistic popularizations of physical theories have conspired to elevate what was originally meant as analogue, to the level of established truth. It would be as if the declaration "Bill is a tower of strength," changed from a statement about Bill's moral character to a literal truth. Bill may be many things, but he is not a tower. No matter how fruitful or powerful the model, reality is ultimately reduced to less than it truly is. The mingling of thought and experience as metaphor may be, on one level, uplifting or successful, but, if taken literally, it becomes deeply disquieting on another. Thoreau would, I think, hardly be happier with Purcell's vision of a snowfield than he was with the explanation of a sunset given by nineteenth-century optics. Here among ourselves during this conference, certain poets have expressed a similar dismay in seeing nature as essentially geometric solids. Purcell's emotions were as genuine as our geometers'. I would suggest firstly a great tolerance for the myriad metaphors which may justly be applied to any single experience or object. Perhaps the happy contention among us will, as with the Hippocratics, prevent any one of them from rising to dogma. But moreover, I would suggest that we may postpone the union and rather practice pure positive and pure negative gnosis. We then may await the union as an act of grace and not one of human fabrication.

We have seen in physics that normal experimentation is thoroughly laden with implicit theoretical assumptions, and that conversely, theory is normally couched in the language and concepts of the perceptual world. Is it possible to separate these two pursuits and to cultivate them separately, at least as a discipline for the soul? I think so.

Plato admonished his students to study geometry as a *propaideutikon* for the mind, as a means of purification and exercise in pure thought. Goethe admonishes science and us to remain with the phenomena, not to replace them with mechanical models, but rather to exalt the phenomenal world itself until it approaches the ideal. I would suggest that we may gain greatly by following the injunctions of both. In what follows I will present a brief introduction to projective or synthetic geometry, not as sacred mathematics but purely as an inner exercise which stresses the perception of invariant relationships under geometric transformations. A second part will consist of an introduction to a science of phenomena as put forth by Goethe. Of particular importance will be Goethe's emphasis on the process of discovery, which allows perception of unity in a multiplicity of phenomena. Indeed, invariance will be a common theme through both sections, otherwise dissimilar.

## Transformation and Invariance

Under that despotism of the eye (the emancipation from which Pythagoras by his *numeral,* and Plato by his *musical* symbols, and both by geometric discipline, aimed at, as the first *propaideutikon* of the mind)— under this strong sensuous influence, we are restless because invisible things are not the objects of vision; and metaphysical systems, for the most part, become popular, not for their truth, but in proportion as they attribute to causes a susceptibility of being *seen,* if only our visual organs were sufficiently powerful.[6]

Proclus tells us of the special character and value of mathematics in his Preface to *Euclid's Elements.*[7] In the neo-Platonic view, study and practice of mathematics lifts the soul from the mundane world to a realm intermediate between our extended, corporeal world and the purely non-spatial, unextended world of duration often termed the archetypal realm. This intermediate or ectypal realm shares the extended character of our world but lacks its substantial nature. The forms of geometry are incorporeal but remain spatially extended and so belong to the

---

6. Samuel Taylor Coleridge, *Biographia Literaria,* quoted in Owen Barfield, *What Coleridge Thought* (Middletown, Conn.: Wesleyan University Press, 1971), pp. 19-20.

7. Proclus, *Diadochus, A Commentary on the First Book of Euclid's Elements,* trans. G.R. Morrow (Princeton: Princeton University Press, 1970).

ectypal realm. According to neo-Platonism there can be no certain knowledge, only opinion, in the mundane world. Knowledge of the ectypal proceeds by a different faculty, *dianoia* or the discursive intellectual capacity. Indeed, the theorems of geometry may stand as a paradigm for that mode of inquiry which can move with complete security from one proposition to the next. An alternative mode of knowing, *episteme,* was demanded if knowledge of the archetypal realm was to be gained. Here it is not a question of sequential steps in a line of reasoning but rather an instant of recognition, of pure intuition which carries with it its own weight of conviction. There is no proof in the geometric sense wherein a faulty step in logic may insert itself. Nor as in the mundane world of opinion must one marshal evidence in support of one's hypothesis. Mathematics then played the tutor to the young philosopher or statesman who would aspire to rise to a higher, more certain vision.

The special character of mathematics, which made it so esteemed in Pythagorean and Platonic thought, also excited the young Novalis, who studied eighteenth-century science and mathematics as deeply as he did poetry and philosophy. Among his fragments we find,

Current mathematics is only the first and simplest revelation of the
    true science of spirit.
It is little more than a special empirical organon or instrument.
True mathematics is the proper element of the Magi.
The life of the gods is mathematics.
Pure mathematics is religion.
In the orient true mathematics is at home. In Europe it has
    degenerated into mere technique.[8]

Novalis also knew the power of mathematics to lift us above the cares of everyday life. He wrote to his ill brother Erasmus:

Your resolve to study algebra is certainly very healthy. The sciences have wonderful healing forces—at least like opium—they silence the pains and raise us into spheres permeated by an external sunlight. They are the most beautiful asylum to which we are granted access.[9]

Let us then explore this pole of our consciousness, one which turns aside from the facts and data of the natural world and concerns itself

---

8. von Hardenberg, *Novalis Schriften,* Vol. II, Fragments on mathematics.
9. Ibid., Vol., IV, p. 177.

with pure forms, relationships and movement. The approach to geometry developed especially during the nineteenth-century as projective geometry is, I think, wonderfully suited to our purpose. The great English mathematician Cayley would declare, "Projective geometry is all geometry and reciprocally." Hankel called it the "royal road to all mathematics." Let us then begin our journey on this road which, perhaps not surprisingly, has grown recently rather narrow with disuse.

At the very heart of projective geometry is the concept of transformation. Indeed the modifier "projective" refers to the transformation which acts as the generative principle in projective geometry, transforming one spatial form into another. The simplest projective transforformation is the mapping of all points on one line to points of a second line by a "perspectivity." Consider Figure 1.

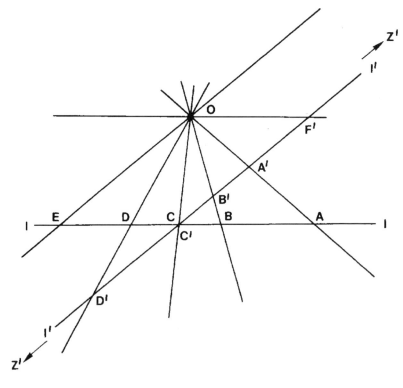

Figure 1

Allow line l to be our original line on which we may identify certain points, for example, A, B, C, D and E. Let us suppose that we wish to place the points of line l into one-to-one correspondence with the points of a second line l'. We may do this by choosing a "center of perspectivity" O and then drawing lines through OA, OB, OC and so on. The points of intersection A', B', C', D', E' and the points corresponding to their unprimed counterparts. In this way we may transform the points of one line to the points of another line in a unique way. Clearly, the transformation depends on the exact relationship between l, l', and O. Notice that we encounter a special case in the transformation of E to E'. If we take OE to be strictly parallel to l', then we expect from Euclidean geometry that these two lines will never intersect. In projective geometry, on the other hand, we say that OE and l' meet in the "point of infinity." That is, we add so-called "ideal elements" to the primitives of geometry. It is thus clear that we may transform any point on our original line to infinity by a suitable choice of O and l'. Reciprocally, the point at infinity on l may be mapped to a point on l' (say F'). We may gain a further insight into the continuous and unbroken nature of the line in projective geometry if we imagine the several lines through our center of perspectivity, O, to be merely the various positions of a single line through O as it rotates about O. As this line swings clockwise it passes through A', B'. . .until it reaches the ideal point E' of the line l'. If we continue, we notice the point of intersection seems now to approach from above, as if the line l' has only one ideal point (Z') which can be reached by moving in either direction along the line. To each line of the plane we may associate an ideal point. All parallel lines share the same ideal point. The locus of all such points becomes the "ideal line" of the plane. Inclusion of ideal elements in geometry allows theorems to be stated simply without exceptional cases and provides for wonderfully mobile transformations, as we shall shortly see. We have seen already how the infinite can appear in the finite and reciprocally.

Ironically, although the metamorphic powers of projective transformation are enormous, the primary objective of the geometer, as enunciated for example by Felix Klein in his Erlangen program,[10] is to seek out the *invariant* properties of geometry. Thus, we must, for example, ask after those properties which are unchanged by a perspectivity. As a concrete instance consider the transformation of a triangle ABC by the center of perspectivity, O, as shown in Figure 2. We draw lines

---

10. Felix Klein, *Elementary Mathematics from an Advanced Standpoint—Geometry*, trans. E.R. Hedrick and C.A Noble (New York: Dover, 1948), Vol. 2.

connecting OA, OB, OC. Any triangle whose three vertices lie on these three lines can be seen to be in perspective correspondence with triangle ABC. Notice that distances are not preserved. That is, the line segment AB is not the same length as A' B'. Neither are the angles at corresponding vertices equal (ABC = A'B'C'). If we had started with a parallelogram instead of a triangle we would also have discovered that two parallel lines are in general transformed into nonparallel lines. It should be stressed that this is in great contrast to the more familiar Euclidean transformations, which are circumscribed by rotations and translations. Under these latter transformations lengths, angles and parallelism are clearly invariants. Under the more general projective transformation such invariants disappear and we must search for other more subtle invariant properties.

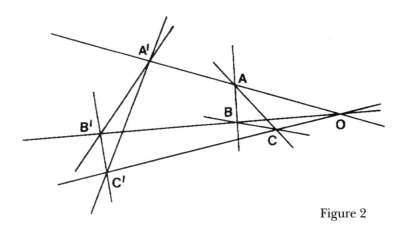

Figure 2

The first such invariant we may notice is that a straight line always ends up as a straight line. In fact, projective transformations are the most general transformations for which this is true; they comprise the most general group of "linear transformations." A second invariant is that points of intersection are always mapped into corresponding points of intersection. Thus the point of intersection for the two lines AB and BC (namely B itself) is mapped into B' which itself is the point of intersection for the lines A'B' and B'C'. From these two invariants we may already begin to gain our bearings in this otherwise extremely dynamic and mobile arena. The spatial notions common to us from everyday experience dissolve, and if we are not to become totally disoriented we must discern the fixed landmarks of our new geometry.

A somewhat more elusive but very deep invariance in projective geometry is that of the "cross-ratio." When projective geometry is elaborated in the explicitly analytic language of coordinates and equations, the cross-ratio often stands as the starting point and cornerstone of the discussion. For our own purposes we may begin synthetically by merely investigating the properties of the "complete quadrangle." As the name implies, the quadrangle possesses four corner or vertices each connected to the three others for a total of six lines, four of which we usually think of as the sides and two as the diagonals of the quadrangle. (See Figure 3.)

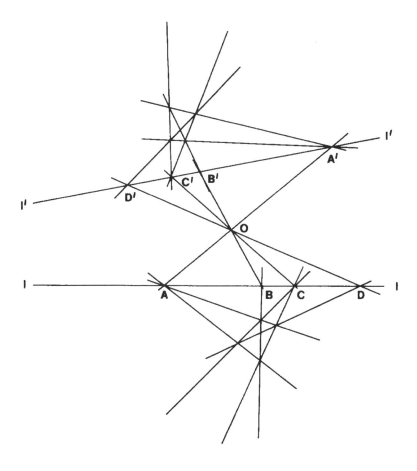

Figure 3

We now construct the line through points A and C, designating the points of intersection of the diagonals by B and D. So far we have been very general in the construction, imposing no restrictions on the specific nature of the quadrangle, yet a very peculiar relationship exists between the four points A, B, C, and D which are said to form a "harmonic set." Let AB, AD and so on designate the lengths of the line segments between points A and B, A and D. . .as measured, say, by an ordinary ruler. If we form the two ratios AB/AD and CB/CD, we find that the cross-ratio AB/AD : CB/CD = -1 or, in terms of multiplication, AB/AD · CD/CB = -1. (One must pay attention in the above to direction in the segment lengths because AB = -BA.) The cross-ratio so defined will always equal minus one for harmonic sets of points as generated by a quadrangle. Moreover, this cross-ratio is exactly preserved under a projective transformation! That is, if we transform line 1 to 1' by a perspectivity (or series of perspectivities) the cross-ratio A'B'/A'D'· C'D'/ C'B' will still equal negative one. We need not make measurements to prove this. Again consider Figure 3. We may merely construct a complete quadrilateral from three points of the harmonic set A'B'C'D'. The last diagonal drawn will always be found to pass through the missing fourth member of the harmonic set. With this we know the cross-ratio has not changed in the slightest!

I have limited our study to the cross-ratio of harmonic sets where the invariance can be clearly seen by our ability to construct a second quadrangle from the set of transformed points. The concept is, however, far more general. (I refer to the extensive literature on projective geometry, for example, to John Wesley Young's *Projective Geometry*[11] or Olive Whicher's book of the same title.[12]) In the cross-ratio we see that although distances themselves are not preserved, ratios of distances are. That is, it is a relationship or pattern which remains constant, not a simple distance or measure. This invariant pattern shows itself in the reappearance of the quadrangle in a metamorphosed form. Thus in projective geometry we cannot hold to distances, which are ever-changing, but must rather train ourselves to perceive invariant patterns of a more subtle and mobile nature. With this I think we begin to sense the real power of mathematics to lift us out of normal, sense-generated concepts to search for deeper unities and invariances in the sense-free

---

11. John W. Young, *Projective Geometry*, Carus Mathematical Monographs, No. 4 (Chicago: Open Court, 1930).

12. Olive Whicher, *Projective Geometry: Creative Polarities in Space and Time* (London: Rudolf Steiner Press, 1980).

domain of pure thought. It can become, as Novalis said, a beautiful sun-lit asylum.

Before passing on to Goethe's science of phenomena, I must spend just a short page or two on one further aspect of projective geometry. So far we have been concerned with transformations which transform points to points in a unique way. Such transformations are termed "collineations" and they comprise one group of projective transformations. There exists, however, another class of transformations termed "correlations," which are not point transformations but rather transformations under which there is a change of the space element. The simplest example is the correlation which establishes a correspondence between the points and the lines of a plane. In this case the *entirety* of a line is placed in correspondence with a single point and reciprocally. To be more specific let us consider the pole-polar transformation with respect to a conic section.

For simplicity we start with the special conic section, the circle (although in projective geometry the circle, strictly speaking, is indistinguishable from the ellipse). We would like to establish a one-to-one correspondence between the points of the plane in which our circle lies and the lines of that plane. This may be done in the following way. Choose a point P, say, lying outside of the circle. (See figure 4.)

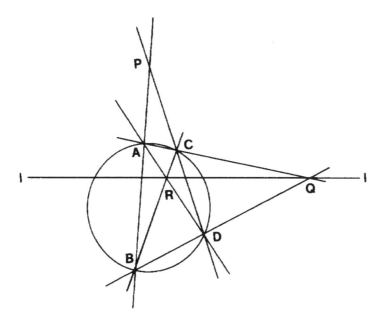

Figure 4

Through P we construct two lines which intersect the circle in the points A, B and C, D. We now complete the construction of the quadrangle inscribed in the conic by constructing the two remaining sides AC, BD and the two diagonals AD, BC. The points of intersection Q and R are the two remaining diagonal points (P was the other). The line l through Q and R is the line corresponding to the point P. In this way, using the inscribed quadrangle ABCD, we may always establish a correspondence between a given point and a line of the plane. If on the other hand we wish to find the point corresponding to a given line we must construct a *quadrilateral* which circumscribes the conic and which has the given line as one of its *diagonal lines*. (See Young, pp. 74-79.)

Let us bring the above considerations into movement. Consider the sequence of drawings in Figure 5.

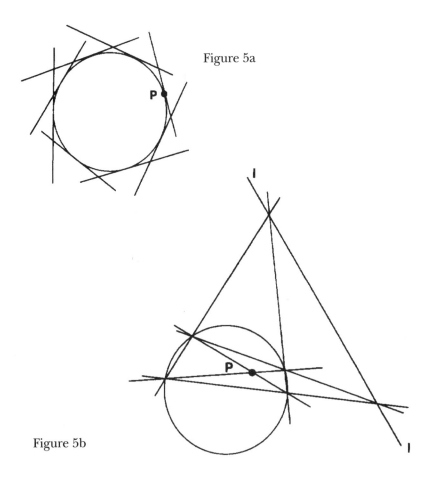

Figure 5a

Figure 5b

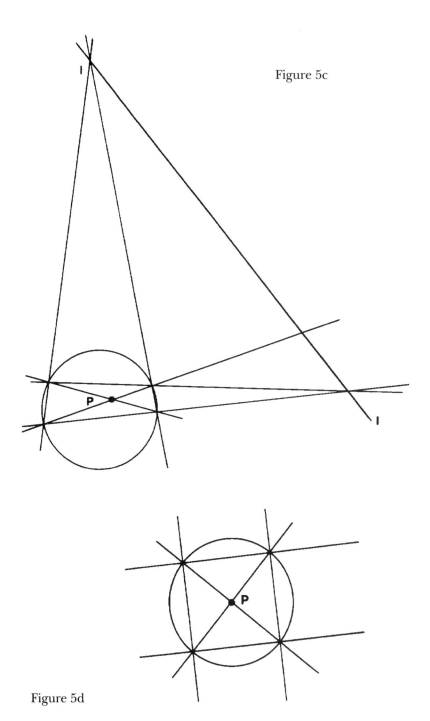

Figure 5c

Figure 5d

For each of four cases, I have established the line corresponding to the point P with respect to a circle. I begin with the "pole," P lying on the circle (Figure 5a). The "polar" line will of necessity be the line tangent to the circle at that point. If we were to move P around the circle, the polar line will follow. Here we may note that an alternative way of considering the circle is made apparent. We are accustomed to considering the circle as that locus of points all a certain distance from a central point. This corresponds to the movement of P around the circle. But clearly we may, with equal justice, consider it as the form embraced, or circumscribed by the family of tangent lines we have drawn. This alternative was first put on a rigorous foundation by the German mathematician and physicist Plucker in the first part of the nineteenth century. The conics, or indeed any form, may thus be considered not as the locus of an infinity of points, but as the form enveloped by an infinity of tangent lines. If the form is three-dimensional, the lines become bounding planes tangent to all parts of the surface.

Return now to Figure 5 and allow the point P to gradually recede from the circle towards its center (Figures 5b and 5c). The line polar to P gradually moves away from the conic so that we may naturally ask what happens when the point P stands at the precise center of the circle (Figure 5d). In Euclidean terms we would say that the opposite sides of our quadrangle now become parallel, the quadrangle thereby transformed into a parallelogram. When we search after the polar line we find that it has quite disappeared because in Euclidean geometry parallel lines never intersect. From the standpoint of projective geometry, however, the sides still intersect, each pair of parallel lines in a unique point. We may, as before, determine the line which passes through the two points (now at infinity). In this manner we establish the correspondence between the center of our circle and the ideal, line-at-infinity of the plane. Thus with respect to the circle the centermost point is connected with the entirety of the most distant line. If we translate this result into three dimensions, as may easily be done, then with respect to a sphere the central point is placed in correspondence with the entirety of the plane-at-infinity.

The symbolic and allegorical richness of such constructions is obvious. We have an extraordinary picture of the macrocosm reflected in the microcosm. More especially, the entirety of the plane may be, as David Bohm might say,[13] "enfolded" in a single point like some Leibnitzian monad. Yet, while the metaphors are many and wonderful, I would

---

13. David Bohm, *Wholeness and the Implicate Order* (London: Routledge & Kegan Paul, 1980).

have us restrain our fanciful visions and merely experience the splendid artistry of these thoughts. Allow such exercises to remain propedeutics for the mind, purifying, strengthening and vitalizing the fabric of our thinking. Let us not rush to a premature mingling of the perceptual world with the forms and thoughts of pure ideation. No matter how marvelous or mystical, the same dangers exist for us as for Edward Purcell. At this point, we would do well, I think, to follow Goethe's injunction:

> Physics must separate itself from mathematics. Physics must remain resolutely independent and seek with all loving, reverent, pious powers to delve into nature and its holy life with no concern for what mathematics performs and does from its side. Mathematics must on the other hand declare its independence from everything external, follow its own grand spiritual course and develop itself more purely than is possible when, as heretofore, it concerns itself with things at hand and seeks to ascertain something from or assimilate something to them.[14]

## The Light of Nature: Goethe's Science of Nature

In the remainder of this article I will attempt to bring before us a picture of Goethe's researches into the phenomena which nature displays before us. I will select a necessarily very narrow cross section of Goethe's investigations and reflections, ones which illustrate the points I have been making. Yet I hope not to distort the intention of Goethe's thought nor to underrate the extraordinary scope of his researches.[15] Nonetheless, I will limit myself to remarks upon his method of research and discovery especially exemplified in his color studies. It was in fact these investigations which he thought would give him a lasting place in the history of human thought.

> As for what I have done as a poet, I take no pride in it whatever. Excellent poets have lived at the same time as myself; poets more excellent have lived before me, and others will come after me. But that in my century I am the only person who knows the truth in the difficult science

---

14. Johann W. von Goethe, *Wilhelm Meister's Journeymanship*, "Observations in the Wanderer's Fashion," Aphorism 134 (translation by Fred Amrine).
15. Rudolf Magnus, *Goethe as Scientist*, trans. Heinz Norden (New York: Henry Schurman, 1949); Rudolf Steiner, *Goethe the Scientist*, trans. O. Wannamaker (New York: Anthroposophic Press); Arthur G. Zajonc, "Goethe's Theory of Color and Scientific Intuition," *American Journal of Physics*, 44 (1976), p. 327.

of colors—of that, I say, I am not a little proud and here I have a consciousness of a superiority to many.[16]

It will prove helpful to know when and why Goethe began his formal study of color. We may safely begin with his journey to Italy in 1786. In contrast to the grey sky and countryside of Germany, Italy appeared as a fairytale land to Goethe: "We remember how harmoniously the sky binds itself with the earth there and its lively shimmer spreads over us...; slowly wandering clouds color themselves in manifold ways and the colors of the heavenly dome distribute themselves to the earth on which we stand in the most pleasing manner."[17] It was in these surroundings that Goethe was often to be found in the company of painters. On such occasions it happened that he was asked his opinion as to how a particular scene should be rendered. Musing on such issues Goethe became unsettled. It seemed clear that there should be an objective aesthetic basis for the use of color in painting, and yet it appeared to depend rather only on the whim of painter or critic. Upon his return to Weimar he attempted to read an orthodox treatise on color and found the theory presented hopelessly difficult and useless. "These difficulties would have discouraged me had I not reflected that pure experience should lie at the root of all physical sciences. . . ." Thus we find Goethe borrowing a case of optical equipment from his friend court counsellor Hofrat Buttner of Jena. Goethe, however, neglected the equipment entirely until the impatient Buttner finally demanded their return. With the messenger in the doorway Goethe resolved to at least see the celebrated phenomenon of colors known to him from childhood play. He took a prism from the case and looked through it at a nearby white wall, fully expecting to see the white broken up into colors according to a Newtonian scheme. Instead, all he saw was an unchanged white wall. The importance of this moment for the rest of his research is probably hard to overestimate. Like a shot he was convinced of Newton's error. Turning to a window he noticed that color did not appear in the window panes themselves but only where the dark latticework crossed the bright windows. Here, where light and darkness met, colors leapt into view: yellow, orange and red on the one side, blue and violet on the other. Buttner's messenger was sent away empty-handed, and Goethe's experimental research was begun.

16. J.P. Eckermann, *Conversations with Goethe,* selected by H. Kohn, trans. Gisela C. O'Brien (New York: Ungar, 1964), entry for Feb. 19, 1829.

17. J.W. Goethe, *Beitr äge zur Optik*(1791) in *Naturwissenschaftliche Shriften,* Erster Teil (Zurich: Artemis-Verlag, 1949), p. 767.

These researches would span twenty years and culminate in the publication of the three volume *Zur Farbenlehre* in 1810. Ideally we should explore the contents of these works, particularly the didactic volume in which Goethe's experiments and reflections concerning color are carefully presented. We should consider not only the result he presents but should follow him in his research, experiencing with him the myriad color phenomena he explores. Yet we do not have the space to do so here. Rather I would have us consider Goethe's color studies by way of his methodology. For it is here that we may gain a full appreciation for his mode of inquiry and its value as a discipline in positive gnosis. We will find ourselves continually admonished to refrain from theoretical flights and mathematical abstraction. Rather Goethe will invoke the phenomena themselves as the theory, when they are rightly seen.

Firstly, let us inquire after how Goethe "explains" the phenomena of color as produced, say, by a prism. This general set of phenomena Goethe classed under the rubric of physical colors. Usually, when we seek the explanation we expect a reply in terms of a normally unseen but actually present mechanism. For example, the generation of color by the prism might be explained by the oscillatory movement of electrons under the action of an electromagnetic wave (light). The formulation may be cast into a mathematical form and the phenomena of refraction and dispersion quantitatively "explained." Notice that in such a case we are engaged in an activity like that of Purcell, wherein the glass prism we hold in our hand is mentally replaced by electrons electrically attracted to a matrix of atoms all driven by an electromagnetic wave (which we naively know as light). This mode of explanation has been the object of a thoroughgoing critique by such philosopher-scientists as Pierre Duhem. It is a mode of explanation which came into conscious dominance after the Renaissance and remains with us to the present. It is essentially a search for what Aristotle termed "efficient causes."

Goethe almost systematically rejected such an approach to nature. He explicitly stated in an essay written for Schiller that "we are not seeking causes but the circumstances under which the phenomenon occurs."[18] In place of the hidden mechanisms underlying nature, Goethe sought the circumstances of appearance, the invariable antecedents or prerequisites for the manifestation of a particular phenomenon. In this sense Goethe sought not mechanical causation,

---

18. J.W. Goethe, *Goethe's Botanical Writings*, trans. Bertha Mueller (Honolulu: University of Hawaii Press, 1952), p. 228.

but rather an invariant pattern or relationship among the phenomena he studied. Aristotle also noted this as one of his four causes, terming it the "formal cause" of a phenomenon. The formal cause of the octave is the mathematical ratio in which the lengths of identically stretched strings stand, namely 1:2. This concept must be generalized and freed somewhat from its mathematical form, but once we do so we may recognize in Goethe's "explanations" a search amongst nature's multiplicity. These unities are always signs or symbols of an inner agency to which we seem denied access. Unities or invariances are, of course, exceedingly important in orthodox science also: its use of mathematics is an attempt to express just these laws of invariance. At least for Goethe, this language could not capture the full content of color phenomena. By reducing the perceived relationship to a mathematical one, nature is necessarily denuded of just those qualities which Goethe, with Thoreau, would not lose. Most especially, a purely mathematical formulation has little room for what Goethe termed the "*sinnlich-sittliche Wirkung der Farbe,*" or roughly, the sensory-moral effect of color. The eighteenth-century view of the cosmos as pervaded by a moral order is foreign to us. To understand it we must take seriously again the idea that the cosmos is a created reality, not an accidental one. We associate moral qualities with the actions of people, not with such things as light or color. Yet if, in some way, color is a reflection of the activity of a being or beings, present or past, then the inner quality of that activity will manifest also in the phenomena of color. Goethe hints at this when he in his introduction to the *Farbenlehre* declares, "Colors are the deeds of light, its deeds and sufferings."[19] At the end of the same work, green and magenta seem to Goethe to be "the earthly and heavenly offspring of the Elohim."[20]

Instead of a mathematical relationship, we must raise, or exalt, the phenomenal world itself, lift it towards the ideal so that through genuine phenomena we may glimpse the principle or unifying agency which expresses itself as law in the natural kingdoms. In botany this will be called by Goethe his "archetypal plant," in color it is the quest for "archetypal phenomena." Whatever the field, the unifying principle is not accessible through the logic of the discursive intellect, but rather we must mount higher and higher by continual study and shifting of phenomena so that the pattern itself is *beheld.* Of course, says Goethe,

---

19. J.W. Goethe, *Goethe's Werke* (Hamburgen Ausgabe: Christian Werner Verlag, 1955), Vol. 13, p. 315.
20. Ibid., p. 521.

"the observer never sees pure [or archetypal] phenomena with his eyes,"[21] but, nonetheless, we must come to know the archetype through the phenomena themselves. To replace the experience of color with words, models or equations carries with it the consequential loss of the "sensory-moral aspect" of color. The scientist, rather, "should form for himself a method in accordance with observation, but he should take care not to transform observations into concepts, concepts into words and to deal and use these words as if they were things. He should have knowledge of the labors of philosophers in order to lead the phenomena up to a philosophic region."[22]

Color Goethe sought to explain in this sense by leading us through countless color effects until we rise, with the phenomena, to an experience of the two archetypal phenomena at the basis of prismatic and atmospheric colors, the sunset with its vibrant oranges and reds, and the blue vault of the heavens. In these two effects one beholds the purest expression of those "deeds and sufferings of light" which we call color. From these and similar considerations Goethe goes on to "explain" the color which first prompted his investigations, those he saw at the boundary of window and latticework.

We have encountered this mode of knowing before. Its likeness to seeing, to beholding of natural law in the phenomena themselves, recalls to us the neo-Platonic *episteme*. There remains, however, an essential distinction. Whereas for Plato and his students the sense world could never act as the source of true knowledge, for Goethe it is the sole trustworthy spokesman for the deepest unities of nature. Whereas Plato would admonish his students to turn their eyes away from the stars to know true astronomy, and ridicule the Pythagoreans for torturing the catgut in search of new harmonics, Goethe would show little patience for the "speculative science," *Naturphilosophie*, which contemporaries like Schelling and Hegel propounded. Eckermann reports a conversation between Goethe and Hegel in which Hegel defined for Goethe his dialectic method. Goethe rejoined that it was fine so long as not misapplied to show true as false.

That is why I prefer the study of nature which does not allow such sickness to arise. For there we have to do with infinite and eternal truth that immediately rejects anyone who does not proceed neatly and honestly in observing and handling his subject. I am also certain that many

---

21. *Goethe's Botanical Writings*, p.227.
22. *Goethe's Werke*, Vol. 13, p. 482.

a person dialectically sick could find a beneficent cure in the study of nature.[23]

Thus we find Goethe advocating a rigorous, positive relationship to natural phenomena. Through such a relationship arises the possibility of profound insight into nature's laws or invariant relationships. Such relationships are to be known not abstractly but through a kind of seeing. Is it any surprise that sight for Goethe was the noblest, almost divine, sense possessed by human beings?

> Sight is the noblest of senses. . . it stands infinitely higher [than the other four], refines itself beyond matter and approaches the capacities of the spirit.[24]

The special place of *episteme* or of "intuitive judgment" (*anschauende Urteilskraft*) in Goethe's methodology simultaneously brings a new element into Western thought. If the logical tracts of Aristotle acted as the texts on which Western consciousness was weaned, then Goethe's scientific writings struggle to inject a new or at least profoundly neglected dimension into human inquiry. Contemporary science espouses two of the three modes of knowing described by neo-Platonists: *dianoia* or rationalism as exemplified by the rigorous mathematical formulation of physics, and empiricism in which evidence is gathered in support of scientific opinion or hypothesis. The third mode, *episteme*, was always the province of mysticism and revelation—that is, of negative gnosis. Yet Goethe in his science strives to bring the most exalted of Plato's cognitive faculties into the sense world. We may find antecedents of this view in Paracelsus and certain alchemists. But Goethe refrained from anticipating or establishing superficial correspondences so common to his more speculative contemporaries, and rather sought to move through the phenomena themselves, searching for the purest expression of an archetype which could then illumine a broad realm of disparate phenomena. The means which the investigator employs is neither purely rational nor purely empirical, but what Goethe termed "rational empiricism." We should not imagine this as merely a mixture or sequential treatment of phenomena first empirically and then rationally as one has in orthodox science. Rather it is a mode of study through which the investigator may gradually unite with the objects he investigates.

---

23. Eckermann, *Conversations with Goethe,* entry for Oct. 18, 1828.

24. Goethe, *Wilhelm Meister's Journeymanship,* "From Makarie's Archive," Aphorism 128 (translation by Fred Amrine).

There is a gentle empiricism that makes itself in the most intimate way identical with its objects and thereby becomes actual theory. This heightening of the spiritual powers belongs, however, to a highly cultivated age.[25]

In place then of hypotheses which are "lullabies that the teacher uses to lull his pupils to sleep,"[26] Goethe advocates a gentle, rational empiricism through which the phenomena themselves, when intimately known, become the theory.

I find it most interesting that certain twentieth-century philosophers, scientists and psychologists are now drawing our attention to the intuitive or imaginative components of science. I may mention Michael Polanyi, who sees all understanding as "tacit knowings," that is, as a kind of intuitive knowing unlike purely analytic or discursive thought. It is by "indwelling"[27] that tacit knowing arises and so "since all understanding is tacit knowing, all understanding is achieved by indwelling."The kinship between Goethe's knowing-as-seeing and Polanyi's tacit knowing could be elaborated at some length, particularly by a study of Polanyi's "subsidiary and focal awareness" and his many examples given in support of this view. We cannot explore those connections or distinctions here, but let me include just a passage which points to the profound connection Polanyi sees between a perceptual act and the perception of coherence (or I would say the perception of an archetype) in a particular phenomenal realm. He states that scientific discovery is the shifting of our awareness from the particulars of observation to their coherence:

This has been my basic assumption. I maintained that the capacity of scientists to perceive in nature the presence of lasting shapes differs from ordinary perception only by the fact that it can integrate shapes that ordinary perception cannot readily handle. *Scientific knowing consists in discerning gestalten that indicate a true coherence in nature.*[28]

A few pages later Polanyi writes:

---

25. Ibid., *Aphorism* 126.
26. Ibid., *Aphorism* 140.
27. Michael Polanyi, *Knowing and Being*, ed. Marjorie Greene (Chicago: University of Chicago Press, 1969), p. 160.
28. Ibid., p. 138.

This act of integration, which we can identify both in the visual perception of objects and in the discovery of scientific theories, is the tacit power we have been looking for. I shall call it *tacit knowing*.[29]

Goethe might have called it *anschauende Urteilskraft*, the faculty which allows one to rise above the particulars to a perception of coherence and relationships within the phenomenal world.

Once we have attained this power or capacity in a particular field of inquiry, then the facts carry with them their own explanation.

> The highest thing would be to comprehend that everything factual is already theory. The blue of the heavens reveals to us the fundamental law of chromatics. One should only not seek anything behind the phenomena: they themselves are the theory.[30]

Here we should rest content, not seek for hidden causes or mechanisms but "let the observer of nature suffer the archetypal phenomena to remain undisturbed in its beauty."

Yet how, we may ask, is such a power of knowing to become ours. Goethe's reply would be, I think, through the process of investigation itself. Nature presents itself to us through ordinary "empirical phenomena."[31] We may, however, engage her and shift and vary the conditions of appearance. In this way we may know her through "scientific phenomena." As the result of all our experience and experiments it is now possible that the "pure phenomenon" or archetype may arise to meet us, not circumscribed by a single isolated phenomenon, but rather as a coherence symbolized or most nearly manifest in one or a few primary experiences. The phenomenal world has become our teacher. As we dwell within it, it shapes organs or capacities within us for knowledge of itself. Just as, "the eye owes its existence to the light," so too the subtle faculties by which we "see" coherences or archetypes are shaped within us by the experiences we undergo.

> Out of indifferent animal organs the light produces an organ to correspond to itself; and so the eye is formed by the light so that the inner light may meet the outer. . . . If the eye were not sunlike, how could we perceive the sun.[32]

---

29. Ibid., p. 140.
30. Goethe, *Wilhelm Meister's Journeymanship*, Aphorism 136.
31. *Goethe's Botanical Writings*, p. 228.
32. *Goethe's Werke*, Vol. 13, pp. 323-24.

In the deepest sense Goethe saw the world as formative. What is true of light is also true of perception more generally. Indeed, each act of careful observation and consideration shapes and stimulates capacities within us.

Every new object, well contemplated, opens up a new organ within us.[33]

Polanyi in his own language speaks likewise of the transformative power which the act of "indwelling" possesses:

Such extensions of ourselves develop new faculties in us; our whole education operates in this way.[34]

Through a gentle empiricism we develop faculties which allow us to see more deeply into nature. Under the quiet gaze of this science we may read, as Novalis writes,

the great Manuscript of Design which we everywhere descry, on wings of birds, on the shells of eggs, in clouds, in snow, in crystal, in rock formations, in frozen water, within and upon mountains, in plants, in beasts, in men, in the light of day. . . .[35]

It is, in Paracelsus' terms, the Light of Nature. But it is not nature known through the intellect alone, but rather also through living Reason which "takes joy in development," which sees in the individual the universal.


WHAT STANDS BEFORE Goethe in imagination, as archetype, can begin to sing as inspiration when the pure-thought organs—exercised, for example, through geometry—wed with the beheld coherences of nature. Perhaps in this way, by a vigorous cultivation of both positive and negative gnosis the loss of Orphism may be redeemed. Through a strict, sense-free thinking and a phenomenology free of mental constructs, the essential, dynamic and ensouled figure of nature can arise first in imagination and then in the sounding of heaven's harmonies, finally to be experienced in selfless, conscious union.

We must be clear that this is not an egotistical quest for self-illumination but rather carries with it a burden of world responsibility. What we have gained through nature must be placed once again at nature's

33. Ibid., p. 38.
34. Polanyi, *Knowing and Being*, p. 148.
35. von Hardenberg, *Novalis Schriften*, Vol. I, p. 79.

service. Novalis, in a few words, placed with us the greatest task when he wrote, "Humanity is the Messiah of Nature."

Rudolf Steiner says it more gently in a verse given to his wife, Christmas 1922, yet the meaning is the same. What once was given to us by the gods must now sound anew from our humanity.

> The Stars once spoke to human beings.
> Their growing muteness is cosmic fate.
> To perceive this muteness can
> cause pain in earthly human beings.

> Yet what humanity speaks to the stars
> ripens within this muted stillness.
> And to perceive this speech
> can become power in spiritual human beings.[36]

---

36. Cf. Rudolf Steiner, *Verses and Meditations*, trans. George Adams (London: Rudolf Steiner Press, 1961), p. 97; Rudolf Steiner, *Truth Wrought Words*, trans. Arvia MacKaye Ege (Hudson, N.Y.: Anthroposophic Press, 1979), p. 31.

*Intently considering once, and reasoning with himself, whether it would be possible
to devise a certain instrumental assistance to the hearing, which should be firm and
unerring, such as the sight obtains through the compass and the rule, or, by Jupiter,
through a dioptric instrument; or such as the touch obtains through the balance, or
the contrivance of measures; — thus considering, as he was walking near a brazier's shop, he heard from a certain divine casualty the hammers beating out a piece
of iron on an anvil, and producing sounds that accorded with each other, one combination only excepted. But he recognized in those sounds, the diapason, the
diapente, the diatessaron, harmony. He saw, however, that the sound which was
between the diatessaron and the diapente was itself by itself dissonant, yet, nevertheless, gave completion to that which was the greater sound among them. Being
delighted, therefore, to find that the thing which he was anxious to discover had succeeded to his wishes by divine assistance, he went into the brazier's shop, and found
by various experiments, that the difference of sound arose from the magnitude of the
hammers, but not from the force of the strokes, nor from the figure of the hammers,
nor from the transposition of the iron which was beaten. When, therefore, he had
accurately examined the weights and the equal counterpoise of the hammers, he
returned home, and fixed one stake diagonally to the walls, lest if there were many,
a certain difference should arise from this circumstance, or in short, lest the peculiar
nature of each of the stakes should cause a suspicion of mutation. Afterwards, from
this stake he suspended four chords consisting of the same materials, and of the
same magnitude and thickness, and likewise equally twisted. To the extremity of
each chord also he tied a weight. And when he had so contrived, that the chords
were perfectly equal to each in length, he afterwards alternately struck two chords at
once, and found the before mentioned symphonies, viz. a different symphony in a
different combination. For he discovered that the chord which was stretched by the
greatest weight, produced, when compared with that which was stretched by the
smallest, the symphony diapason. But the former of these weights was twelve
pounds, and the latter six. And, therefore, being in a duple ratio, it exhibited the
consonance diapason; which the weights themselves rendered apparent. But again,
he found that the chord from which the greatest weight was suspended compared
with that from which the weight next to the smallest depended, and which weight
was eight pounds, produced the symphony diapente. Hence he discovered that this
symphony is in a sesquialter ratio, in which ratio also the weights were to each other.
And he found that the chord which was stretched by the greatest weight, produced,*

*when compared with that which was next to it in weight, and was nine pounds, the symphony diatessaron, analogously to the weights. This ratio, therefore, he discovered to be sesquitertian; but that of the chord from which a weight of nine pounds was suspended, to the chord which had the smallest weight [or six pounds,] to be sesquialter. For 9 is to 6 in a sesquialter ratio. In like manner, the chord next to that from which the smallest weight depended, was to that which had the smallest weight in a sesquitertian ratio, [for it was the ratio of 8 to 6], but to the chord which had the greatest weight, in a sesquialter ratio [for such is the ratio of 12 to 8]. Hence, that which is between the diapente and the diatessaron, and by which the diapente exceeds the diatessaron, is proved to be in an epogdoan ratio, or that of 9 to 8. But either way it may be proved that the diapason is a system consisting of the diapente in conjunction with the diatessaron, just as the duple ratio consists of the sesquialter and sesquitertian, as for instance, 12, 8, and 6; or conversely, of the diatessaron and the diapente, as in the duple ratio of the sesquitertian and sesquialter ratios, as for instance 12, 9, and 6. After this manner, therefore, and in this order, having conformed both his hand and his hearing to the suspended weights, and having established according to them the ratio of the habitudes, he transferred by an easy artifice the common suspension of the chords from the diagonal stake to the limen of the instrument, which he called chordotonon. But he produced by the aid of pegs a tension of the chords analogous to that effected by the weights.*

*Employing this method, therefore, as a basis, and as it were an infallible rule, he afterwards extended the experiment to various instruments; viz. to the pulsation of patellae or pans, to pipes and reeds, to monochords, triangles, and the like. And in all these he found an immutable concord with the ratio of numbers.*

IAMBLICHUS, *Life of Pythagoras*

# 8 | Apollo: The Pythagorean Definition of God

................................................*Anne Macaulay*

THERE ARE MANY MYSTERIES surrounding Pythagoreanism: Where did Pythagoras get his wisdom? What is the connection between Pythagoras and the subsequent Pythagoreans in Athens—Plato, Socrates, etc.—with whom there was no direct intermediary? Why did Pythagoreans "worship" Apollo when their philosophy was "beyond" religion? What is the nature of Apollo? These are unanswered questions. More may be formulated about sacred practices thought to come from the Middle East and India: Where did mantric practices come from? Was there a sacred alphabet from which the vulgar one was derived? How is it related to Kabalistic practices? How is this all connected with Pythagoreanism?

To all this jumble of questions, a single answer emerges in the nature of Apollo. When this is revealed, many outstanding features come to light, in particular the very essence of the Apollo, which can also be seen as a description or definition of god, one that is valid and acceptable today since it stands up to scientific principles.

When I began my researches, I had no intention of entering these areas concerning Apollo and religion. I started by exploring the history of the modern guitar to try to discover where it had come from. What I found was that the guitar was derived from the cithara, the ancient Greek instrument invented by Apollo. The music, then, can be seen to be an integral part of Pythagoreanism: using standard archeological methods, along with the music, all the "tools" of the Pythagorean culture were considered together, which led back in time eventually to the source of Apollo in the West of Europe in the megalithic period. The musical side was essential to unraveling these mysteries, first because the music defines the background to the whole culture in time and space, and second because it demonstrates the relation to Pythagorean geometric practices; third and not least, it shows how we in the extreme West of Europe are still so strongly connected to the ancient roots.

The argument is in three parts. The First section is purely musicological or, more strictly, organological (the study of the morphology of musical instruments). In the Second section the relation between the music of the cithara and Pythagorean geometric practices is explored, then connected with the tools of Pythagoreanism, leading to the hypothesis of the nature of the sacred (preliterary) alphabet. The Third section is the testing of this hypothesis using the name Apollo, which reveals both the nature of Apollo and the basic background of Pythagoreanism.

BEFORE STARTING SOMETHING NEEDS TO BE SAID about the historical background into which this research falls. The trail leads back into Britain at a very early period when the megalithic structures were being built (Stonehenge, etc.). With the new calibration of carbon dating, the age of these megalithic sites is now seen to be far older that had previously been thought. (See Chronological table.) The consequence of this new dating is that it is now realized that the Western European megalithic culture could not have been derived from Eastern sources, as it predates anything comparable in the East by millennia; e.g., the first megalithic stone structures go back to 4700 B.C. and the stone setting at Callanish in the Hebrides to 3700 B.C.; the first use of stone in Egypt, at the time of Zoser, is after 2700 B.C. Incidentally, Imhotep, Zoser's architect, is thought by some to be an outsider who came from the West.

This new historical sequence derived from carbon dating has invalidated the old well-known theory of the diffusion of culture from the East to the West. This has led to a renewed interest in British archeology, and many excavations are now being carried out in order to get material for dating. The results are gradually putting the dates further and further back, for example the unexpectedly early date recently procured for Callanish, 3700 B.C. The period of most activity, when well over a thousand rings were erected, was from c. 3200 to 1500 B.C., after which the use of large stones (megaliths) ceased; by c. 1400 B.C. Stonehenge was abandoned for some unknown reason. At much the same time some other megalithic sites were also abandoned, but at others there was continued occupation with developing pottery stiles, metal technology, etc., right on into the Iron Age and the coming of the Romans. This continuity is very important. All the traceable artifacts show an unbroken line of development through the mesolithic period into historical times; there were intrusions, e.g., the beaker peoples, but these are now seen as the spread of new cultural ideas rather than wholesale invasions as thought before.

| | CHRONOLOGICAL TABLE | | |
|---|---|---|---|

| | BRITAIN | GREEK WORLD | EGYPT |
|---|---|---|---|
| 4700 | French magalithic sites | | |
| 4500 | British megaliths | | |
| 3700 | Callanish | | |
| 3200 | | | The First Dynasty |
| 3100 | New Grange | | |
| 2800 | Maes Howe | | |
| | First stage at Stonehenge | | |
| 2700 | | | First use of stone in building |
| 1800 | | New palaces in Crete Before 1700: | |
| 1700 | | First Apollo seal | |
| 1450 | | Second Apollo seal Eruption of Thera First evidence of cithara | |
| 1400 | Stonehenge abandoned | | |
| | Appearance of the Alphabet in Eastern Mediterranean | | |
| 1350 | | | Moses, Akhenaten? |
| 1200 | | Troy | |
| 1150 | | Collapse of the palace system | |
| 800 | | Colonization in Asia Minor Later colonization in Italy Homer | |
| 600 | | Founding of Marseilles | |
| 6th C | Hecataeus visits Hyperborea | PYTHAGORAS End of Archaic Period | |
| B.C. | | | |
| A.D. | Romans break continuity in England | | |
| 400 | Celtic Church in Ireland | | |
| 600 | Celtic missions into Europe | | |

MEGALITHIC PERIOD (label spanning 3100–1700 on timeline)

CONTINUITY (label spanning 800–6th C on timeline)

# I. The Music

The starting point is the modern guitar. The question is, where did it come from? The guitar has been taboo in many circles, and when I started about fifteen years ago to trace its history, it was almost unbelievable; there were only a few very shallow sources available, all of which were contradictory and so superficial that I realized they could be discarded. So I had to start from scratch. The most fruitful source of information, I discovered, was to examine the actual instruments, quite a large number of which have survived from as early as the Renaissance. Before that time the best source proved to be pictorial evidence from paintings, carvings, sculptures and drawings in early manuscripts.

The guitar first comes into history about A.D. 1500. This is the point from which the first record of the tuning has survived. We don't really know at what pitches these instruments were played, but for all the plucked-string instruments there are records describing how to tune them. The pitch was controlled by the quality of the first string: the instructions read, "Put your first string on and tune as high as it will go without breaking, and then tune the other strings to the first one." This then is the standard! I choose to write all the tunings at the pitch of the modern guitar, which shows the relationship of the string and tunings as well as any other method.

The basic guitar in the Renaissance had seven strings tuned in four courses. The top string was single and tuned in "E," the second was a double-strung course with both strings in unison in "B," the third course was also double and tuned to "G" but with an octave separation and the fourth course was also double with an octave separation in "D." The double courses were an archaic feature and are a crucial part of the evidence.

So there were seven strings on the guitar. The demands of the new music in the Renaissance led to extending the number of strings; the guitar types had extra strings added below the standard tuning, while the lute and vihuella, both having identical tunings to the guitar, had as well as the strings below an extra melody string added above. It is this extended guitar that is the father of the modern instrument—in about 1800 the double courses were eliminated, leaving the six single strings as we know them today.

The basic tuning of all these instruments, the lute, the vihuella, the guitar, etc., has an interval of a fourth, then a major third, then another fourth; this is known as 4-3-4 tuning, which is the typical Western European tuning found on all indigenous European instruments. There were (and still are) other tunings that had been imported from the East along with the actual instruments; e.g., the mandolin.

The term "Spanish" which has been applied to the guitar since the time of Henry VIII is derived from the popularity of Spanish music at that period. Spain grew wealthy as the result of the discovery of America, and there was an artistic flowering. Musically there was also an ebullience, and it coincided with the development of printing; Spanish books of music thus travelled with their form of guitar. The Spanish guitar was then very like the modern guitar, but in the rest of Western Europe there were also guitars with the same tuning but very different body construction. The Spanish form of the instrument was both easier to make and more robust than other forms, hence the comparative rapidity with which it was adopted.

Musical instrument makers are extraordinarily conservative, and to find such widely varying body shapes on the guitar in the Renaissance indicates that the guitar had been in the West in all these countries for a very long time. The archaic double courses can be seen as a feature that must have been derived from a much earlier stage. It is fair to presume that the guitar was in fact a Western European instrument, not a peculiarly Spanish one nor derived from the Arab world.

Something must be said about where the guitar types were used. Apart from the Welsh Bardic schools, all music was taught within the Church until the Reformation. And the lute or guitar was the compulsory instrument for all would-be musicians, just as the piano is the compulsory instrument today for all musical studies. All the harmony was worked out on these plucked-string types. As one goes back in time, more and more of the information about the guitar comes from Church associations.

Going backwards from the Renaissance, traces of the guitar can be picked up from several sources. A number of guitar-related names occur in literature such as Chaucer; the proper name was "cithara" but a variety of corruptions of this name appear: *crwth*, which is the Celtic form, cittern, guittern, etc. These many derivatives of the name indicate that the instrument must have been in Western Europe for a very long time.

The names of instruments don't tell you that much about them. A more informative source is in paintings, and happily in the early Renaissance religious subjects were popular; many musicians were shown, and groups of angelic musicians were a common feature. Yet another source is the carvings on Gothic cathedrals, where musicians were a common feature.

But going even further back, information can be found in early manuscripts in which, apart from main illustrations, there are delightful little drawings at the edges of the script; much detail about musicians is learned from this source. Most of these early manuscripts were written in church scriptoria, thus showing where the guitar was known and used. An art historian, Winternitz, has traced pictures in a psalter written in Germany and shown the transition between the cithara-lyre type of instrument, which has arms and seven strings, and the protoguitar, which is this lyre with a fingerboard on it. This ninth-century drawing is thought by the style to have been copied from an earlier drawing which takes the date back to the eighth century. All this proves that the guitar types that are well-known from later times were derived from a seven-stringed lyre in use in Western Europe at an early time.

The eighth-century date takes us back to the early days of Christianity, when much of Northwest Europe was re-Christianized by Celtic missions. This allows a longer view to be taken; from Celtic sources, both from the Welsh Bardic tradition and instruments and from Celtic legend, it is found that the *crwth* is the instrument of the Druids and Bards. The Celtic Church was founded within the Druidic stream in Ireland, so it is logical that the Druid instrument should continue to be the source of music when Christianity arrived. (The Irish insist that the harp is their Druidic instrument, but the harp was introduced into Ireland by the Vikings after the Church was formed.)

One can skip the Romans as being a possible source for the Western cithara. They were notoriously bad musicians, and if they could not learn to play an instrument in three easy lessons they altered the instrument! The cithara that the Romans had acquired from Greece as a seven-stringed lyre was made into a four-stringed instrument in the Roman world. If they had reduced their cithara to a four-stringed instrument, it cannot be the source of the Western seven-stringed cithara, called the *crwth* in the Celtic world. The cithara was in Druid hands in spite of the Romans, not as a result of them.

Having traced the protoguitar back to the Druids in pre-Roman times, one would imagine that this is as far as could possibly be hoped, but there is a surprise. Diodorus Siculus (Book II, ch. 47) quotes earlier sources, one of them being Hecataeus of Miletus, who was a sixth-century B.C. Greek geographer and traveller. He visited the land of Hyperborea, which in this instance is Britain, and described the local Apollonian priests who played the cithara. The Greeks were fastidious about naming objects, and as there were other names in Greek for the different types of lyres, one can presume that the instrument he encountered was the same as the Greek cithara. The whole of this quotation from Hecataeus is of immense interest, and other parts of it are used later in the argument.

This point is as far back in time as one can go, using conventional sources, in tracing the protoguitar in Western Europe; note however that Hecataeus' visit to Britain was very soon after the first Greek settlement in the West (Marseilles), so one can also assume that the Greeks had not had time to have introduced their cithara to the Hyperboreans;—it must therefore have been a long-established "native" instrument.

Though the protoguitar can be traced in name back to the sixth century B.C. in Britain, there is insufficient evidence to give any clues as to how this seven-stringed instrument was tuned at this early date. However, as Hecataeus equated the Hyperborean form with the Greek cithara, it is legitimate to explore the early Greek musical sources to try to find out more about the British instrument.

*Greek Music*

There is much information available about Greek music from surviving books, but most of the records come from the time later than Hecataeus, who lived in what is termed the archaic period, around 600 B.C. After this time there were a great many changes during the classical period, but the later alterations have nothing to do with the Western connection, so we have to restrict the search to the archaic period.

In this early period, c. 600 B.C., the cithara was used by the Bards and the aristocracy; they sang to it, they danced to it, and it was associated with Apollo, to whom legend ascribed its invention. At this time cithara music was guarded with religious scruple, and it was punishable by death to change the tuning or the number of strings; and it was, despite what the musicologists say, the most important musical instrument. This is justified not only by the connection of the cithara with Apollo, but by the legend that Apollo competed with Marsias who played the aulos (flute)—Apollo was claimed the victor, whereupon he flayed Marsias.

What is the historical position of the Greek cithara? The Greeks believed that the cithara had come into Greece as a three-stringed lyre in the ninth century and that it had been developed in Greece itself. This is one of the many fallacies that must be abandoned, because from pictorial evidence the seven-stringed lyre can be traced back to Minoan Crete, c. 1450 B.C. There are indubitable illustrations of the cithara in Crete, depicting an instrument slightly more curved than the later ones, with carved swans' heads on the ends of the arms. In view of the fact that Apollo is ascribed with inventing the cithara and that in later times his main symbols were the cithara and the swan, to find the two together in Crete indicates a full Apollo awareness there.

After a long period of development in Crete, there had been a new phase starting, about 1800 B.C., with the rebuilding of the palaces. This was the great Minoan period. But disaster struck. Around 1450 much of Crete was damaged by the eruption of the island of Thera; then there was Mycenean dominance, followed by further interwarring in the Greek world, resulting in the siege of Troy, c. 1200 B.C. Shortly after this event, about 1150 B.C., there was an ill-understood event which brought about the complete collapse of the palace system. The Greek world took a long time to recover; about 800 B.C. the Greeks started colonies in Asia Minor and a little later in Italy. They did not make contact with the Western Celts until the founding of Marseilles in c. 600 B.C. This long period of inter-Greek warring had an effect on the art world. As far as music is concerned this type of political stress has a reliably standard reaction: there are no new developments and the existing music becomes very conservative. The religious vigor with which cithara music was preserved into the end of the archaic period was the final stage of the preservation of Minoan musical practices, i.e., the tuning and playing methods of the cithara at this time were identical with Minoan practices.

Having placed the cithara in its Greek historical context, we can now turn to the question of whether there is any relationship between the music of the Greek form and the Renaissance guitar. There is a strange gap in the musicological world, in that the guitar has not been considered a respectable instrument and was not acceptable as a qualification for musicological studies until very recently. As a result, the Greek texts relating to the cithara, which is a plucked instrument, have only been examined by wind-instrument players and to a lesser extent by bowed-instrument players, none of whom knows how a plucked instrument behaves in practice. This leaves the Greek texts on the cithara uninterpreted, though all are translated and ready to be examined. Though not a musicologist, I have played the guitar, and the practical information gained from this type of familiarity has enabled me to work out how the cithara was played.

The playing method of the cithara hinges on the uses of harmonics in a certain way so clearly shown in hundreds of paintings of citharists from Greek vases. The cithara was held on the left side of the player's body, kept in position with a strap over the left shoulder. The left hand was held behind the strings. The first string, which was furthest from the player, was the top of the scale. The second string was played on the third harmonic, using the little finger. The third, fourth and fifth strings were played open like the first and seventh, and the sixth string was played on the third harmonic, using the thumb. This is the standard playing position that is so often pictured. This left hand position produced the scale. (I prefer to call the series of notes a scale as I believe the Greek term "mode" implies more than the scale itself.)

Curt Sasch has worked out what the various Greek modes or scales were, and we learn from other sources that cithara players preferred the Lydian mode. This is the ancient Lydian mode of 600 B.C., which is not the same as the Lydian mode of early church music. Further, there is a report from the end of the archaic period in which we learn that the archaic scale sounded strange since it had a gap in the middle, a feature that had been eliminated by the extension of the scale to eight notes.

Knowing the scale, and that it had the middle note missing, it can now be aligned with cithara techniques to discover the tuning of the cithara in the archaic period. The ancient Lydian scale is the same as our modern major scale, give or take fractionally for natural temperament. Written at the same pitch as the guitar, in descending order it is:—G, F$^\#$, E, D, B, A, G, *with the middle note c missing*. From the playing technique it is known that the second and sixth notes were derived as harmonics. The F# is the third harmonic of the note B and the A is the third harmonic of the note D. So the Greek cithara tuning is:

| String: | 1st | 2nd | 3rd | 4th | 5th | 6th | 7th |
|---------|-----|-----|-----|-----|-----|-----|-----|
| Played: | open | 3H | open | open | open | 3H | open |
| Tuning: | g' | B | e' | d' | b | D | g |
| Scale: | g' | f#' | e' | d' | b | a | g |

The tuning therefore is made up of one E, two B's, two G's, and two D's. This can immediately be recognized as the same tuning as that of the basic seven-stringed guitar at the time of the Renaissance. Frankly, I was shattered when I discovered this tuning; I had never dreamt that it could have survived so completely over so long a period of time.

In confirmation of this tuning, there is the statement ascribed to Pythagoras himself that has been taken out of context: he said that the four fixed notes of the scale were the interval of a fourth and a fifth. He made this remark specifically in relation to the scale obtained on the cithara, which was the Pythagoreans' instrument and on which their musical theory was worked out. From the musicologist's point of view, it has been asked why he only quotes four notes in the scale when it is well enough known that an extended scale had been in use for some time before Pythagoras' statement. Look at the tuning of the cithara: it is made up of only four notes; the top g' is merely the octave of the lower g. The B and D on the second and sixth strings are not part of the scale, thus leaving the notes e', d', b, g as the only fixed notes in the scale. And g to d' is a fifth, and b to e' is a fourth. This tuning is explored further later on. But it must be emphasized again that the cryptic remark by Pythagoras about the fixed notes of the scale is completely explained by the cithara tuning; there is no mystery about it.

Having seen the continuity of the tuning, I looked again at the Western information and realized that there had been one single alteration to the ancient tuning; this alteration looks more like a deliberate development rather than an erroneous change, and as such it would have to be placed at some point before the Romans moved West because it was spread throughout Western Europe from Spain northwards. As development of this nature must be associated with a cultural "high," it must be associated with such an event in the West. We know so little about pre-Roman Western Europe that it is difficult to pinpoint that period.

The alteration to the tuning in the West involved the raising of the pitch of B on the second string to b, which is the pitch of the scale. I call this the Celtic tuning. There is evidence from the medieval period of the seven-stringed lyre being played with a single harmonic on the sixth string. This altered tuning produces the pentatonic scale with the second lowest note, a, being derived as the third harmonic of the note D. This scale still survives in Scottish and Irish folk music.

The Celtic tuning is g, D, b, d', e', b, g', and this was the form that was paired over the fingerboard in the eighth century. So the Celtic tuning paired is e', bb, g'g, d'D. Comparing this with the three known Renaissance guitar tunings:—

| Phalaise: | e' | bb | gG | dD |
|---|---|---|---|---|
| Bermuda: | e' | bb | g'g | d'd |
| Mudarra: | e' | bb | gg | dD |

In all these three known tunings, the two b's are at the same pitch. The high pitch of the g' and the d' have been retained by Bermuda, but this high level of the bass string must have confused the melody. All the tunings have retained the octave separation of at least one of the bass courses from the original Celtic tuning.

The Celtic pentatonic tuning forms the answer to the question of why the double courses were used on the cithara-type plucked strings in Western Europe. And the three tunings quoted show how the musicians were trying to retain the old feature of the double courses and adapt them to suit the new music that was in fashion in the Renaissance and later.

The extraordinary length of time involved in which this basic cithara tuning has survived, from at least early Minoan times till today, is quite unique in the musical world. One wonders how such a sophisticated tuning could have survived intact for so long. One reason why it survived in Western Europe through the Dark Ages was that it was firmly within the Church; it had been in the Church since Christianity first arrived, and the Church was probably the only institution in the West that could have preserved such a sophisticated art form in those troubled times.

There is, however, another reason for its survival that is inherent in the tuning. In the Greek cithara, the top three strings played open and together play the E minor chord, and the four lower strings played open produce the G major chord; this is the relative major of the E minor chord. This is full-blooded harmony, not contrapuntal harmony but complete major and minor triads. In the Celtic tuning, when the second string was raised to the pitch of the scale, this note was now superfluous to the scale but it was not eliminated; the result was that the same E minor and G major chords could still be achieved as in the Greek form. Then in the eighth century, when the seven strings were paired over the fingerboard, this was done in such a way that the top three courses still played the E minor chord and the lower three courses the G major chord. These two chords thus emerge as a necessary feature of cithara music; if the musicians and the audiences were used to this form of music, it could not be discarded, and it looks as if the demands of this particular harmony are the reason this ancient tuning has remained intact so long.

So the major triad combined with its relative minor triad is an essential feature of the cithara and is thus part of the Greek canon of music. Perhaps this is a good place to say something about the word harmony. The Greeks used this word to imply anything that fitted together to make a whole, e.g., the parts of a boat. It did not necessarily mean musical harmony in the sense that we use the same word today. If these musical triads are a basic feature of the cithara, there is the implication that the word cithara itself implies musical harmony; in fact in the West of Europe all the instruments with the 4–3–4 tuning were properly called the cithara, as was the harp which of course with its many strings was also capable of playing major and minor triads. If this is correct, then the use of the word harmony in Greek texts does not necessarily imply musical harmony in the modern sense, but the word cithara does.

The subject of the cithara has been fairly well covered except for the question of its origins. The Greeks and their seven-stringed cithara were comparative newcomers to the Eastern Mediterranean in the Minoan

Era. After c. 1450 B.C., the Greeks were so preoccupied with catastrophes and wars that they were not in a position to introduce musical instruments to the Hyperboreans; how then did the Hyperboreans come to have the same instrument, as described by Hecataeus? The answer is that there must have been a common cultural source that flourished before 1450 B.C. which gave the same cithara instrument to both the Greeks and the Hyperboreans in the West of Europe.

Before 1450 B.C. there are many known civilizations in Egypt and the East, but it is also known that in none of these places was the cithara used, nor was the god Apollo known. Apollo is, however, thought to have come from the North; and looking at the British datings, the appearance of Apollo's lyre in Crete c. 1450 B.C. is also about the time that Stonehenge was abandoned, along with some other megalithic sites. This date is the end point of the long and brilliant megalithic period which had lasted for nearly three millennia. Considering all the factors—the presence of cithara music in the West before the Greeks came, the details of the Hecataeus quotation relating how he was told in Hyperborea that Apollo had been born in their land, the limiting date of 1450 B.C. from the Greek end, the abandonment of Stonehenge and the presence of so much Pythagorean-type geometry in the megalithic rings (Thom)—it is beginning to look as if the cithara, the god Apollo and the Pythagorean way of thought all came from the megalithic West of Europe. The sheer size and spread of the megalithic culture both in space and time make it a suitable cradle for the development of these features. This is now a very promising picture, but there is not enough evidence to prove anything at this point.

In order to try to find more evidence, I then turned to archeological practices. From archeological remains, specific cultures are identified by the presence of a unique set of tools, which may occur at several places, thus demonstrating the spread of that culture. The next step is therefore to examine the whole culture surrounding the cithara in the Greek world and identify the Pythagorean tools.


## II. The Cithara and Pythagorean Geometry

*Cithara Tuning and Geometry*

The basic notes of the cithara tuning are E, B, G and D, which are the same notes that make up the top four strings of the guitar today. G to D is the interval of the fifth and B to E is the fourth, hence Pythagoras' remark that the four fixed notes of the scale were made up of a fifth and a fourth.

This tuning can also be put into Pythagorean terminology which describes musical intervals in terms of comparative string lengths:

e' to b is a fourth, which is equal to 3/4
b to g is a fifth, which is equal to 4/5

In both these statements the note b has the value 4, so the relationship of this group of three notes is the set 3:4:5.

The use of extended sets of proportion in a musical context is not recorded in Greek literature, but from Euclid there is massive evidence of this practice in their mathematics. Not only did they use extended sets, but they also used the inversions of those sets. It is justified therefore to convert this musical set to its inversion:

3:4:5 converts to 1/3:1/4:1/5

This inverted set represents musically the differentials at the third, fourth and fifth harmonics of a resonating string. If the basic string is taken as G, then the differentials are d, g, b—i.e., the second inversion G major chord. So the tuning of the cithara is made up of the set of proportions 3:4:5 combined with the inversion of the same set.

The value of the note D can be worked out in actual figures. To remove most of the fractions in 1/3:1/4:1/5, multiply throughout by 20, which is the value of G:

20/3:20/4:20/5 = 6.666:5:4

The Pythagoreans were known in their time as musical theorists, and they were the ones who defined this numerical method of describing musical intervals. The most famous piece of geometry ascribed to Pythagoras is the theorem about the triangle with sides in the proportion 3:4:5, and there can be no doubt that the Pythagoreans were aware of the musical sounds of this triangle. But the theorem involves the squaring of the sides. What is the music of the resultant figures?

$3^2$ = 9, which is close enough to 2 x 4.45, the note A
$4^2$ = 16, which is the note B
$5^2$ = 25, which is very close to the note $D^{\#}$

The chord $D^{\#}$:B:A = 25:16:9 is the dominant seventh, the interval $D^{\#}$ to A being the tritone. (Note: The relationship of the tritone is very close to root 2.)

Having put the actual proportions on the notes of the tuning, it is now possible to produce a complete set of proportions for the scale that is derived from this tuning. In descending order,

g' = 2.5, i.e., the note g = 5 divided by the octave factor 2
$f^{\#}$'= 2.666, i.e., the note B = 8 divided by 3 (third harmonic)
e' = 3
d' = 3.333
b = 4
a = 4.444, i.e., the note D = 13.333 divided by 3
g = 5

When this set of proportions is multiplied throughout by 3 x 3 x 2, it becomes 45:48:54:60:72:80:90, and this is a familiar set of musical proportions known from late classical Greek literature.

The set of proportions of the scale comes up later on.

From the foregoing it is clear that music and geometric practices are integrally related in Pythagorean practice. There is a further significance, however, because the cithara was described as the invention of Apollo, the god of the Pythagoreans who used the cithara itself in their discussions and played it.

From the musical evidence, it has been seen that the tuning of the cithara must have been the same both in Minoan Crete and in the earlier source that is possibly Hyperborean Britain. As Apollo is implied in the Minoan swan-headed cithara, and is also implied in the early megalithic source in Britain from Hecataeus' remarks, the question can be formulated if the Pythagorean type of philosophy was also complete in Minoan Crete and the early megalithic period.

To try to answer this question the various "tools" of Pythagoreanism are now going to be collected in an attempt to trace the culture by its unique complex of artifacts.

In one sense, the cithara and its tuning were tools of the philosophy, as also was geometry. The Pythagoreans were astronomers and coined the phrase "the music of the spheres," thus connecting music with astronomy; they worshipped Apollo and had a philosophy related to numbers.

Turning now to megalithic Britain, which of these tools can be identified there? From Hecataeus' report we know that the cithara was established there before the Greeks came and that these Hyperboreans believed that Apollo had been born in their land. The musical facts that I have aligned justify the belief that the cithara was in Britain before 1450 B.C. From the megalithic sites, the next three tools are well established by the work of Thom: the extended use of astronomy; the use of Pythagorean-type geometry in the plans of the sites; the significance of whole numbers for circumferences, i.e., a philosophy of number.

What other tools did the Pythagoreans use? While I was musing on the situation so far, new perspectives began to emerge. In the evidence from megalithic Britain, the astronomically oriented sites are designed on Pythagorean-type geometry, and they also include devices to achieve circumferences with whole numbers. Thus in what appears to be a proto-Pythagorean manifestation, geometry and a concern for whole numbers are integral.

Number and geometry; . . . then it struck me that the Pythagoreans were unique in that they used the letters of the alphabet both as numerals (a feature common to all early alphabetic usage) and as geometric symbolism. Geometry in the well-known Pythagorean form is unique to the Greek Pythagoreans, so the next thought was whether the alphabet in a preliterary sacred form was at the root of the megalithic culture.

The use of the letters of the alphabet for geometric symbolism is not well recorded, but there are crumbs to be picked up here and there. This idea makes the alphabet into a numero-geometric system which was also used for the basic elements of speech (vowels and consonants). If there had been an earlier sacred form, then it would not have been used to write vulgar language; the Pythagorean attitude to geometric theorems, which they held in some way sacred, gives the clue to the purpose of the sacred form: it was used to create names for their figures.

So now this hypothetical sacred alphabet can be described and can be defined. The sacred alphabet is an ancient system in which the numerals and geometric elements were represented by geometric symbols; to each of these signs a single sound (vowel or consonant) was added, in order to create names appropriate to their significant geometric figures.

This sacred form can also be termed the numero-geometric alphabet. (Note: The alphabet is that unique system of writing where each symbol represents a single sound [vowel or consonant]. Latest research has shown that these letters were first used as gradual inclusions in the syllabary in Cyprus. From Cyprus this system passed into the Semitic work in its complete form. At the point in time under consideration, about the middle of the second millennium B.C., there were strong Minoan influences and the founding of Greek bases in Cyprus. The Cypriot syllabary is closely related to the Minoan and Mycenean linear scripts.)

At this point in the exploration there is still no proof of any of the ideas that have been raised, but there is a great deal of encouraging background evidence, and the historical positions and datings of all the areas concerned make these seem more possible, as they all fit in beautifully.

The attractive thing about the sacred alphabetic hypothesis is that it can be tested—so this testing forms the next section.


## III. Testing the Alphabetic Process

To test the hypothesis about the nature of the sacred alphabet, a suitable name must be found and the numero-geometric values of the letters of that name must be determined, then used to create a figure; i.e., the values of the letters are taken as the "given" parts of a Greek geometric theorem.

In the context that has arisen, the name that is to be tested is at once obvious, APOLLO. There is no definitive etymology for this name: Apollo was the god of the Pythagoreans; he invented the cithara whose geometry and proportions have been fully explored.

### APOLLON

A = alpha. This is the first letter of the alphabet and represents the number One. In the Pythagorean philosophy of number, one was totality and it was depicted as a circle with diameter Ten units. So:—A = a circle with diameter ten units.

P = pi, which was the seventeenth letter of the alphabet. Later it was used to denote the factor of the relation of the circumference to the diameter of the circle. A factor cannot be used in a geometric construction. The geometric value of this letter has to be guessed but, as you will see when it arises, there is very little choice for a regular figure with the proportion seventeen other than a circle whose circumference is seventeen.

P = a circle with circumference seventeen.

O = omicron, which is the sixteenth letter. It was used to denote a circle and is taken as

O = a circle with circumference sixteen units.

L = lambda, the twelfth letter. It is taken as a rectangle with sides three by four.

N = nu, the fourteenth letter. Was this letter anything more than a grammatical grace? The Romans did not retain it: if however it is taken as a circle with circumference fourteen, its diameter is 4.4545, using pi = 22/7, which is the Greek value.

These geometric parts defined by the letters of the name Apollo are now treated as the given elements in a typical Greek theorem and are constructed into a single figure.

*Step One*
There are two lambdas side by side in the name Apollo, so these can be drawn as such. AB = BE = DC = CF = 3, AD = BC = EF = 4, with the angles at 90 degrees.

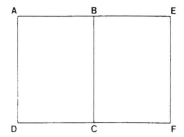 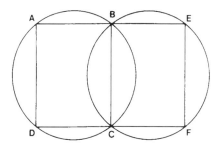

*Step Two*
The two omicrons are either side of the lambdas in the name Apollo. A circle with circumference 16 has a diameter 5.0909. This is so close to the length of the diameters of the lambda rectangles that the error is ignored, and the two omicron circles are placed with their centers on the midpoints of the diagonals AC and CE. The first circle cuts A, B, C and D, the second cuts B, C, F and E.

*Step Three*
The alpha totality circle presumably encloses but does not cut the rest of the construction. The radius of a circle with a diameter 10 is 5 units. But in the figure AC = DB = CE = BF = 5, so the center of the alpha circle can be either B or C. As the figure is symmetrical, it does not matter which. Let it be placed on B. This alpha circle will now touch the construction at D and F.

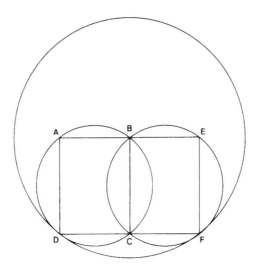

*Step Four*

The letter pi. How is the value 17 to be included? There now seems little choice, and it is taken as a circle with circumference 17 and placed with its center on CB extended, touching but not cutting the alpha circle at G.

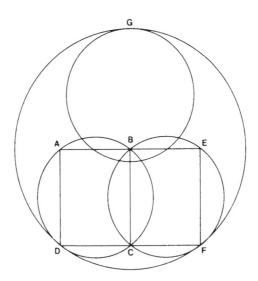

*Step Five*

This is being treated like a Greek theorem. After the given elements have been defined, significant intersections are joined. Join the two points where the pi circle cuts the omicron circles above the line ABE, and extend this line to cut CA extended at K and CE extended at L. Join the two points where the pi circle cuts the omicron circles below line ABE and extend it to cut AC in M and CE in N.

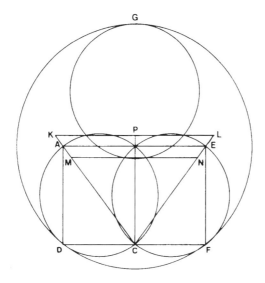

What now is to be done with the last letter nu? The diameter of a circle with circumference 14 is 4.4545. On measurement, and from accurate calculation, the length from C to P, the midpoint of KL, is this value. In a sense this dimension defines the significant area of the figure. It does, however, confuse the design, and I choose to omit it from the drawing.

The APOLLO geometry is now complete.

The first surprise about this exercise is that the numero-geometric values of the letters of the name Apollo form a concise and well-defined figure: there is no other obvious way in which these geometric parts could be put together. Now, however, a more precise examination must be made.

The measurements of the figure are:

AB = BE = DC = CF = 3 (by the construction)
AD = BC = EF = 4 (by the construction)
AC = CE = 5 (by the construction)
KP = 3.3 (from measurement)
MN/2 = 2.6 (from measurement)
PC = 4.5 (from measurement)

Compare this with the set of proportions derived from the cithara scale. (Note: It is already apparent that the measurement of the dimensions is too crude and a mathematician has calculated the lengths for me.)

| The Scale | Proportions of the Scale | Measurements of the Figure |
|---|---|---|
| g' | 2.5 (i.e., 5/2) | |
| f#' | 2.6666 | 2.692 = MN (calculated) |
| e' | 3 | 3 = AB, BE, DC, CF |
| d' | 3.333 | 3.343 = KP = PL (calc.) |
| b | 4 | 4 = AD, BC, EF |
| a | 4.444 | 4.459 = PC (calculated) |
| g | 5 | 5 = AC, BD, CE, BF |

Considering the strict limitations in the construction of the Apollo figure, which are defined by the numerical position of the letters of the alphabet, the resultant musical proportions in such accurate detail form the proof of the sacred alphabet hypothesis.

*Further Proof*

The music has pointed to the existence of proto-Pythagorean philosophies in Minoan Crete. So I went to Crete to search for the Apollo geometry. Most of the Minoan archeological finds are exhibited in the museum at Heraklion, and there I found amongst the many beautiful engraved seal stones two which have the Apollo geometry on them. The earliest is dated before 1700 B.C. and is a small button type with the three circles, having three featherings in one circle, four featherings in the second and five featherings in the third. The second stone is dated before 1400 B.C. and is a tiny crystal bob, again with the three Apollo circles on it. Many of these seals have beautiful geometric devices, and many others depict swans, the attribute of Apollo.

These two Apollo seals from Minoan Crete prove the Greek section of the knowledge of Apollo at an early date there and also the presence of the sacred alphabet in Crete, coinciding with the arrival of the first Greek-speaking peoples there. The date of the earliest seal is totally satisfactory since the alphabet as a means of writing vulgar speech did not appear in Cyprus until after the middle of the second millennium, when there was a strong Minoan and Greek presence.

*Evidence from Megalithic Britain*

Professor Thom has worked for many years on the designs of the megalithic rings. There are many variations of involved geometry in their plans, but very many are devised from the starting point of one of the Pythagorean right-angled triangles at the center; most often this is the triangle with sides in the proportion 3:4:5. The precise Apollo geometry has not come to light, but the exact circle of the Apollo geometry has no irregularities to be traced, so the exact circles may represent Apollo. However, the geometry that Thom has worked out is so similar that one of the designs he quotes can be read off from the sacred alphabet as A TH O L L O. These similarities of type are too strong to be discarded.

But there are, surprisingly, written records to support the claim that Apollo was devised in Hyperborean Britain. The same reference from Hecataeus that is quoted by Diodorus, and has been used above, states: "Moreover, the following legend is told concerning it [Hyperborea]: Leto [the mother of Apollo] was born on this island, and for that reason Apollo is honored among them above all other gods" (Loeb edition).

If Apollo was known in Minoan Crete (and there is more evidence for this other than what I have shown), then the birth of Apollo in Hyperborea must antedate the appearance of Apollo in Crete, which is no later than 1450 B.C. by conventional sources. This again places Apollo firmly in the megalithic period.

There is yet further proof however. It has been clearly demonstrated that the megalithic sites were used to define calendrical dates from astronomical events; i.e., the builders were astronomers. Does Apollo have any astronomical significance?

Apollo was equated with the sun and his twin sister with the moon. This is a promising start but is insufficient information to connect with the geometry. However there are two specific astronomical events recorded in Greek literature in association with Apollo. The first comes from the same Diodorus quotation. Hecataeus arrived in time to find the Hyperborean priests celebrating the return of Apollo at the end of the 18.5 year moon cycle. The second event is well recorded but ill understood. Apollo was supposed to leave Delphi in the autumn, spending the winter in Hyperborea, from whence he returned in the spring. Since Apollo's main attributes are the swan and the lyre, I realized that this belief could refer to the movements of the constellation Cygnus, the swan, and its neighboring group, the lyre, which are only visible in the Greek world in summer. This constellation is circumpolar in Britain, which means that it is visible throughout the year.

The next step was to ask an astronomer to check this suggestion and, viewing the Apollo geometry as a star guide with the point G as North and the great circle as the horizon, to determine whether it had any relation to astronomical events in the year 2600 B.C. (There are other reasons not mentioned here that seem to place Apollo at about this date.) Taking this date into account, the astronomer found that at the latitude of Stonehenge the points D and F in the Apollo geometry would have marked the rising and setting positions on the horizon of the moon at the end of the 18.5 year moon cycle. Does the pi circle define the movement of Cygnus throughout the year? He was doubtful of this, since this constellation is such a large object, but he did discover that the second brightest star in Lyra was at its zenith at midnight on Midsummer Day in 2600 B.C., i.e., it was lying on the line CP, which he thought significant.

So the answer to the question is yes, the Apollo geometry is related to the astronomical events associated with him in ancient times. (Note: In the Apollo geometry, the circumpolar stars are defined by the pi circle. It is interesting to find that in ancient China, c. 1100 B.C., the Emperor wore as a symbol of his office a jade circular ring called the "Pi" and this object was used to tell the time by observing the circumpolar stars. See Keith Critchlow, *Time Stands Still*.)

All ancient astronomers, as far as is known, considered the circumpolar stars as the most sacred part of the heavens.

Thus we can conclude that Apollo is the name derived through the sacred numero-geometric alphabet from a geometric figure which was itself derived from astronomical observations of the circumpolar stars and the moon. The secondary dimensions of the figure are the set of proportions of the scale and basic acoustic laws.

## IV. Final Remarks

The impetus to this research was the question "Where did the guitar come from?" and the answer is that it was derived from the seven-stringed lyre called the cithara, which had originated in megalithic Britain c. 2700 B.C.

There is, however, a strange twist to this work; in order to find more evidence to confirm the musical suggestions, the whole culture surrounding the cithara was examined, and the idea of the sacred alphabet emerged. When this was tested by using the name Apollo, the very basic nature of the god also emerged.

The edges of history. Nothing so far is known about the megalithic builders from the archeological evidence, but it is now possible to say that these peoples were proto-Greek-speaking wise men with a proto-Pythagorean philosophy. As the inventors of the alphabet, the megalithic culture can now be termed a civilization, and the geometric patterns built into the circular temples can be considered as writing which still requires further decoding. So history is now pushed back. A nice feature is that the megalithic remains demonstrate not the progress of kings, battles and conquests, but the development of a way of thought: these peoples were indeed civilized.

There is a great deal of room for speculation, but I tend to think that the proto-Greek language that these Apollo originators spoke was never a natural language but one artificially constructed within the schools; it perhaps started as an "Esperanto" of the native tongues, but within the schools the wisdom language developed with the addition of many new words derived from the sacred alphabet. If this idea is right, then the use of this language in the Greek world can be explained as an explosion of interest in the Apollo wisdom which became so general after c. 1400 B.C. that it evolved into the common tongue and ousted the indigenous Luvian language almost completely. This would make Greek stand as a wisdom language devoid of any racial associations.

Where did Pythagoras receive his training?

With the revelation of the nature of Apollo, it is clear that all the facets of Pythagoreanism were present in megalithic Britain and that all the separate aspects are of an integral nature. There were several important Apollo sites in the Greek world and the wisdom must have been kept alive down the years within these establishments; Pythagoras' training must therefore have been within the Greek Apollo tradition.

The name Pythagoras must be a conferred name, for it means "pithia," Apollo's temple and "agoras," the place. As the Apollo establishments were in a crisis point at the time of Pythagoras, it would appear that he was commissioned to make the secret wisdom public for the first time.

The existence of this stream of Apollo wisdom explains the problem of why the later teachers, Socrates and Plato, etc., were known as Pythagoreans in their day but there was no direct intermediary who could have passed Pythagoras' teaching on to them. The relationship is that they were all teaching aspects of the Apollo wisdom in public.

*The Apollo Wisdom and the Alphabet*

It is apparent that the wisdom from the West of Europe filtered eastward from very early times. There are traces of it in Egypt c. 2700 B.C. and in Asia Minor a little later. These early stages are more elusive, but by the middle of the second millennium B.C., with the appearance of the alphabet, it is easier to trace the spread of the Apollo wisdom that went with the alphabet. It is generally accepted that "monotheism followed the alphabet." But perhaps it is the other way round; the spread of the wisdom brought the alphabet with it.

Soon after the alphabet arrived in the Semitic world, Moses for the first time in the Bible, ordered that this shall be written down. Moses however came from Egypt where at his time there were many Minoans: Moses introduced monotheism.

Akhenaton too in Egypt caused something of a revolution and proclaimed monotheism, and he also was at the time of the spread of the alphabet. His work was erased in Egypt, and the alphabet was not adopted there for a very long time.

It would seem that monotheism was a feature of the Apollo wisdom at this stage and that it moved with the alphabet into the East and India; the progress of the wisdom can be traced by following the alphabet itself.

Judging from what is well recorded in much later times, the numeric associations of the letters assumed the most important philosophic aspect of the alphabet after it first emerged into the open. In these ancient times, mathematics was a sacred study for the most part, and the arithmetic that was used for trade, etc., was of a completely different nature, even using different signs for the numerals. Mathematics, then, was a subject set apart, possibly used in a manner similar to the alchemists' use of chemistry. The laws of mathematics were seen as absolute laws or the design of God. As the mathematics developed, larger numerals were required and the original system, with each letter representing the numeral of its position in the alphabet, had to be expanded. I suspect that the first form had only nineteen letters, which were used for the numerals from one to nineteen. When the system first appeared in the Semitic world, it had already been extended to include hundreds, and thousands, but in the Greek world a conservative shorter form was preserved.

At about the time of Pythagoras the Greek alphabet was revised by a group of wise men; Simonides, a greatly revered poet, was one of those involved. It is on record that he included a seventh vowel, omega, "so that there was a separate vowel for each string of the cithara." This revised alphabet was eventually adopted officially by Athens c. 415 B.C. and is the classical Greek alphabet as known today.

This revised form had now been extended so that it was comparable to the Semitic form and had sufficient letters to cover the same numerical range. It is this form that was used both in the Old Testament texts and in the Gnostic writings; in the Greek world this system flourished in the Christian Gnostic writings.

In India more of the geometry seems to have survived, as there are some surprisingly early scripts relating to cubic geometry, the square altar, etc. It was also in India that the so-called Arabic numerals were devised.

In the period when Apollo was devised, the letter A was the number one and meant totality; as already stated it was depicted as a circle with diameter ten units. In the New Testament Jesus says, "Not a jot or a titlte shall go unnoticed." The jot is the translation of the Greek "iota," which is the tenth letter and incidentally was not in the Hebrew alphabet. It is clear that the iota is the littlest bit and was depicted then as an upright stroke, as it is today.

The use of these two letters is interesting. In the words Macrocosm and Microcosm we all know what is meant. The only difference, however, is the interchanging of the "A" and the "I." Note also that Apollo's music is cIthara and his healing is cAthara, i.e., harmony in its essence and harmony within totality. Now look again at the "Arabic" numerals. The symbol for "one=totality" has been demoted to the zero, and the "iota=ten=the littlest bit" has been given pride of place as number one.

I feel sure that the ancient form with one=totality is at the root of the monotheism that seems to be associated with the early alphabet. I also believe that the alterations that make up the "Arabic" system are closely related to the rot that set in with Aristotle, etc. It has taken a long time to work its way through, but I think that the egotism and self-centeredness that are so prevalent today are related to the way we think of numbers. In the old form, if the individual is the microcosm, his relation to totality is a conceivable relation of one to ten, but with the symbol for totality reduced to nothing, how can one relate to the whole?

Returning now to the statement that Simonides created a seventh vowel so that there could be a separate vowel for each string of the cithara, it is interesting that when the sacred alphabet was vulgarized and taken to the Semitic world no vowels were disclosed; extra signs had to be used for these. Was this because the vowels were the most sacred part and were considered by all to be too holy to defile? There is a description of Greek priests in Alexandria singing as if they were the cithara, on the vowels only. Powerful stuff indeed, and the implication is that this was an ancient practice associated with the origins of the cithara. It is also learned that the Pythagoreans thought that a man healthy in body and mind was like a well-tuned cithara. How much closer can you get to the association of pitch and the vowels with the chakras? As no form of writing other than the alphabet distinguishes the vowels, surely the Yogic practices using pitch and vowels to tune up the chakras must be derived from the Apollo wisdom. And this leads on to all mantric practices. The Egyptian hieroglyphs were sacred, but they did not define sounds as they are in the alphabet; such a sacred set of sounds is required to define sacred mantras.

The sacred Apollo sites were marked with a stone which was thought of as the navel of the world, where God is connected to earth. And these stones are called OMPhali.

AND FINALLY LET US RETURN TO APOLLO. It came as a shock to me to find that this god was derived from a geometric figure. This is no deified hero nor an archetypal godlet, but a synthesis of observed facts about the relation of the stars, the moon and the sun to earth; it is a time piece and a calendar; it is a statement of the laws of the heavens in terms of geometrical and mathematical elements which themselves exhibit absolute laws; and these laws also apply to music: this must surely be the music of the spheres. The concept is total and the harmonic nature of the music demonstrates the great harmony of creation. Apollo can thus be seen as the logos or in another sense as the definition of the absolute god.

Perhaps the most important message from Apollo to us today is to become aware again in practice of the harmony which pervades all being.

*Pythagoras, however, did not procure for himself a thing of this kind through instruments of the voice, but employing a certain ineffable divinity, and which it is difficult to apprehend, he extended his ears, and fixed his intellect in the sublime symphonies of the world, he alone hearing and understanding, as it appears, the universal harmony and consonance of the spheres, and the stars that are moved through them, and which produce a fuller and more intense melody than anything effected by mortal sounds. This melody also was the result of dissimilar and variously differing sounds, celerities, magnitudes, and intervals, arranged with reference to each other in a certain most musical ratio, and thus producing a most gentle, and at the same time variously beautiful motion and convolution. Being therefore irrigated as it were with this melody, having the reason of his intellect well arranged through it, and as I may say, exercised, he determined to exhibit certain images of these things to his disciples as much as possible, especially producing an imitation of them through instruments, and through the mere voice alone.*

IAMBLICHUS, *Life of Pythagoras*


*The followers of Pythagoras and Empedocles, and most of the Italian philosophers, say that there is a certain community uniting us not only with each other and with the gods, but even with brute creation. There is in fact one breath pervading the whole cosmos like a soul and uniting us with them.*

SEXTUS EMPIRICUS, *Advanced Mathematics*

# 9 | Blake, Yeats and Pythagoras[*]

............................................................*Kathleen Raine*

THE TWO POETS WHO HAVE MOST RADICALLY called in question the premises of Western materialism are Blake and Yeats. Both challenged the scientific premise that the only object of knowledge is the phenomenal world of nature, assumed to have an existence in independence of mind, which passively receives impressions from a material and lifeless universe. Both challenged the premises of materialism, and both poets held mind itself to be the "place" of the apparently external universe. Yeats was Blake's first editor and greatest disciple; it is therefore necessary, before discussing two poems in which Yeats speaks of Pythagoras, to understand how Blake understood the part played by the half-legendary founder of the Western speculation of nature through number which has led to the "reign of quantity" in which we live, and which many, not least among the scientists and mathematicians themselves, are now beginning to call in question.

However, albeit an incomplete gnosis, it would be the merest prejudice to dismiss the great achievement of Western thought, the numerical speculation of the natural universe whose beginnings go back to Platonic and Pythagorean mathematics. We can but marvel at the coherence and diversification down to the limits of investigable matter, of that gnosis. We must remember also that the modern merely quantitative concept of number is far removed from that of Pythagoras himself or of the Greek philosophers. Pythagoras taught through symbols; and Berkeley, writing of the "Aegyptians" (from whom Pythagoras himself learned the mysteries of number), noted that they thought of "God and nature making one whole, or all things together as making one universe." To restore this

---

* A revised version of this paper was published in *Yeats the Initiate: Essays on Certain Themes in the Work of W. B. Yeats* (Mountrath, Ireland: the Dolmen Press, and London: George Allen and Unwin Limited, 1986).

ancient philosophical understanding of number was the avowed intent of Thomas Taylor the Platonist, contemporary and one-time friend of Blake, who was a mathematician before he was a philosopher and whose first important work was a translation of Proclus's commentaries on Euclid; who leads us straight back to Pythagoras. Taylor appears in Blake's *An Island in the Moon* as "Sipsop the Pythagorean." Blake must have had long conversations with Taylor on the mysteries of number for Taylor seems to have persuaded Blake (for he was fired with no less zeal to convert his contemporaries to the perennial wisdom than was Blake, but in its Platonic not its Christian tradition) to take some lessons in Euclid; but without converting him to the worship of the Divine Tetraktys. The record of this episode is in the journal of William Meredith, an architect and friend of Taylor. The entry is as follows:[1]

> T. Taylor gave Blake, the artist, some lessons on mathematick & got as far as the fifth proposition which proves that ye two angles at the base of an isosceles triangle must be equal. Taylor was going thro the demonstration but was interrupted by Blake exclaiming 'ah never mind that—what's the use of going to prove it. Why I see with my eyes that it is so, & do not require any proof to make it clearer.'

The story is characteristic of both men—Taylor the Platonic theologist, Blake who held that the living Imagination is the spirit that knows all things, by immediate perception. Whereas the Greeks start from nature, the object of knowledge, Blake starts from the principle of perception itself—spirit.

In one of his earliest writings—dating probably from the time he was seeing Taylor—Blake wrote his tractates *There is No Natural Religion*. Here he argues his case that "He who sees the Infinite in all things, sees God. He who sees the ratio only, sees himself only." "The true faculty of knowing must be the faculty which experiences. This faculty I treat of," he writes; and from the beginning of his life to the end he strove to make clear to others what was so clear to himself, that mind—the faculty which experiences—is the ground of all that we know objectively as "nature." Sense (Blake wrote near the end of his life in the margins of Berkeley's *Siris*) is the eye of the Imagination. He must have remembered his sessions with Taylor many years before, and his allusion to Pythagoras is clear when in another marginal comment he writes "God is not a mathematical diagram." The allusion is to the Tetraktys, and it was not Blake's

---

1. Quoted in a paper on "The Meredith Family, Thomas Taylor and William Blake," by James King, published in *Studies in Romanticism*, X. Spring 1972, no. 2.

way to make such comments without chapter and verse. On his Laocoon engraving, made at about the same time as the Berkeley marginalia, he wrote "The Gods of Greece & Egypt were Mathematical Diagrams—see Plato's works." He had doubtless read the *Timaeus* in Taylor's translation, but those lessons in mathematics are not to be forgotten.

In the Berkeley marginalia he goes to the root of the matter—his own reason for rejection of the mathematical ground of reality:

> Harmony and Proportions are Qualities & not Things. The Harmony & Proportion of a Horse are not the same with those of a Bull. Every Thing has its own Harmony & Proportion. Two Inferior Qualities in it. For its Reality is its Imaginative Form.

This is the form which can be apprehended immediately by sense, the eye of the Imagination; and Blake makes this also clear:

> Knowledge is not by deduction, but Immediate by Perception or Sense at once. Christ addresses himself to the Man, not to his Reason. Plato did not bring Life & Immortality to Light. Jesus only did this.

—Here we must remember that for Blake Jesus *is* the Imagination—the two words are for him synonymous—the living principle itself.

Blake goes on to say that "Jesus supposes every Thing to be Evident to the Child & to the Poor & Unlearned. Such is the Gospel." And his last marginal comment on Berkeley is unambiguously antiphilosophic: "What Jesus came to Remove was the Heathen or Platonic Philosophy, which blinds the eye of Imagination, the Real Man."

This is, of course, unfair to the Platonic theology, from which besides (especially from Plotinus) Blake has borrowed large parts of his system. But he has a point, for Blake a central one. Berkeley truly writes that

> Plato and Aristotle considered God as abstracted or distinct from the natural world. But the Aegyptians considered God and nature as making one whole, or all things together as making one universe.

Berkeley's "Aegyptians" refers above all to the *Hermetica*. Blake comments only on the first half of Berkeley's statement:

> They also consider'd God as abstracted or distinct from the Imaginative World, but Jesus, as also Abraham & David, consider'd God as a Man in the Spiritual & Imaginative Vision.

—Man being, of course, for Blake, a living spirit; he is not referring to the physical "garment," the material body. He continues:

> Jesus consider'd Imagination to be Real Man & says I will not leave you Orphans and I will manifest myself to you; he says also, the Spiritual Body or Angel as little Children always behold the Face of the Heavenly Father.

It is clear that Blake suspected the Greeks, including Pythagoras himself, founder of Western mathematics, as being responsible for what he calls the "wrenching apart" of Nature from the living Imagination. He writes specifically about harmonics, and in this challenges the Pythagorean element in Greek thought.

The allusion to harmonics comes in a passage three times repeated in Blake's Prophetic Books; from which we may judge the importance he attached to it. In this passage Blake is putting his case against Locke and his school who held that all knowledge comes through the senses; a view which survives in modern Behaviorism and the like. The corollary to this belief that all knowledge comes through the senses is that the only "knowledge" is of the external, quantified world of "nature." According to this view (Blake set it forth in his early Tractates against Natural Religion)

> Naturally man is only a natural organ subject to Sense.
> Man cannot naturally Perceive but through his natural or bodily organs.

In considering the Five Senses he is at pains to argue that we do not see with them, but through them: it is the True Man, the Imagination, who is the perceiver. Plato had himself written that we see through the eye, not with it: a phrase repeated in many contexts by Blake. In his *Auguries of Innocence* he wrote that

> We are led to Believe a Lie
> When we see With Not Thro' the Eye
> Which was Born in a Night to Perish in a Night . . . .

"I question not my Corporeal or Vegetative Eye any more than I would Question a Window concerning a Sight. I look thro' it & not with it"— so he concludes his notes on *A Vision of the Last Judgment*: which Judgment is, for Blake, precisely and specifically the awakening from natural to Imaginative perception.

The passage on the natural senses is as follows:

> Ah weak & wide astray! Ah shut in narrow doleful form,
> Creeping in reptile flesh upon the bosom of the ground!
> The Eye of Man a little narrow orb, clos'd up & dark,
> Scarcely beholding the great light, conversing with the Void;
> The Ear a little shell, in small volutions shutting out
> All melodies & comprehending only Discord and Harmony;
> The Tongue a little moisture fills, a little food it cloys,
> A little sound it utters & its cries are faintly heard,
>
> . . .
>
> Can such an Eye judge of the stars? & looking thro' its tubes
> Measure the sunny rays that point their spears at Udanadan?
> Can such an Ear, fill'd with the vapours of the yawning pit
> Judge of the pure melodious harp struck by a hand divine?

—and so with the other senses. Such is the world to those who look not through but with eye and ear and the other bodily organs. The sense of hearing can register, Blake notes, harmonics (discord and harmony) but not melody—"shutting out all melodies" because harmonics are a physical phenomenon whereas melody belongs to the Imagination, and exists only in terms of meaning and imaginative experience. Yet when he writes of "the pure melodious harp struck by a hand divine" he might well have been thinking of that Lyre of Apollo whose origins go back to Pythagoras himself. Taylor comments that

> This harmony of the spheres is admirably unfolded by Simplicius in his commentary on the second book of Aristotle's *Treatise on the Heavens*, as follows: 'The Pythagoreans said, that an harmonic sound is produced from the motions of the celestial bodies; and they scientifically collected this from the analogy of their intervals; since not only the ratios of the intervals of the sun and moon, and Venus and Mercury, but also of the other stars, were discovered by them'.

But then Simplicius writes of Pythagoras' alleged faculty of hearing that music, that this was not heard in the mortal body. The sound of divine bodies is not audible to terrestrial ears;

> . . . but if any one, like Pythagoras, who is reported to have heard this harmony, should have his terrestrial body exempt from him, and his luminous and celestial vehicle, and the senses which it contains purified . . . such a one will perceive things invisible to others. . . .

Pythagoras, however, seems to have said that he heard the celestial harmony, as understanding the harmonic proportions in numbers, of the heavenly bodies, and that which is audible in them.

It is likely that Blake had read Taylor's notes on the Lyre of Apollo; that the beautiful symbol touched his imagination but that he was repelled by Taylor's mathematical explanation. For the materialist could well argue that, yes, music affects us because our bodies are attuned to the harmonics of the universe through the structure of the sense-organs: music is no more than a physical sensation evoking a physical response. For Blake music is something else altogether; and this is why he makes his distinction between harmonics and melody—the "pure *melodious* harp"—melody being pure meaning; considered physiologically it has no existence. Therefore Blake writes that the heavens are themselves only an instrument upon which is played the music of the Imagination.

I touch the heavens as an instrument to glorify the Lord! For Blake the question is, who plays the harp?

In the last plate of Blake's Job engravings Job and his family are all playing upon musical instruments, Job himself on a harp, whose meaning is very clear. And note that Blake chose the instrument of the Jewish tradition—the harp of David—rather than the lyre of Apollo and Pythagoras.

WE FIND THE THEME OF THE LYRE and the music of the universe in the writings of other Romantic poets, notably Shelley and Coleridge. Shelley, a Platonist, writes of the breath of the Spirit, that touches and awakens the lyre of the universe:

Make me thy lyre, even as the forest is:
What if my leaves are falling like its own!
The tumult of thy mighty harmonies
Will take from both a deep autumnal tone,
Sweet though in sadness. Be thou, spirit fierce,
My spirit! Be thou me, impetuous one!

We must not suppose that Shelley is speaking metaphorically of this spirit of life striking the tuned lyre of the created world. The so-called "pathetic fallacy" is an invention of the nineteenth century (Ruskin coined the phrase so popular thereafter among literary critics) which accepted as a matter of course the post-Cartesian view that still holds good in our Universities that the universe is a mechanical structure without life, which operates according to mechanical laws. To attribute life to such a universe (the "pathetic fallacy") is presumed to be a sentimental personification of what is really lifeless. This may be so in the case of certain rationalist poets (one thinks of Erasmus Darwin) who do hold a mechanistic view of the universe and who just for fun or for some other effect personify its elements; but this was never the case with Shelley or Keats, Coleridge or Blake, all of whom followed a more philosophically venerable tradition of the *unus mundus*, in which nature and informing spirit are one and indivisible. By no poet is this made more clear than by Coleridge, who in *The Aeolian Harp* expresses this one life:

> O! the one Life within us and abroad,
> Which meets all motion and becomes its soul,
> A light in sound, a sound-like power in light,
> Rhythm in all thought, and joyance everywhere. (1.26-9)

The light in sound and sound-like power in light suggests the Pythagorean harmony that governs the whole universe; and the Lyre of Apollo appears even more clearly in later lines:

> And what if all of animated nature
> Be but organic Harps diversely fram'd.
> That tremble into thought, as o'er them sweeps
> Plastic and vast, one intellectual breeze,
> At once the Soul of each, and God of all? (1.44-9)

Coleridge is very close to Blake; and is it of deliberate intent that he too speaks rather of harp than lyre? And both Shelley and Coleridge use the Biblical image of the "wind" of the spirit, the "breath" of life without which the "organic Harps" are silent.

As to Pythagoras, his last appearance in Blake's writings is still an ambiguous one. In *Jerusalem* (plate 73) there is a list of the names of the men of God sent to "preserve from eternal death" the secular world-rulers. Los, eternal spirit of prophecy, creates

> Adam, Noah, Abraham, Moses, Samuel, David, Ezekiel,
> Pythagoras, Socrates, Euripides, Virgil, Dante, Milton.

—So Blake wrote; but then he changed his mind and deleted the classical philosophers from Pythagoras to Milton. It seems that, finally, he had concluded that these were not agents of the spirit, the Imagination, but of the ratio—natural reason. He was doubtless in this unjust not only to Pythagoras himself but to the Platonic metaphysics; and yet it is certainly true that the course history has taken in the West, from Pythagoras by way of Plato and Aristotle, has been to a purely quantitative scientific measurement of the Universe, with a consequent loss of that spiritual vision it was Blake's prophetic task to restore. Blake had a battle to fight and had to state his case without any trace of ambiguity.

FINALLY to Yeats.

In a sense one picks up the thread of Blake's thought, his affirmation of the Imagination as against positivist science, in Yeats, as if a single mind ran through both poets. And indeed they did both alike draw upon Tradition whose teaching is the same at all times throughout all its formulations. Yeats had evidently read Iamblichus and the other Pythagorean texts; and like Blake he was a metaphysician, for whom poetry was the language of spiritual knowledge.

One thinks, in relation to Pythagoras, of two poems especially: "Among School Children" and "The Statues." The occasion of "Among School Children" is a visit Yeats, "A sixty-year-old smiling public man," pays to a convent school for girls. He thinks of his old love Maud Gonne—as she must have been as a child; and of his own youth. Now they are both old:

> Her present image floats into the mind—
> Did Quattrocento finger fashion it
> Hollow of check as though it drank the wind
> And took a mess of shadows for its meat?

The name of Plato, introduced in the second stanza, introduces the myth of Leda, mother of Helen of Troy, to whom he had long ago compared Maud Gonne, not only in respect of her beauty but because she, like Helen, had been one through whom blazed the events of history:

> Was there another Troy for her to burn?

Dublin was Maud Gonne's Troy, whose Troubles had by now had as outcome the Republic of Ireland of which Yeats, once a young revolutionary, is now himself a senator. From Leda's other egg Castor and Pollux had hatched; and Yeats, himself an astrologer and born under the sign of the Twins, considers Maud Gonne and himself as born into history out of the same egg, "the yoke and white of the one shell," their fates and their lives united from before birth. Theirs is the intimacy of Isis and Osiris in the womb, love's closest conceivable union here suggested.

"Among School Children" moves from a consideration of generation into a time-world (which the poet considers in terms of the Neoplatonic tradition especially) to the paradox which has troubled humankind since the Epic of Gilgamesh, how to reconcile the soul's immortal nature with the mortality of the body that moves from birth to death so inexorably. It is essential, always, to read Yeats's poetry against the background not of current positivist humanist ideologies but of the Sophia Perennis, for which the soul is a reality and an eternal spiritual world soul's native country. Plotinus on The Soul's Descent into Body (*Ennead* IV.8) well describes this knowledge which underlies Yeat's poem; mythologized by Porphyry in his *De Antro Nympharum* (On the Homeric Cave of the Nymphs) to which Yeats alludes in the fifth stanza. Without this paradox of mortal self and immortal soul the profound inner tension of the poem could not exist; for it is no mere lament over mortality but a wrestling with far deeper questions.

First of these is generation itself, introduced in the symbol of the egg of Leda, and elaborated later in allusions to Porphyry and to Plato. "Leda and the Swan" appears in Yeats's *Collected Poems* on the page before "Among School Children," and the symbol of the egg (one he was later to elaborate in *A Vision*) is there presented with great power. Both Orphic and Indian cosmology, and also Blake, speak of the world-egg, the world as a womb into which generating souls "descend" from a discarnate eternal world. Whence do the souls come? Why do they come? Who sends them on their journey and for what purpose? In "Leda and the Swan" the paradox of divine and carnal begetting is united in the image of Zeus himself in the guise of a swan ("the brute blood of the air") and Yeats asks what the girl—Leda—can know of the event of which she is the agent, or its historic import. To this theme of the profound mystery of the relation between superhuman cause and human event we shall later return.

Once generated the heaven-born soul must pass through the time-world, become the "sixty-year-old smiling public man" and the hollow-cheeked image of Botticelli's Magdalene. Yeats felt much bitterness about old age, passionately evoked in the contrast between the thought of Maud Gonne as a child and "her present image":

> And thereupon my heart is driven wild. . .

What he felt can be assumed; but that feeling is but the starting point for a search for meaning in the journey of what Blake calls "the worm of sixty winters" from cradle to grave. The answer he seeks is not the facile humanist lament over mortality. "More! More! is the cry of a mistaken soul; less than All cannot satisfy Man," Blake had written; and "The desire of Man being Infinite, the possession is Infinite & himself infinite" (*There is no Natural Religion*). The human situation being now stated, Yeats establishes the foundations of his search: from Leda's egg to "a comfortable kind of old scarecrow," his image of old age; and we think of those other bitter lines, from "Sailing to Byzantium":

> An aged man is but a paltry thing,
> A tattered coat upon a stick, unless
> Soul clap its hands and sing and louder sing
> For every tatter in its mortal dress.

In that poem he goes to learn of the sages of Byzantium; here he will question the Greek philosophers.

The Neoplatonic situation of the poem is established in the fifth stanza by his allusion to Porphyry:

> What youthful mother, a shape upon her lap
> Honey of generation had betrayed,
> And that must sleep, shriek, struggle to escape
> As recollection or the drug decide,
> Would think her son, did she but see that shape
> With sixty or more winters on his head,
> A compensation for the pang of his birth,
> Or the uncertainty of his setting forth?

If the reference to Porphyry and to the Platonic doctrine of the descent of souls into generation is understood this stanza is of perfect clarity, which makes the heavy weather made of it by Academics unwilling to look at the whole body of thought which was for Yeats the ground of his life and his writings seem absurd. According to Plato himself (*Republic* X) souls about to enter generation must cross the river Lethe and there drink the forgetful draught of *hyle* (matter) before their arrival in the world of generation. They are warned not to drink too deeply of the material draught because those who do so will forget eternity; whereas those who drink less deeply are able to recollect their anterior state. Those "drugged" with matter are what the Neoplatonic writers call "sleepers"; and those who recollect the eternal world "shriek, struggle to escape" when they find themselves bound into a mortal body. This theme is recounted in mythological form by Porphyry, who adds the detail that "honey" is the sweet lure of sexuality through which the process of generation is set in motion. There may be a glance towards Wordsworth's lines about the generating soul "trailing clouds of glory" as it comes from God into this world where that vision will "fade into the light of common day"—itself a Neoplatonic theme. There is an account of a session with the medium Eusapia Palladino, related by Flammarion, in which just this confrontation did occur—the young spirit-mother recalled by her aging son was saddened by his aged aspect.

Yeats then philosophizes: is Plato's answer the true one, that only the eternal world, of which nature and the time-world is only a mutable image, is real? Or that of "soldier Aristotle," whose pupil was the world-conqueror Alexander, and whose philosophy is the real basis of Western materialism? Or that of Pythagoras, who had discerned the great universal harmony?

> Plato thought nature but a spume that plays
> Upon a ghostly paradigm of things;
> Soldier Aristotle played the taws
> Upon the bottom of a king of kings;
> World-famous golden-thighed Pythagoras
> Fingered upon a fiddle-stick or strings
> What a star sang and careless Muses heard:
> Old clothes upon old sticks to scare a bird.

Pythagoras' golden thigh, which he showed to Abaris, a priest of the Hyperborean temple of Apollo, was taken to indicate that he was the God himself, or his avatar. The naming of Abaris establishes a link with Ireland of "that ancient sect"—the Pythagoreans—mentioned in the later poem, "The Statues"; while the lines that follow refer to Pythagoras' gift of listening to the music of the spheres ("what a star sang"). Yeats habitually embodied profound thought or recondite allusion in the airy-light vesture of images. At a first reading we may enjoy such images without full understanding; but examination will show them to be firmly and accurately established in the sources from which the poet had himself gained his knowledge; he had his share of "blear-eyed wisdom out of midnight oil" but it is a poet's task to embody his metaphysics in symbolic images, "a little song about a rose," as Yeats himself wrote. But the "hard symbolic bones" are never absent. He had evidently read in Iamblichus' *Life of Pythagoras* this passage:

. . .employing a certain ineffable divinity, and which it is difficult to apprehend, he extended his ears, and fixed his intellect in the sublime
symphonies of the world, he alone hearing and understanding, as it appears, the universal harmony and consonance of the spheres, and the
stars that are moved through them, and which produce a fuller and
more intense melody than any thing affected by mortal sounds. This
melody also was the result of dissimilar and variously differing sounds,
celerities, magnitudes and intervals, arranged with reference to each
other in a certain musical ratio, and thus producing a most gentle, and
at the same time variously beautiful motion and convolution.

Taylor (whose translation of Iamblichus Yeats as well as Blake would
have read) favored, as we have seen, a rational explanation of that
music—that Pythagoras did not really "hear" sounds but apprehended
a mathematical harmony. But in Pythagoras' teaching music was central;
and the music of the Pythagorean rituals was a transcription of the heavenly harmonies.

Being therefore irrigated as it were with this melody, having the reason
of his intellect well arranged through it, as I may say exercised, he determined to exhibit certain images of these things to his disciples as
much as possible, especially producing an imitation of them through instruments, and through the mere voice alone. For he conceived that by
him alone, of all the inhabitants of the earth, the mundane sounds were
understood and heard, and this from a natural fountain and root. . .
. But he apprehended that other men ought to be satisfied in looking to
him, and the gifts he possessed, and in being benefitted and corrected
through images and examples, in consequence of their inability to com-
prehend truly the first and genuine archetypes of things. (Ch. XV)

Pythagoras had temples built to all the Muses; whom Yeats here calls
"careless" perhaps in an ambiguous sense, as signifying that they had no
concern for human affairs, and also that they only carelessly and inade-
quately recorded the celestial harmonies in their "imitation through
instruments"; a poor second-best. The "fiddle-stick or strings" refers of
course to Pythagoras' discovery of the numerical harmonics of the dia-
tonic scale. The "fiddle- stick" is the monochord on which he "fingered"
these harmonic intervals; and the "strings" tuned to give sounds in the
same harmonic scale, the lyre, associated with Apollo and signifying, as
we have seen, the numerical harmony of the universe.

Why then is Pythagoras himself rejected by Yeats along with too
abstract Plato and too concrete Aristotle as just another scarecrow? It

would seem because all three make a separation between the mortal life of the body, and the life of the immortal soul. Pythagoras taught his disciples to scorn whatever has to do with the body and to discipline themselves continually in an asceticism alike of body and of laborious intellectual studies. Yeats had long ago learned from Blake that "Man has no Body distinct from his Soul; for that call'd Body is a portion of Soul discern'd by the five Senses, the chief inlets of Soul in this age" (*Marriage of Heaven and Hell*). He doubtless included the "sacred code" of Pythagoras and the Platonists in his condemnation of all those responsible for the error "That Man has two real existing principles: Viz: a Body & a Soul." Yeats too was looking for a principle of the unity of all things and failed to find it in any of the Greek philosophers here dismissed.

In the seventh stanza the Christian teaching is also, by implication, dismissed for similar reasons. The paradox of the relation of mortal body and immortal soul, so poignantly experienced by the "youthful mother" of the child whose journey of life must lead to sickness, old age, and death, confronts the nuns in another form:

> Both nuns and mothers worship images,
> But those the candles light are not as those
> That animate a mother's reveries,
> But keep a marble or a bronze repose.
> And yet they too break hearts—O Presences
> That passion, piety or affection knows,
> And that all heavenly glory symbolise—
> O self-born mockers of man's enterprise.

Human bodies are but images of the soul; and the "images" of saints and holy persons themselves serve only to remind their worshippers of the distance between earth and heaven; which the nuns seek to attain, as it is said in the next stanza, by bruising the body to "pleasure soul." The gods (the "self-born") who embody themselves in the holy images are "mockers of man's enterprise." Thus Yeats dismisses virtually the whole of the Western tradition on account of this separation of body and soul.

Now comes Yeats's resolution of the paradox in his unifying image of the great Tree of Life, the "chestnut-tree," perpetual manifestation of creation ever-flowing, as Iamblichus wrote of the music Pythagoras heard, from "a natural fountain or root." There is nothing in the Greek or the Christian—Western—imagery hitherto employed to prepare us for this image of the tree; and we shall see that it is in fact taken from a different tradition which Yeats here deliberately places in contrast with all the "bibles and sacred codes" of Western thought. We here have a transition from Platonic to Vedantic thought; for it was to the wisdom of India that Yeats was to turn increasingly in his later years, finding in the teachings of the Upanishads (which he was in his last years to translate) an answer which sufficed him. The image of the chestnut-tree marks such a transition—tree and dancer alike come, as we shall see, from India, where alone the resolution of the paradox of body and soul is to be discovered.

I happened by a fortunate chance to have put into my hands, during the Lindisfarne Conference on Pythagoras, a little collection of "versions" by Robert Bly of poems by Kabir. In one of these was the image of the chestnut tree developed in terms so closely resembling Yeats's image that it seemed evident beyond all doubt that here was Yeats's source. Robert Bly had made his versions from Rabindranath Tagore's and Evelyn Underhill's *One Hundred Poems of Kabir* (a book that I subsequently discovered to be in Yeats's library), published in 1915. He confessed that "chestnut-tree" was his own addition; doubtless he too had, consciously or otherwise, discerned the similarity of Yeats's poem and Kabir's. I hastened to look up Tagore's original translation, and there can be no doubt that this was a book Yeats had read and treasured, for in it are several unmistakable and important sources of other poems besides "Among School Children." In order to establish this I shall here digress.

The first unmistakable allusion to Kabir is in "Wild Swans at Coole," published in 1919. Kabir had written

Tell me, O Swan, your ancient tale.
From what land do you come, O Swan? to what shore will you fly?
Where would you take your rest, O Swan, and what do you seek? (xii)

The swan, world-wide emblem of the soul, is a migrant from world to world; and this doctrine underlies Yeats's lines also:

But now they drift on the still water,
Mysterious, beautiful;
Among what rushes will they build,
By what lake's edge or pool
Delight men's eyes when I awake some day
To find they have flown away?

Yeats had implied the immortality of the swans in the previous lines:

> Their hearts have not grown old;
> Passion or conquest, wander where they will,
> Attend upon them still.

And may we not say that the answer to Yeats's rhetorical question with which he ends the poem is answered by Kabir:

> Even this morning, O Swan, awake, arise, follow me!
> There is a land where no doubt nor sorrow have rule: where the
>     terror of Death is no more.
> There the woods of spring are a-bloom, and the fragrant scent
>     "He is I" is borne on the wind:
> There the bee of the heart is deeply immersed, and desires no
>     other joy. (xii)

Here unity of being is expressed in the "He is I" so characteristic of Sufi poetry, and in that of Kabir, who was born into a Moslem family but who then became the disciple of a Hindu teacher, thus uniting the two traditions.

This background to Yeats's poem—for such I believe it to be—suggests a richness of meaning, certainly implicit in Yeats's vision of the swans at Coole, which raises the poem from the level of personal sentiment into a metaphysical statement. He had long ago deliberately abandoned all exotic imagery (from Arcadia or from ancient India) and it would have been in keeping with his practice to transpose Kabir into terms of Irish landscape and a symbolism which conforms completely with the images of his own country.

At the end of his life he was, I believe, thinking of another of Kabir's poems—and, again, as a reconciling image of unity—when he wrote

> Cast a cold eye
> On life, on death.
> Horseman, pass by!

Kabir had written

> Look upon life and death: there is no separation between them.
> The right hand and the left hand are the same. (xvii)

It is after all no secret that Yeats had in his later life committed himself to the Indian mystical and metaphysical tradition in which he had found what he had long sought in vain in the West. In the light of this background, lines that to the secular reader might seem bitter had for Yeats, initiate of the perennial wisdom, another sense altogether, that of unity and harmony. This view of death is altogether in keeping also with his view of the history of the discarnate soul, long studied, and recorded in *A Vision*.

Returning, then, to the symbolic image of the chestnut tree, which so suddenly, without bridge or preparation, bursts in its affirmative glory in the last stanza of "Among School Children," we see that it too is established in the Indian unitive tradition. It is here placed in contrast with all the "old scarecrows" of the West who make a separation between body and soul.

> Labour is blossoming or dancing where
> The body is not bruised to pleasure soul,
> Nor beauty born out of its own despair,
> Nor blear-eyed wisdom out of midnight oil.
> O chestnut-tree, great-rooted blossomer,
> Are you the leaf, the blossom or the bole?
> O body swayed to music, O brightening glance,
> How can we know the dancer from the dance?

The reader's sense of release in these lines is Yeats's sense of release from Western dualism in all its forms. He has found another tradition, that expressed in Kabir's poem:

> When He Himself reveals Himself, Brahman brings into manifestation
> that which can never be seen.
> As the seed is in the plant, as the shade is in the tree, as the void is in
> the sky, as infinite forms are in the void—
> So from beyond the Infinite, the Infinite comes; and from the Infinite
> the finite extends.
> The creature is in Brahma, and Brahma is in the creature; they are ever
> distinct, yet ever united.
> He Himself is the tree, the seed, and the germ.
> He Himself is the flower, the fruit and the shade.
> He Himself is the sun, the light, and the lighted.
> He Himself is Brahma, creature, and Maya.
> He Himself is the manifold form, the infinite space;
> He is the breath, the word, and the meaning.

He Himself is the limit and the limitless: and beyond both the limited
    and the limitless is He, the Pure Being.
He is the Immanent Mind in Brahma and in the creature.
The Supreme Soul is seen within the soul.
The Point is seen within the Supreme Soul,
And within the Point, the reflection is seen again.
Kabir is blest because he has this supreme vision! (vii)

This undisclosed background of the great Indian spiritual tradition, as
expressed in Kabir's poems, removes all obscurity from Yeats's lines; and
at the same time makes it clear that he is in this poem contrasting two
traditions of wisdom, that of the objective mind of the West with the unitive mind of the East, in which the poet found his own long-sought
resolution.

One or two points remain to be clarified; the tree is called "great-
rooted" because its root is in God, and here if anywhere there is a point
of reconciliation with Pythagoras, who heard the music of the spheres
issuing from a "natural fountain and root." The image of the dancer, not
present in the poem we have quoted, appears in many others in the
same volume; and indeed the dance and the dancer are the Indian symbol par excellence; Shiva dances, and Kali, and all things dance; as in
this poem:

. . . .
He is pure and indestructible,
His form is infinite and fathomless,
He dances in rapture, and waves of form arise from his dance.
The body and the mind cannot contain themselves, when they are
    touched by His great joy.
He is immersed in all consciousness, all joys, and all sorrows;
He has no beginning and no end;
He holds all within His bliss! (xxvi)

There are many other references to the Dance:

Before the Unconditioned, the Conditioned dances:
'Thou and I are one!' this trumpet proclaims. (xxviii)

—and again

Mad with joy, life and death dance to the rhythm of this  music.
The hills and the sea and the earth dance. The world of
man dances in laughter and tears. (xxxii)

But enough has surely been said to recreate the background of Yeats's Tree:

> There is a strange tree, which stands without roots and bears fruits
> without blossoming;
> It has no branches and no leaves, it is lotus all over.  (xlvii)

(Note: Two other images call for comment, and what is here suggested is speculative only. First, why "chestnut-tree"? I suggest that Yeats needed a blossoming tree but that the too strong symbolic associations of apple, rowan or hawthorn were unsuitable. There are not so many large, flowering trees which are native to the British Isles, but the chestnut-tree provided what he needed.

The "brightening glance" of the dancer is something that must strike anyone watching the classical Indian dancers. Dr. Santosh Pall, herself a dancer whom I have had the pleasure of watching many times, has explained to me that the use of the eyes follows a strict rule in which "the eye follows the hand, and the mind follows the eye." I know of no other dancing tradition in which the eyes themselves form part of the dance in this way.)


WHEN IN "The Statues" Yeats returns to the theme of Pythagoras and the Western tradition, the confrontation with Eastern thought is explicit. This poem must be taken to express Yeats's own last thoughts upon Pythagoras and the objective knowledge of the West, based upon number. To Yeats, as to Blake, the mystery lies in the relationship between number and immeasurable meaning. The paradox is announced in the first stanza; number, as such, is objective and impersonal:

> Pythagoras planned it. Why did the people stare?
> His numbers, though they moved, or seemed to move
> In marble or in bronze, lacked character.

The statues here introduced suggest those which, in "Among School Children," "keep a marble or a bronze repose." In the earlier poem these are said to be

> . . . Presences
> That passion, piety or affection knows,
> And that all heavenly glory symbolise—
> O self-born mockers of man's enterprise

They are spiritual presences, "self-born" in the sense that they are not made by human knowledge or skill. How are we to reconcile this view with the statement that "Pythagoras planned it"? The face of the statue is "plummet-measured" as though knowledge of the correct proportion could give the secret of beauty; as if the "calculations that look but casual flesh" were in themselves the Presences of supernatural beauty that awaken human passion. And this is surely indeed what the Pythagoreans meant when they said that the Gods are numbers—the assertion challenged by Blake when he retorted that "God is not a mathematical diagram." Nature may be a great numerical harmonic structure, but what of melody, meaning, beauty, qualities known only to the living spirit, the Imagination? Yeats's statement goes on:

> But boys and girls, pale from the imagined love
> Of solitary beds, knew what they were,
> That passion could bring character enough,
> And pressed at midnight in some public place
> Live lips upon a plummet-measured face.

I doubt whether Blake would have accepted this; for him the proportions of horse and bull are secondary, and he would surely have said that the imagined face of the beloved precedes, and does not originate in, the plummet-measurements. Calculations, Blake would have said, can never account for beauty which is experienced in the unity of its imaginative image, "For its reality is in Its Imaginative Form," the "self-born" Presence.

In the earlier poem the marble and bronze "Presences" (Yeats's use of the capital surely implies the presence of a person, a living being) could break hearts: they can be loved and worshipped. And here again the paradox that numerical harmony can arouse love and recognition is even more insistently stated. Dr. Santosh Pall ("A Study of W.B. Yeats's use of Symbols with particular reference to the Dancer," thesis submitted to the University of Delhi for the degree of Doctor of Philosophy, 1979) finds in the phrase "character enough" the implication that the "character" projected upon the statues by dreams of love is in fact only just enough and no more—it suffices but does not fully realize the dream of the soul which asks not for images but for the thing itself. Here it is the "imagined love" that is the thing itself, the archetype which the statues merely reflect. Pythagoras was only able, after all, to teach a way of making "copies" of the divine originals. Yeats is here amplifying the earlier theme of the "idle Muses" who could only imitate on lyre or dulcimer the heavenly music itself. In the first poem the "numbers" were expressed in musical, in the second in mathematical harmony.

The argument of the second stanza is that it was not the naval victory of the Greeks at Salamis that determined the rise to supremacy of Western civilization but the school of Greek art to which the Pythagorean knowledge of number gave rise. Phidias is "greater than Pythagoras" because his "calculations that look but casual flesh" were embodiments of dreams. And yet the conquest of Apollonian order over "Asiatic vague immensities" can only be the knowledge of number and harmonics of which Pythagoras, not Phidias, was the author.

> No! Greater than Pythagoras, for the men
> That with a mallet or a chisel modelled these
> Calculations that look but casual flesh, put down
> All Asiatic vague immensities,
> And not the banks of oars that swam upon
> The many-headed foam at Salamis.
> Europe put off that foam when Phidias
> Gave women dreams and dreams their looking-glass.

The many-headed python of chaos was slain by Apollo, God of number and order; the symbol of the seven-headed serpent which seeks to draw down the Sephiroth of divine manifestation from a spiritual to a material order is one also familiar to Yeats through his Cabbalistic studies as a member of the Society of the Golden Dawn.

In the "Long-legged Fly," also published in Last Poems but apparently written after "The Statues," Yeats takes up the theme of the looking-glass of dreams:

> That girls at puberty may find
> The first Adam in their thought,
> Shut the door of the Pope's chapel,
> Keep those children out.
> There on that scaffolding reclines
> Michael Angelo.
> With no more sound than the mice make
> His hand moves to and fro.
> *Like a long-legged fly upon the stream*
> *His mind moves upon silence.*

Nothing here about number or calculation: the mind of Michael Angelo moves upon the current of the flow of a deeper, unknown mind. The painted image emerged not from the known but from the unknown.

Having in the second stanza paid tribute to the Apollonian principle of number, order and calculation, Yeats in the third introduces the contrast of Western and Eastern thought already noted in "Among School Children." Here it is not the Hindu dance of life but the Buddhist "emptiness" which is set in contrast with the positive Western philosophy for which knowledge is measurement of an external universe. The verse opens with an allusion to the Hellenistic influence—specifically the representation of Apollo—which, by way of the early Gandhara sculptures led to the typically oriental icon of the Buddha seated in contemplation:

> One image crosssed the many-headed, sat
> Under the tropic shade, grew round and slow.
> No Hamlet thin from eating flies, a fat
> Dreamer of the Middle Ages. . . .

The Indian Prince Siddhartha, who received enlightenment through contemplation seated under a Bo-tree, is here contrasted with that type of the Western prince, Hamlet. Hamlet grew thin from "eating flies" as cats are said to do, catching at these teasing tormentors always seen as external to himself, as Western "knowledge" is, typically, a piecemeal knowledge of external nature; "in fortuitous concourse of memorys accumulated & lost," as Blake says (J.33.8). (This is a speculative interpretation for I find no apparent link between Hamlet and cats other than this slender one of feeding on the wrong diet.) I am again indebted to Dr. Santosh Pall for the interpretation of the Buddha's roundness as the inner plenitude of those whose knowledge is within; the subjectivity of consciousness itself as contrasted with the Western objectivity.

> . . .Empty eyeballs knew
> That knowledge increases unreality, that
> Mirror on mirror mirrored is all the show.
> When gong and conch declare the hour to bless
> Grimalkin crawls to Buddha's emptiness.

The theme of the eyeballs is one about which Yeats has written in *A Vision*. It was the Romans, he writes, who

> . . .made a discovery which affected all sculpture to come. The Greeks painted the eyes of marble statues and made out of enamel or glass or precious stones those of their bronze statues, but the Roman was the first to drill a round hole  to represent the pupil, and because, as I think, of a preoccupation with the glance characteristic of a civilization

in its final phase.... May it not have been precisely a talent for this alert attention that had enabled Rome and not Greece to express those final *primary* phases?

(The primary phases representing for Yeats objective knowledge, the antithetical subjective knowledge.) The passage concludes:

> When I think of Rome I see always those heads with their world-considering eyes, and those bodies as conventional as the metaphors in a leading article, and compare in my imagination vague Grecian eyes gazing at nothing. Byzantine eyes of drilled ivory staring upon a vision, and those eyelids of China and of India, those veiled or half-veiled eyes weary of world and vision alike. (p.275-7)

There are Gandhara Buddhist sculptures that seem to catch, as it were, the open eyes of the Greek Apollo in the very act of closing, of turning inwards from the Western scrutiny of an external, to the Eastern contemplation of an inner world. This change in representation accompanies an interiorization of knowledge itself; the plenitude of mind itself replaces speculation of nature. The Platonic and Pythagorean cosmology itself becomes, in the Indian metaphysical perspective, interiorized, relativized, a *Maya* which is in no sense a reality, being only an appearance: "Knowledge increases unreality." In one of his unsurpassable condensations of metaphysics into an image Yeats describes all knowledge as merely images reflected from a finally unknowable source:

> Mirror on mirror mirrored is all the show.

Beyond the measurable lies the immeasurable, "Buddha's emptiness," nirvana. Yeats's own choice of the Eastern, not the Western wisdom is implicit in the last two lines of the stanza. The "hour to bless" is known to Buddha and declared with "gong and conch." To this supreme enlightenment Grimalkin (the cat "grown thin with eating flies") must humbly crawl. Dr. F.A.C. Wilson suggests that the cat image refers to the Egyptian cat-goddess and above all to that supreme cat-goddess the Sphinx. Since it was from Egypt that Pythagoras learned his mathematical "mysteries" the implication would seem to be that quantitative Western knowledge must make its final submission to the East, where spirit, not matter, is the ground and first principle.

Would Blake have been satisfied to crawl to Buddha's emptiness? I doubt it; for although he himself describes nature as a "veil" of appearances, a *maya*, he sees this veil as woven by the Imagination, ever-changing according to the imaginings of the weavers. He too saw the relativity of natural appearances, but for him Imagination is by no means nirvana, but a plenitude of imaginative forms. Nirvana would have meant nothing to the poet who wrote:

> Many suppose that before the Creation All was Solitude & Chaos. This is the most pernicious Idea that can enter the Mind, as it takes away all sublimity from the Bible & Limits All Existence to Creation and Chaos, To the Time & Space fixed by the Corporeal Vegetative Eye, & leaves the Man who entertains such an Idea the habitation of Unbelieving demons. Eternity Exists, and All things in Eternity, Independent of Creation . . .

This describes Plato's intellectual world but not nirvana; and Blake's Platonic indebtedness is clear in such passages as

> There Exist in that Eternal World the Permanent Realities  of Every Thing which we see reflected in this Vegetable Glass of Nature.

"To the Eyes of the Man of Imagination, Nature is Imagination itself" is nearer to Kabir, who made no separation between real being and manifestation, than to "Buddha's emptiness."


IN THE LAST STANZA Yeats comes back to Blake's question—who strikes the music from the lyre of the universe?

> When Pearse summoned Cuchulain to his side,
> What stalked through the Post Office? What intellect,
> What calculation, number, measurement, replied?

A "Presence" of the superhuman is here invoked with an effect of chilling terror. Like "the brute blood of the air" that engenders the Trojan War in the loins of Leda this impulse comes from beyond number and measurement; these "reply" to the supernatural impulsion but do not initiate. In "The Statues" the passions to which the numbers "reply" are Love and War—the young lovers and the women who find in works of art the looking glass of dreams; and the warrior Cuchulain, spirit of 1916 and the Irish rising, the Irish Ares. These are the antinomies whose contrary powers set the world in motion between the two contrary gyres of history, as described in *A Vision*. In "A Dialogue of Self and Soul," "Sato's ancient blade," the sword of the *samurai*, and

> That flowering, silken, old embroidery, torn
> From some court lady's dress

are "emblematical of love and war." Elsewhere Yeats writes of the super-human that sets the events of love and war in motion as incalculable and transcendent. It is Zeus who begets Helen of Troy with all the consequences that followed:

> A shudder in the loins engenders there
> The broken wall, the burning roof and tower
> And Agamemnon dead.

Over the awe-inspiring and incomprehensible mystery of generation the human agent—the "staggering girl"—has little control. And so with the generation of Jesus Christ, the contrary principle of love, whose birth is

> The uncontrollable mystery on the bestial floor. ("The Magi")

In "A Stick of Incense" the Divine Humanity (to use Blake's term) is begotten in an act of mere stupid lust. Whether God-begotten or lust-begotten (the paradox is that these are united in the symbol of God in the form of bird or bull or shower of gold) the mystery stands beyond reason or that numerical order Apollonian Pythagoras can understand by "calculation, number, measurement." It seems that for Yeats, as for Blake, "God is not a mathematical diagram" but a living mystery.

And yet at this time when in Othello's words "chaos is come again," Yeats summons his compatriots to remember their Pythagorean birthright, the "ancient sect" of the Hyperborean Apollo whom he supposes to have existed in bronze-age Ireland:

> We Irish, born into that ancient sect
> But thrown upon this filthy modern tide
> And by its formless spawning fury wrecked,
> Climb to our proper dark, that we may trace
> The lineaments of a plummet-measured face.

Is Yeats giving, then, the last word to Pythagoras? The concluding lines seem ambiguous, for it is in "our proper dark"—the inner world of the soul—that the "plummet-measured face" is to be traced; the inner universe behind the Buddha's "empty eyeballs." Love and war are

> . . . emblems of the day against the tower
> Emblematical of the night.

In "A Dialogue of Self and Soul" self summons to the world of day, of action, of love and war, soul to

> That quarter where all thought is done:
> Who can distinguish darkness from the soul?

It is

> . . . ancestral night that can,
> If but imagination scorn the earth
> And intellect its wandering
> To this and that and t'other thing,
> Deliver from the crime of death and birth.

It seems that it is within the darkness of the soul that we are to "trace" the "lineaments" of that face Pythagoras with his plummet could measure. In "A Dialogue of Self and Soul" he describes that ascent into the soul's darkness:

> I summon to the winding ancient stair;
> Set all your mind upon the steep ascent,
> Upon the broken, crumbling, battlement,
> Upon the breathless starlit air,
> Upon the star that marks the hidden pole;
> Fix every wandering thought upon
> That quarter where all thought is done:
> Who can distinguish darkness from the soul?

It might seem that In "The Statues" Yeats bids us ascend into the soul's darkness, above the chaos of the "filthy modern tide," the "many-headed" chaos Apollo's avatar had mastered at the beginning of Western civilization. That is not I think the whole meaning; for Yeats the alternation of the gyres runs, as for Plato and the pre- Socratics, for ever. Self refuses (in its dialogue with soul) the negative solution:

> I am content to live it all again
> And yet again, if it be life to pitch
> Into the frog-spawn of a blind man's ditch,
> A blind man battering blind men. . .

and having found and accepted unity beyond the contraries the poet experiences the beatitude of which Kabir had spoken:

> So great a sweetness flows into the breast
> We must laugh and we must sing,
> We are blest by everything,
> Everything we look upon is blest.

We must remember that it was not Buddhism with its empty nirvana that Yeats in his last years embraced but the religion of the Upanishads, the plenitude of Hinduism which embraces both life and death in a single, unceasing dance. We need not assume that in "The Statues" Yeats is regarding "Buddha's emptiness" as a complete answer to Pythagorean number—on the contrary, it is Kabir's ever-blossoming tree of the universe that he chose as reconciling symbol.

The scorn and bitterness of the last stanza of "The Statues" notwithstanding, there is a certain note of triumphant wisdom that, again, suggests the resolution of the antinomies; a note he had sounded in "The Gyres." Yeats, here placing his faith in his own symbol of the Gyres (itself grounded in Plato and the pre-Socratics) of a perpetual alternation of ages, gold giving place to iron, but then again, of necessity, iron to gold, is able to master his bitterness by that symbol:

> Conduct and work grow coarse, and coarse the soul,
> What matter? Those that Rocky Face holds dear,
> Lovers of horses and of women, shall,
> From marble of a broken sepulchre,
> Or dark betwixt the polecat and the owl,
> Or any rich, dark nothing disinter
> The workman, noble and saint, and all things run
> On that unfashionable gyre again.

"Nothing"—Buddha's emptiness, or even perhaps the many-headed chaos itself—is called "rich" and "dark," the fertile source whence Apollonian order itself flows out of the "natural fountain and root." Yeats's majestic acceptance transcends, finally, all antinomies, even that of Pythagorean ordering of nature and "Buddha's emptiness" of spirit, each to itself the sole reality, to its contrary, unreality. There we must leave the question at the farthest point to which the poet can lead us.

. . . . . . . . . . . . . . . . . . . . . .

*Plato and the Pythagoreans think that being and unity are not something else, but that this is their nature; namely, that their essential being is just to be one and to be being.*

ARISTOTLE, *Metaphysics*

ROBERT LAWLOR is the author of *Sacred Geometry*; *Earth Honoring*; and *Voices of the First Day: Awakening in the Aboriginal Dreamtime*. After training as a painter and a sculptor, he became a student of the Yoga of Sri Aurobindo, and lived for many years in Pondicherry, India, where he was one of the founding settlers of Auroville, the international spiritual community. It was in India that he discovered the works of the French Egyptologist and esotericist, R. A. Schwaller de Lubicz. This led him to a deep exploration of the principles and practices of ancient sacred science. An artist, lecturer, film maker, and translator (he has translated works of Alain Daniélou and R. A. Schwaller de Lubicz), Lawlor now lives on Flinders Island, off the coast of Australia, where he works with the Aborigines.

KEITH CRITCHLOW is the author of (among others) *Order in Space*; *Islamic Patterns*; and *Time Stands Still*. Trained as a painter, Critchlow discovered geometry intuitively. A period of intensive geometric practice (and work with Buckminster Fuller) led him to the recognition that the universal principles of geometry are revealed and confirmed both by the area of design where art and mathematics meet and in the study of nature and ancient and medieval sacred cosmological Stone, Temple, Cathedral, and Mosque architectures. Keith Critchlow has been a senior lecturer at the Architectural Association in London, and has taught Islamic Art at the Royal College of Art. He has also participated as geometer in various sacred architectural projects, and is a co-founder of *Temenos: A Review Devoted to the Arts of the Imagination*, and of *Kairos*, a society whose object is "to investigate, study and promote traditional values of art and science." Keith Critchlow is presently Director of Research of the Prince of Wales Institute of Architecture.

ARTHUR ZAJONC is Professor of Physics at Amherst College, where his research has concerned the nature of light and the experimental foundations of quantum mechanics. He has also taught and written extensively on interdisciplinary aspects of science, the history of science, culture, and spirituality, especially the work of Johann Wolfgang von Goethe and Rudolf Steiner. He is the author of the book *Catching the Light: The Entwined History of Light and Mind* (Bantam, 1993). Arthur Zajonc has been a visiting scientist at many laboratories, including the Ecole Normale Supérieure, and the Max Planck Institute for Quantum Optics. He was a Fulbright professor in Austria in 1993. He is a fellow of the Lindisfarne Association and the Fetzer Institute.

ANNE MACAULAY lives in Scotland where she has, for many years, studied the origins of the alphabet, the history of the guitar, the figure of Apollo, and other mysteries surrounding Pythagoreanism. Mrs. Macaulay has lectured at RILKO (Research into Lost Knowledge Organization) and has been a trustee of the Salisbury Center in Edinburgh.

KATHLEEN RAINE is a British poet, with an international reputation as a scholar of the Imagination. A renowned student of William Blake, a penetrating critic, and a profound autobiographer, the following are some of her many works available in English: *Selected Works of Thomas Taylor, the Platonist; Blake and Antiquity; The Human Face of God; Yeats, the Initiate; Defending Ancient Springs; Golgonooza, Blake's City of Imagination; Selected Poems; The Presence; Living with Mystery.* The first three volumes of her autobiography have recently been reissued in one volume by Skoob Books and George Braziller, while a fourth volume, *India Seen Afar,* was published by Green Books in 1991. Kathleen Raine is a co-founder and the editor of *Temenos.* She is also the founder of the Temenos Academy of Integral Studies.

CHRISTOPHER BAMFORD (the editor) is co-director of Lindisfarne and Anthroposophic Presses and author of books and articles on Celtic Christianity, Platonism, Romanticism, and Hermeticism.